# Civil–Military Relations in the Islamic World

# Civil–Military Relations in the Islamic World

## Paul E. Lenze Jr.

LEXINGTON BOOKS
Lanham • Boulder • New York • London

Published by Lexington Books
An imprint of The Rowman & Littlefield Publishing Group, Inc.
4501 Forbes Boulevard, Suite 200, Lanham, Maryland 20706
www.rowman.com

Unit A, Whitacre Mews, 26-34 Stannary Street, London SE11 4AB

British Library Cataloguing in Publication Information Available

**Library of Congress Cataloging-in-Publication Data Available**

ISBN: 978-1-4985-1873-4 (cloth: alk. paper)
ISBN: 978-1-4985-1875-8 (pbk.: alk. paper)
ISBN: 978-1-4985-1874-1 (electronic)

∞™ The paper used in this publication meets the minimum requirements of American National Standard for Information Sciences Permanence of Paper for Printed Library Materials, ANSI/NISO Z39.48-1992.

Printed in the United States of America

# Contents

# Acknowledgments

A book is a huge, solitary undertaking for the writer, but it would not be possible without tremendous support. My thanks to my editors at Lexington Books, Joseph Parry and Emily Roderick, for their assistance shepherding this book to print. A huge thank you to Firecreek Coffee for all the excellent coffee that fueled a lot of the writing throughout the last two years.

At Northern Arizona University, the Department of Politics and International Affairs has been a wonderful place to teach for the last six years. To my chair, Lori Poloni-Staudinger, thanks for giving me a teaching schedule that allowed me to complete the research and writing of the manuscript. She also offered excellent advice over the years about all things related to the academe. Many thanks to my colleagues in the department for their support over the years; a special thanks to Glenn Phelps for his advice and stories over lunch, and Sean Parson and John Hultgren for their friendship. John Hultgren and Maiah Jaskowski also took time out of their busy schedules to look over parts of the manuscript, which was much appreciated. Fred Solop and Nancy Wonders offered advice and support and made me feel at home in Flagstaff from day one. A huge shout out to my undergraduate research class on civil–military relations in the Middle East—Sydney Cheifetz, Dakota Cunningham, John Kelly, Astrid Price, Sara Rodriguez, Sarah Takesian, and Kierstin Turnock—whose research and final papers helped me refine my arguments and improve the book. My cousin, Ryan Benjamin, came through in the clutch and lent me his ASU login so I could complete some last minute research. Parwez Besmel, Rob Knox, Haleigh Parkinson, Kevin Redmond, Samantha Schommer, Evan Welty, Mary Witlacil, and Spencer Young were my TAs and GAs the past two years while I researched and wrote this book; their hard work allowed me to devote more time to writing. Luis Fernandez helped me understand the ins and outs of the publishing business while also providing excellent counsel. I'm glad I could keep his book proposal template's record going and will miss not having an office next door to his.

Finally, this book would not have been completed without the love and support of my friends—Ross Caldwell, Wil Figueroa, Michelle Mellinger, Jessica Moore, Joe Mullenix, Dan Ball, Crystal Ball, Jess Farwell, Julie Beard, Justin Hopkins, Sara Hopkins, Cyndi Salsman, Adriane Stocking, Nisha Marvel, Luke Marvel, Sheena Kriekenbeek, Jeff James,

Padraic Jordan, Justin Taft, Crystal Sturm, Eric Breshears, Jenny Breshears, Sam Rosenberg, Joanne Levy, Gibson Magill, Mary Magill, Brian Giubardo, Mayte Giubardo, Bill Martinchuk, Sherrie Martinchuk, Ginger Christenson, Luis Fernandez, Mare Schumacher, David Lipinski, Eric Nolan, Jason Minos, Joe Huseby, Glen Smith, Joy Smith, Pete Collins, Sancheen Collins, Katie Searles, John Nickerson, Corrinne Olson, Kassi Schwartz, and Chelsea Piper. There are many other friends whom I have met over the years, but space doesn't allow me to thank you all, so to you and anyone else I may have forgotten, thank you.

My family is my biggest supporter. Thank you to my cousins John and Terrina Guempel for letting me stay for a month the last two summers to work on the book and spend time in the city I love. To my cousin Bridget Blanchard, thank you for always being there for me. To all the Lenze, Horan, and Guempel families, thanks for all the fun times over the years that allowed me to get my mind off work. Aunt Gustie, you were my biggest champion and a mentor, I've accomplished all I have because of you. To my Mom and Dad, thanks for imparting a love of reading at an early age. Finally, to my sister, Jennifer, and my nephews, Dylan, Noah, and Brody, this book is dedicated to you, because you have shown me what matters most in life. I love you all.

# Abbreviations

ALGERIA

| | |
|---|---|
| ALN | *Armée de Liberation Nationale* |
| ANP | Armée Nationale Populaire |
| PPA | Parti du Peuple Algérien |
| AML | Amis du Manifeste et de la Liberté |
| CRUA | Comite Revolutionnaire d'Unite et d'Action |
| CNRA | *Counseil National de la revolution algerienne* |
| CCE | *Comité de coordination et d'exécution* |
| UDMA | Democratic Union of the Algerian Manifesto |
| FLN | *Front de Liberation Nationale* National Liberation Front |
| FIS | *Front Islamique du Salut*, or Islamic Salvation Front |
| FFS | Front of the Socialist Forces |
| MSP | Movement for Society and Peace |
| MTLD | Movement for the Triumph of Democratic Liberties |
| RND | National Rally For Democracy |
| RCD | Rally for Culture and Democracy |
| PT | Worker's Party |

## EGYPT

| | |
|---|---|
| FJP | Freedom and Justice Party |
| MB | Muslim Brotherhood |
| RCC | Revolutionary Command Council |
| SCAF | Supreme Council of the Armed Forces |

## PAKISTAN

| | |
|---|---|
| CMLA | Chief Martial Law Administrator |
| ISI | Inter-Services Intelligence |
| JM | Jaish-e-Mohammad |
| JI | Jamaat-I-Islami |
| LeJ | Lashkar-e-Jhangvi |
| LeT | Lashkar-e-Taiba |
| MQM | Muhajir Qaumi Mahaz |
| MRD | Movement for the Restoration of Democracy |
| NWFP | Northwest Frontier Province |
| PML | Pakistani Muslim League |
| PPP | Pakistani People's Party |
| SSP | Sipah-e-Sahaba Pakistan |

## TURKEY

| | |
|---|---|
| DP | Democrat Party |
| AKP | Justice and Development Party |
| MSP | National Salvation Party |
| NUC | National Unity Committee |
| CHP | Republican People's Party |
| TGNA | Turkish Grand National Assembly |

# ONE

## Introduction

The clock strikes 4:00 a.m. Over the radio a code word is transmitted. Upon hearing this signal, two armored brigades and one infantry brigade move out from their barracks just outside the city limits. Within minutes, troops have cordoned off the capital and the state's two other major cities, surrounding the state television, radio station, airport, and major roads. Units move toward the offices of the president or prime minister and the residences of the party leaders. The military junta—consisting of the chief of the general staff, various generals, and a handful of field rank officers fan out to key government offices, the television and radio stations.

At this point, the junta announces over the air that the government has been relieved of its duties for excessive corruption and conduct threatening the security of the state. Over the next few weeks and months, the junta establishes connections with bureaucrats within the massive state bureaucracy, as well as with compliant politicians from one, or possibly both, political parties. In fact, one of the ultraconservative members of the junta might reach out to a friend in a far right (read: Islamist) party to curry favor essentially to appear to allow this party the opportunity to oppose the operation. This accomplishes two objectives: (1) The junta will attempt to gain support of those political forces which fear the other parties more than the military junta; and (2) The junta will attempt to step forward and fight other groups after associating them as extremists or terrorists. Finally, the junta and their allies in government declare martial law to ensure that control can be maintained as "reforms" are implemented throughout government and society.

The scenario described above is commonly known as a military intervention or *coup d'état*. Generally, this term is used to refer to the military assuming control of the rest of a country's state institutions. It is not a

1

new phenomenon; it has been in existence for more than three hundred years, since the rise of the modern state (Luttwak 1968, 29). The military played an important, if not central role, in the process of nation-building and state formation in the developing world. As Kees Koonings and Dirk Kruijt (2002) argue, "In the majority of nation-states that have emerged and . . . consolidated during the nineteenth and twentieth centuries, military politics was the rule rather than the exception" (1).

These cases of military involvement in politics share a few common features: "strong identification of the military with the fate of the nation and its core values, emphasis on the theme of order and especially the protection of the integrity of the state, national strength and development, and a military doctrine that links the destiny of the nation and the interests of the people to the historic mission of the military" (Koonings and Kruijt 2002, 10). Furthermore, "national values derived from prevailing religious or ideological paradigms (Christianity, Islam, nationalism, socialism) are invoked to lend 'higher support' to the intervention," since the military is seen as defender of the nation and, in the postcolonial developing world, the military was created with economic assistance from international actors (Koonings and Kruijt 2002, 10). This creates a military culture reliant upon international economic and military assistance to maintain its interests.

Historically, militaries are reluctant to rule directly and seek to "return to the barracks." In the literature this has been known as military withdrawal or military disengagement from politics. A military's "return to the barracks" is defined as the level and nature of military involvement in politics having moved from military control to military participation, or from military participation to military influence in politics (Welch 1987). Since the end of colonialism, there has been a proliferation of states in Europe, Asia, Latin America, and the Middle East that have been subject to military interventions and withdrawals.

Many states in these regions were successful in their democratic transitions, but in the Middle East, authoritarianism has prevailed over democracy. To better understand why states in the Middle East and South Asia have not experienced the same progress as other regions in terms of democratization, it is important to gain an understanding of the various factors that influenced military interventions and withdrawals in this part of the world. This book asks: How do civil–military relations in the Middle East and South Asia contribute to coups, democratic transitions and democratic consolidations during the Cold War and post-9/11 era?

In a special edition of the journal *Comparative Politics*, Eva Bellin did a survey of twenty-one states in the Middle East and found that the failure of democratization in the region is not a result of a lack of a strong civil society, a lack of market economies, adequate income and literacy levels, a lack of democratic neighbors (with the exception of Turkey), and a lack of democratic culture (Bellin 2004, 141). By no means is the Middle East without these features; the problem is their continued repression by the state. Specifically, Bellin (2004) argues that these Middle Eastern states' coercive capacity is fostering robust authoritarianism and prohibiting a transition to democracy (143).

What does the state's coercive capacity look like? Essentially, the answer lies in the strength of the state. Bellin (2004) quotes Theda Skocpol (1979), "'If the state's coercive apparatus remains coherent and effective, it can face down popular disaffection and survive significant illegitimacy, 'value incoherence,' and even a pervasive sense of relative deprivation among its subjects'" (143). The strength, coherence, and effectiveness of the state's coercive apparatus "'distinguish[es] among cases of successful revolution, revolutionary warefare and nonoccurrence'" and could be applied to democratic transitions to see if the state's coercive apparatus had the will or capacity to crush the democratic process (Bellin 2004, 143). In other words, the democratization process examines contestation or consensus between the state's coercive apparatus and civil society. Therefore, to better understand the democratic transition and consolidation process in the Muslim World, an understanding of the military, and its role as the coercive institution of state, is important in a post-Arab Spring Middle East and South Asia, the regions currently experiencing conflict between the military, politicians, and society.

In 2012, Bellin reassessed her argument on the endurance of authoritarianism. She argues that the Middle East "was not singularly authoritarian because it was exceptionally lacking in the prerequisites of democratization (whether cultural, socioeconomic or institutional). . . . [W]hat distinguishes the Middle East was not the absence of democratic prerequsities but rather . . . the presence of an exceptionally muscular coercive apparatus endowed with both the capacity and will to repress democratic initiatives originating from society" (Bellin 2012, 128). The coercive apparatus refers to the military and Bellin (2012) argues four factors contribute to the ability to repress:

> 1) the fiscal health of the coercive apparatus, especially robust in many countries thanks to the access many states had to petroleum, gas, geostrategic, locational and secondary rents; 2) the maintenance of international support networks, successfully retained by many Middle Eastern states even in the post-Cold War era because of their potential service to security interests. . . .; 3) the low level of institutionalization of the coercive apparatus; and 4) the low level of popular mobilization that could typically be assembled to confront the coercive apparatus in the name of political reform. (128–29)

Put simply, the first two factors determine the military's capacity to repress, while the latter two factors are crucial to determine the will to repress (Bellin 2012, 129). Therefore, this book seeks to test Bellin's (2004; 2012) robustness of authoritarianism argument on the key states of the

Middle East and South Asia. Doing so will allow for the development, and more complete understanding, of an Islamic civil–military relations.

## CIVIL–MILITARY RELATIONS, MILITARY INTERVENTIONS, AND WITHDRAWALS

Civil–Military Relations (CMR) is concerned with the study of militaries and their relationship with political leaders. The study of CMR traces its origins to the classic study by Samuel Huntington (1957), *Soldier and the State: The Theory and Politics of Civil–Military Relations*. Huntington argues that professionalism is the key to military autonomy and maintaining objective control of the military, focusing on Western democracies. What is objective control of the military? Politicians provide strategic direction, give orders, and the military executes the order. The military cannot argue against the order; they must implement the order at the tactical and operational level to meet the policy objective.

Generally, scholars have asked the following questions regarding the relationship between military officers and political development: Why do militaries engage in *coup d'etats*? and How do military dictatorships influence democratic transitions? There are three theoretical schools of thought regarding military intervention in these states' politics. One group puts more emphasis on the organizational dynamics within the army then on outside forces influencing states. Morris Janowitz (1964 [1977]) is the leading scholar of this view. He examined the structure of the military and concluded that the military's organizational unity, cohesion, and control over the "'instruments of violence'" allowed it to intervene in politics more readily than civilians (27–28, 31–32).

Huntington's (1968) *Political Order in Changing Societies* also addresses military intervention in politics and argues that intervention is a result of general politicization of social forces and institutions. The inability of political institutions to cope with increasing social mobilization causes disorder and chaos, thereby increasing the likelihood of military intervention (196). Huntington (1968) argues that the military as an institution is "the advance guard of the middle class," which promotes social and economic reform, and national integration (222). The weakness of civilian institutions and civilian politicians to deal with their state's problems causes the military to become politicized.

The second group focuses on society as reason for military rule. In *The Man on Horseback: The Role of the Military in Politics*, Samuel Finer (1976) examines how the military intervenes in politics and concludes that the form military intervention takes is different for each society. Specifically, he looks at subjective and objective factors, which he calls the disposition and opportunity to intervene in politics. In short, a military's disposition to intervene in politics comes from the following reasons: the national interest, corporate self-interest, social (especially ethnic or class) self-interest and individual self-interest (chapter 4). The military sees its political duty as being the custodian of the national interest. This role throughout history has taken a number of forms. On one hand, the military overtly rules the nation and establishes a political agenda. On the other hand, the military is seen as an arbiter or veto that will intervene if a decision or policy by civilian politicians is perceived as a threat to the permanent interest of the nation (31). Intervening on behalf of the national interest is often used by militaries as justification to hide their real motives, that of self-interest and corporate interest. Both terms are highly related, in that the military is considered a professional organization and issues such as pay, military spending, and national security matters are considered the purview of the military. As such, Finer (1976) argues, "Anxiety to preserve its autonomy provides one of the most widespread and powerful of the motives for [military] intervention" (41). In essence, the disposition to intervene for Finer is an emotion "and though it is true that some armed forces, like some individuals, act blindly on their emotions, most people make some kind of rational calculation before doing so" (63). In making the decision to intervene, Finer argues that the objective conditions on the ground in a particular state must be taken into account; these are the "Opportunities to Intervene."

Finer's discussion of "Opportunities to Intervene" includes: an increased civilian dependence on the military, the effect of domestic circumstances, and the popularity of the military. As discussed above, the military is generally viewed as a professional organization with an ethos and is often deferred to in regards to national security and foreign policy issues. Finer contends this dates back to the Cold War era. The context of foreign policy decisions at the time involved large military expenditures, a nuclear threat, and the increasing technicality of warfare, making decisions by civilian leaders a lot harder since not all of them would be able to competently assess military tactics and strategy (66). Next, some examples of domestic circumstances for intervention would be crisis situations, labeled as overt, latent, chronic or power-vacuum situations, in which the military is asked or ordered to intervene as a police force. This breakdown in domestic security tends to feed the population's dislike for civilian politicians. The popularity of the military increases with the perception of civilian incompetence and the military as the nation's savior (73).

Taken together, both the disposition and opportunity for intervention coalesce around the strength or weakness of the civilian population's attachment to civilian institutions. Finer calls this the level of political culture and argues that the higher the level of culture, the fewer opportunities are open for militaries to intervene in politics; and if it tries to intervene anyway, the less support it will receive. Conversely, a lower political culture affords more opportunities for intervention and greater likelihood of public support (75–76). Interestingly, though, the longer the military stays in power after intervention, the more the level of political support will wane and turn public opinion against the military (one influence for a military withdrawing from politics and returning to the barracks). The military's return to the barracks will be discussed shortly, but first a discussion of military elites' self-interest and military corporate interests is in order.

The third group of interventionist scholars focuses on internal dynamics of military hierarchy, corporate interests, personal ambitions, and idiosyncrasies of particular military elites. Scholars such as Eric Nordlinger (1977) and Amos Perlmutter (1977) are concerned with how the military as an institution influences military elites. Nordlinger's (1977) *Soldiers in Politics: Military Coups and Governments* defines military corporatism as the protection and enhancement of the military's own interests through adequate budgetary support, autonomy in managing their internal affairs, the preservation of their responsibilities in the face of encroachments from rival institutions and the continuity of the institution itself (65). For Nordlinger, military corporatism is the number one explanation for why militaries intervene. Another important question asked by Nordlinger is "when do soldiers intervene?" To answer this question, Nordlinger examines civilian governments' performance failures and the resulting loss of legitimacy. In effect, Nordlinger argues, "The officers can more easily rationalize and justify their coups when acting against incumbents whom they see as incompetent or corrupt. More important, performance failures lead to the deflation of governmental legitimacy within the politicized stratum of the civilian population. It is this factor that encourages and allows the officers to act upon their interventionist motives" (64). Perlmutter (1977) would concur with Nordlinger's argument and would add that the decision to intervene is purely a political decision involving: political readiness and the nature of the coup's leadership (102).

## MILITARY WITHDRAWAL FROM POLITICS

Scholars who have studied military intervention have also looked into military withdrawals from politics. Finer (1977) argues that military disengagement occurs as a culmination of three conditions: the disintegration of the original conspiratorial group, the growing divergence of interests between the junta of rulers and those military who remain as the active leaders of the military branches, and the political difficulties of the regime (174). Nordlinger (1977) argues further that the most important factors behind why militaries disengage are: the desire to retain governmental power and its related privileges is less strongly felt by military than by civilian incumbents, when the military feels civilian governments would not overturn their policies, and to return to life as a professional soldier to preserve the military's reputation (147).

Claude Welch (1987) is looking at whether factors specific to a single country (leadership, idiosyncratic historical factors), factors characteristic of a large number of countries or a single geographic region (ethnic diversity, historical patterns of civil–military relations), or factors found universally (economic development, levels of social mobilization) account for varying paths of disengagement (26). Furthermore, Welch (1987) posits six hypotheses on why militaries disengage from politics: 1) Military elites questioning their further involvement in politics; 2) Funding and internal management of the military; namely, that the military will withdraw when they feel that their interests will be respected by civilian governments; 3) the role of the military in protecting the nation or its use in international peacekeeping efforts; 4) to avoid or reduce internal conflict (i.e., strikes, protests or ethnic tensions); 5) the downturn in the economy; and 6) political conditions whereby a civilian political official that is deemed acceptable to the military is found (21–23). Each of these factors is examined in selected states of Africa and Latin America.

Welch (1992) argued that a typology has yet to develop regarding a military's return to the barracks despite there being over eighty cases of military disengagement between 1940 and 1980 (324). In 1992, research regarding military disengagement was linked to broader themes such as the breakdown of authoritarianism and democratization. Most of the research was done on a region-by-region basis through case studies. Patterns were identified in a number of the case studies that were done across Latin America and Europe—namely, the speed and nature of military withdrawal from direct political roles, the relative extent of liberalization and democratization, and the impact of military professionalism on political change (325). In short, these patterns as presented in case studies have, "given the flux, dynamism and uncertainty about the basic phenomena being considered," by presenting disengagement, liberalization and (re)democratization "more as random events than as manifestations of (potentially) broader currents of change, globally or regionally" (Welch 1992, 324). Accordingly, Welch (1992) also shows "areas of disagreement or uncertainty" in military training and attitudes, economic impacts, internal disorder, and gradual versus revolutionary change. He argues, "The respective roles of civilians and officers in the process of disengagement, liberalization, and democratization remain disputed" (Welch 1992, 337). Furthermore, Welch (1992) acknowledges, theoretically, the importance economic factors play, as well as the relative merits of gradual change versus revolutionary transformation, saying that evidence of the latter is "mixed and inconclusive" (337).

Finally, Welch (1992) discusses the gaps he sees in the disengagement literature reflecting an absence of research by Third World scholars, knowledge of intramilitary attitudes, political culture, and the need for case studies in conjunction with hypothesis testing. In short, Welch (1992) is an overview of causal phenomena leading to military disengagement, but empirical examples grounded in theory were absent as Welch threw down the gauntlet for future researchers to take up this cause in the search for "exciting, policy-relevant research across a wide variety of political, economic and social settings" (Welch 1992, 339). Since the events of the Arab Spring, the Middle East and South Asia have garnered renewed interests from policymakers and scholars alike necessitating the exciting, policy-relevant research Welch (1992) called for in comparative politics.

Since the 1950s and 1960s, regimes in the Middle East were studied for a number of reasons; namely, debates on the causes and consequences of military coups, modernization, and early studies of nationalism and post-colonial state building. However, since the 1980s, scholarship on the Middle East been marginalized within the study of developing countries and, even more, in the broader field of comparative politics (Posusney 2004, 127). The literature during the 1980s and 1990s was influenced by the successful democratic transitions occurring throughout Southern and Eastern Europe and Latin America but studying cases that symbolized the persistence of authoritarianism in the Middle East were "almost completely absent from the most important works on political transitions, including those that explicitly focus on the developing world" (Posusney 2004, 127).

This endurance of authoritarianism is the subject of a book by Council on Foreign Relations scholar Steven Cook (2007) titled *Ruling But Not Governing: The Military and Political Development in Egypt, Algeria, and Turkey*. The author examines the Egyptian, Algerian, and Turkish militaries' use of democracy as a façade to prolong their rule. Each state has used, according to Cook (2007), "A democratic façade of elections, parliaments, opposition press, and the ostensible guarantee of basic freedoms and rights in these countries' constitutions [to] . . . provide dedicated counter-elites (in the present cases Islamists) the opportunity to advance their agendas" (x). Although, at the first sign of success by the Islamists, the military regimes step in to nullify the results. Cook (2007) argues this pathological pattern of including and excluding Islamists reflects the stability of these regimes (15). To best understand why democratization has not taken hold in the Middle East, Cook (2007) highlights the relationship between what he calls the military enclave of military elites and civilian politicians in Egypt, Algeria, and Turkey and proscribes what external actors could do to influence this relationship.

For Cook (2007), the military is an organization with varied interests and because of its "high modernist" nature it is the only institution with the necessary skills needed for modernization (15). There are a hierarchy of interests—lesser-order interests, core-parochial and institutional interests, and existential interests—which influence the military's relationship to civilian elites. Encroachment on these interests by civilian elites are met with varied responses by the military enclave, especially if the military's core interests relating to the economy, foreign and security policy, the political and state apparatus, and nationalism are infringed upon. These are considered core interests because:

1. For military elites, economic independence is the best way to achieve economic development;
2. The military is an institution in Egypt, Algeria and Turkey where the formulation and execution of security policy remains the sole province of the officer corps;
3. The military enclaves have embedded within these political systems various means of control and have demonstrated that protecting the integrity of these tools is of primary importance;
4. The military uses nationalist narratives to depict officers as the vanguards of a struggle against colonialism, external aggression, and the realization of the "national will" (Cook 2007, 18–28).

Furthermore, a democratic façade is established that allows the military to "rule but not govern" as the military uses "the presence of pseudo- or quasi-democratic institutions allow[ing] authoritarian leaders to claim that they are living up to their oft-invoked principles about democratic governance with practice" (Cook 2007, 134–35). In describing the Egyptian, Algerian, and Turkish cases, Cook (2007) highlights the friction between Islamists and the military and says that predicting precisely when a military will exert its influence is difficult. Ultimately, the author is defining the unfolding battle over control of state institutions in the Middle East and the endurance of authoritarianism in the region.

Since the Arab Spring, scholars have sought to bring the Middle East and South Asia into a broader discussion of military involvement in politics. Zoltan Barany (2012) is one such scholar who took a comparative approach examining the role militaries play in democratic transitions. In *The Soldier and the Changing State: Building Democratic Armies in Africa, Asia, Europe, and the Americas*, Barany does a large-N study of the aforementioned, differing political environments and geographic regions. He examines how a variety of countries democratized after war, regime change, and state transformation arguing that democratic civil–military relations is a fundamental prerequisite of democratic transition and consolidation (Barany 2012, 10–11). However, Barany does not discuss any of the Arab States affected by the Arab Spring and only briefly discusses Pakistan and its efforts in the postcolonial years.

The events of the Arab Spring inspired Barany (2016) to undertake another comparative study in *How Armies Respond to Revolutions and Why*. There are two central arguments: 1) The success or failure of a revolution is dependent upon the army's response to the uprising; and 2) the army's response can be guessed at, or even predicted in some cases, if we under-

stand the army, its relationship to state and society and the external environment (Barany 2016, 5). Barany details the variables influencing military behavior and uses these variables to develop a model for academics
and policymakers to predict military behavior in future revolutions. He
argues in descending order of importance: 1) the military establishment,
2) the state, 3) society, and 4) the external environment influence military
leaders' behavior during a revolution. This discussion of military behavior toward revolution is quite similar to the literature on military intervention and, more specifically, its discussion of military and elite interests. Therefore, this book applies Barany's (2016) comparative framework
to show military intervention and disengagement from politics are dependent on similar variables, albeit with the order of importance altered
slightly.

Conflict within Middle Eastern civil–military relations can be studied
comparatively through an examination of 1) the external environment, 2)
the military establishment, and 3) state and society. The army's response
to revolution is influenced by threat of foreign intervention and its relationship with states providing military aid (Barany 2016, 24). This aid
serves dual purposes, as Bellin (2012) contends, to protect the security
apparatus of the state and promote security interests of the superpower. I
argue that the Algerian, Egyptian, Pakistani, and Turkish military establishment's behavior was directly affected by military aid received from
the United States and/or the Soviet Union/Russia. The threat of foreign
intervention would be more influential in the Pakistani case and influence military elite behavior. The study of the military establishment, a
critical condition for Barany (2016), involves studying the attributes, conditions, and composition of the armed forces (24). Understanding a state
and its society involves how the state treats the armed forces, its record of
governance, directions to the military during revolution, and the relationship the military has with politicians and civil society groups (24). Each
state discussed herein had prominent groups develop within civil society
during the post-colonial era.

Accordingly, this book will examine the cases of Algeria, Egypt, Pakistan, and Turkey highlighting the confrontation and consensus present
between their militaries, politicians and society. The militaries in these
states have used nationalism to justify their interventions into politics
while ensuring that withdrawal would only occur if national identity
were protected. The choice of these cases allows for a comparison of
states that have experienced a similar historical trajectory, briefly experi-
mented with democracy, and had the military become a dominant institution in the state. Interestingly, all four countries differ in the levels of
ethnic conflict, importance placed on the country by the international
community, and internal security concerns. As a result, the military will
take a keener interest in politics and be more reluctant to disengage.

Despite there being over eighty cases of military disengagement from politics between 1940 and 1980, there has yet to be a typology developed regarding a military's return to the barracks (Welch 1992, 324). Many of the hypotheses that were developed in the past were done so on a regional basis but "they have neither coalesced into a generally accepted paradigm nor served to guide collection of data on a wider basis" (Welch 1992, 324). These cases have been selected because they represent the most recent occurrences of military interventions and withdrawals worldwide. After World War II, decolonization and national independence movements occasioned an increase in the role of the military in the Developing World.

More specifically, the military is generally the strongest institution in a new state due to the former colonial powers' monetary and training assistance. More often than not, politicians would be fighting for power often with motives that contradicted those of the military. According to Koonings and Kruijt (2002), "The conduct of national affairs is too important to leave to civilians, especially in situations of crisis: collapse of governability or legitimacy of the existing regime, severe socio-economic problems and contradictions, internal conflicts or violent upheavals" (21).

Therefore, due to conflict between politicians over how to rule the state, this gives the military pretext to intervene in politics. The officers take it upon themselves to be the defender of the national interest. Subsequently this foray into politics creates conditions on the ground, which exacerbates conflict between politicians and the military thereby giving rise to internal societal actors—communists and Islamists—and their efforts to challenge the military's influence in politics. In return, the military "use nationalism" to defend the nation. Put simply, when a military uses nationalism it is using its position in the state to develop and implement an ideology to ensure the survival of the state and protect the military's interests.

However, not every individual in a state identifies primarily with a nation. Throughout the Middle East and South Asia, ethnic conflict abounds and the military, as the strongest institution, used nationalism to build the nation. Nationalism for the Algerian, Egyptian, Pakistani, and Turkish militaries is an ideology used to paper over ethnic and linguistic differences of regional groups within the state. In a sense, this constructed nationalism by the military is not used to strengthen the Algerian, Egyptian, Pakistani, and Turkish nation-state; instead, it strengthens the Algerian, Egyptian, Pakistani and Turkish praetorian state.

Therefore, the end of colonialism and the sway of powerful international hegemons' influence on politicians and the militaries of Algeria, Egypt, Pakistan, and Turkey offer compelling evidence that three conditions define civil–military relations in the Islamic world: 1) Persistant conflict between military elites and political parties or social groups; 2) Reliance on international economic and military aid; 3) Reluctance to withdraw from politics unless military interests are protected in any democratic transition. This book comparatively examines four important states in the Islamic world, to illuminate the importance militaries will continue to have in political development.

## PLAN OF THE BOOK

The influence of the military in the politics of the Islamic World, especially the Middle East and South Asia, garnered renewed attention since 9/11. As the United States is now winding down its nation-building mission in Afghanistan, understanding military intervention and withdrawal is important because democratization and nation-building cannot happen unless one addresses the failure of political institutions. Understanding how conflict between politicians and the military manifests itself in Algeria, Egypt, Pakistan, and Turkey offers insight into how we might begin to understand what factors will end the endurance of authoritarianism in the Islamic world.

From the early years of the Cold War through post-9/11 the United States and Soviet Union played an important role influencing the political development of the Middle East and South Asia. In fact, during the 1950s in the Middle East, this was known as the "Arab Cold War," which "pitted Arab nationalists against conservative, Western-backed Arab states . . . in vicious political warfare" (Lynch 2014, 368). In the 1960s and 1970s, the superpowers provided political, economic and military assistance as a "realpolitik dynamic set in as states established their internal dominance over one another" (Lynch 2014, 368). The 1980s and 1990s would see both the rise of inter-state conflict, but sectarian conflict as well, with Iraq and Iran engaged in war for the better part of the 1980s. Moreover, the rise of Islamism and Salafism in the 1990s was a direct challenge to the United States' unipolar moment. Since 9/11 and the U.S. invasion of Iraq in 2003, the increase in sectarian conflict has influenced regional politics with Iran and Saudi Arabia each striving for regional hegemony. In short, states in the region were able to use the international ideological context of the Cold War or War on Terror to seek economic and military assistance from the United States or the Soviet Union/Russia. This assistance "provides allied regimes with dual use domestic surveillance and security capabilities that could equally be used to meet domestic terrorist threats as well as to track, monitor, and punish domestic opponents" (Brynen, et al. 2012, 276).

This study uses Alexander George's controlled comparative case study method. This method is a qualitative one that employs a structured focused comparison in which cases are selected that are relevant to the data requirements and research objectives of the study in question. According to George and his co-author Andrew Bennett, there are four strong advantages of case methods that make them valuable and particularly useful for theory development: "Their potential for achieving high conceptual validity; their strong procedures for fostering new hypotheses; their value as a useful means to closely examine the hypothesized role of causal mechanisms in the context of individual cases; and their capacity for addressing causal complexity" (19).

In addition, general questions are asked of each case as a way "of standardizing data requirements so that comparable data will be obtained from each case" (George and Bennett 2004, 86). Questions are asked in a general nature to be relevant across all cases that are selected. Additionally, this method does not prevent investigation of individual characteristics of one or more characteristics, nor does it prevent the exploration of idiosyncratic features of specific cases that may be relevant for theory development or future research (George and Bennett 2004, 86). Put differently, this method allows for a study useful for students and policymakers alike to see the development of conflict in civil–military relations in the Muslim world.

Chapters 2 through 5 are the case studies of Algeria, Egypt, Pakistan, and Turkey, respectively. There are a number of similarities and differences across these four dynamic cases. Accordingly, these cases are an examination of the extent conflict is present in the civil–military relationships throughout each state's history based on the levels of military corporatism, military institutional interest, military elite interests, and bureaucratic conflict between military and civilians. The cases will be organized around the following themes: history, the military establishment, civil–military relations, and regional and international relations.

These cases offer the most recent examples of military intervention and withdrawal from politics worldwide. In addition to an examination of secondary sources on civil–military relations and the politics of each of the respective case study countries, primary sources such as speeches, party manifestos, country constitutions were consulted to determine elite and institutional interests under examination. The sensitive nature of an army's internal politics in this region makes interviews infeasible, but with the Internet there's an increasing availability of material on the militaries of the region, and since 2011 especially, interviews conducted with prominent military and political elites.

Therefore, taking the cases of Algeria, Egypt, Pakistan, and Turkey as a whole, this book will show that within the Islamic world one can argue that militaries intervene in politics because of the conflict that is present between political elites and the military plus the reliance on foreign economic and military assistance from the United States or the Soviet Union/ Russia. Alternatively, the military will withdraw from politics only when military interests are protected. In short, the international environment has influenced the political environment of these states and influenced the generals' decision making regarding whether to intervene and their perceptions of politicians', as well as politicians' and society's, views of the military.

Chapter 6 ties everything together and highlights which causal factors predominate the civil–military relationships in the Islamic World necessitating "men on horseback" coming to the aid of the nation and stunting democratization. Finally, policy recommendations will be provided to afford the reader a better understanding of the importance of the military as an institutional explanation for enduring authoritarianism in the Middle East and South Asia and how democratization efforts in Indonesia, the largest Muslim democracy, could provide lessons learned for the Middle East regarding how to establish civil–military relations in an Islamic democracy.

# TWO

## Algeria

Algeria is a state with a history marred by violence. From 1954 to 1962, Algerians waged their War of Independence against French colonialism. The war became a defining period in the development of the Algerian state. Algerians coalesced around the *Front Liberation Nationale* (FLN), or National Liberation Front, as the vanguard of the Algerian nationalist movement. The FLN was not one unitary organization, but more of an umbrella organization for a number of different factions or clans. As part of the FLN, the *Armée de Liberation Nationale* (ALN) played a dominating role in Algerian politics as the only effective powerbroker at independence.

During the authoritarian regime of Colonel Houari Boumedienne from 1965 to 1978, the ALN was a "people's army" that was "depoliticized" in 1988 with the introduction of a multi-party system. At this point, multiple factions formed political parties to run in democratic elections. After the Islamic Salvation Front (FIS) won the first round of local elections, the ALN stepped in to cancel the second round of elections to prevent an Islamist party from coming to power. This military coup may have prevented an Islamist party from coming to power, but it sparked a civil war claiming hundreds of thousands of lives during the 1990s.

In the years after the civil war, the state of Algeria would hold elections but the participants and outcome would be influenced by the military. Moreover, the economy has been dependent on oil revenues and, at times, foreign aid from the Soviet Union and the United States. Below, this chapter will examine the domestic and international influences that affected the conflicts between the various factions and clans, political parties and the ALN. Algerian civil–military relations are based on populism; however, a democratic civil–military relations will be difficult to

achieve due to the secular versus Islamist conflict which engenders a
military-civil relationship since the Algerian civil war.

## HISTORY

Algeria, a French colony from 1830 to 1962, is a state of approximately
thirty-five million people with a majority Arab population and minority
Berber population. Approximately 75 percent of the population speaks
Arabic with Berber spoken in the mountains (Addi 2014, 429). Given
Algeria's status as a colony, French was also spoken and, today, government business is conducted in both Arabic and French. Algeria's relationship with France would last for 132 years and serve "as a reference point
to all citizens of the modern republic: nationalists and Islamists, modern-
ists and traditionalists, Arabs and Berbers. The history, or perhaps more
often, the mythology, of this period underpins the consciousness to shape
the unconscious of the country's vast youth" (Stone 1997, 30). Therefore,
before further discussing French influence in Algeria, it is important that
we ask: Who are Algerians?

There are two dominant elements of Algerian society: Islam and the
tribe. Islam has been a part of Algeria since the seventh century. Although there are tiny Christian and Jewish communities in Algiers and
other northern cities, nearly all Algerians are Muslims. Also, Algeria is a
youthful society, since 75 percent of the population is under the age of
thirty (Stone 1997, 7). According to Martin Stone (1997), "Under the rule
of the Arabs, the local Berber kingdoms and later the Turks, the inhabi-
tants of what is now Algeria fused their own pre-Islamic beliefs with the
mainstream Sunni rite to create their own particular brand of Islam" (12).
At independence, Islam's influence was relatively weak in towns and
cities but more widespread in the countryside. With the mass migration
of the rural populations in the 1960s and 1970s to the cities, tensions
developed between the conservative, poorer newcomers and the liberal
elite. Simultaneously, the government sought to use Islam for its own
purposes to mobilize the population against its enemies. This effectively
helped spur the rise of political Islam in the 1980s and 1990s.

The next important element of Algerian identity is the tribe. In the
Arab areas the primary unit was the *ayla* (family), whose members descended through male landowners. Furthermore, clans "are a collection
of lineages descended from an even more remote common ancestor; clans
joined together to form tribes based on common . . . ancestors or for their
mutual benefit" (Stone 1997, 14). Prior to independence, tribes operated
independently but during times of war, invasion, or threat did not hesitate to form larger confederations. However, after independence, the traditional dynamic of kin vs. non-kin was given up in favor of promoting a
common predicament—in this case, the revolution. New tribes and clans

continued to emerge, be it the Berbers, Kabyle, or the senior military elite. Interestingly, these senior military elite used the revolutionary war to rally the public to their cause of building a strong Algerian state free of the French. Consequently, William Zartman (1973) argues:

> Those who participated in the war expected things to be better after it was over: in a typically ambiguous set of feelings, they expected to be rid of the disruptive and humiliating foreigner in order to return to their life undisturbed but also in order to benefit from social change and economic improvement. In addition they expected an immediate inheritance of the visible goods of modern life in Algeria and accession to the newly vacated positions of power, prestige, and employment (211).

In other words, modern Algeria was founded through populism that was evident across the Developing World during the colonial era.

Due to Algeria's early history as an integral part of France, the aforementioned populism developed into three separate strands of Algerian nationalism: a religious movement founded by Sheikh Abdulhamid Ben Badis, the revolutionaries founded by Messali Hadj, and the liberals of Ferhat Abbas. The religious movement is associated with a group known as the Association des Ulema. Founded by Ben Badis, the movement believed that Algeria must return to Islam to "regenerate" (Horne 2006, 38). Ben Badis and the Ulema resembled the Wahabi sect of Islam and were devout Muslims who believed in the power of Islam to transform society.

Consequently, Messali Hadj and his "revolutionaries" stepped in to provide an alternative to the Ulema. Messali became president of a political group of Algerian workers called the Etoile Nord-Africaine, which "came to have a proletarian character superimposed over its nationalist and religious doctrines" (Horne 2006, 39). In effect, Messali was one of the first to bring in popular socialism to the revolutionary movement that would later influence the FLN and the socialist policies of the Ben Bella regime.

Abbas and the liberals believed assimilation into the French political community in Algeria would result in social and economic equality from the French. While complete independence may not have been envisioned, in effect, the policy of assimilation was a point of contention that historian John Ruedy (1992) has called a watershed in the nation's history. For the first time "lower middle-class, working-class, and even poor rurual Algerians joined alongside the elites for the first time in challenging the status quo" (139).

The conflicts between these three movements influenced the development of modern Algeria. Factionalism developed due to each nationalist movement's competing visions for postcolonial state. The Blum-Viollette Plan was created by France to offer French citizenship with full political

equality to certain classes of the Muslim elite, including university gradu-
ates, elected officials, army officers, and professionals, which totaled approximately twenty-five thousand Algerians (Toth 1994, 38). This attempt
at unity would be short lived because although Abbas and Badis welcomed the Blum-Viollette Plan, Messali attacked the Plan as "'a new
instrument of colonialism aimed at dividing the Algerian people, by usu-
al French methods of separating the elite from the masses'" (Horne 2006,
41). The *Pied Noirs* took exception to the Blum-Viollette Plan, because
these French citizens of Algeria would be subject to living in a Muslim-
majority state (Toth 1994, 39).

Finally, disillusioned by the failure of the Blum-Viollette Plan, Abbas
became convinced that autonomy was preferable to assimilation for Algerian Muslims. As Quandt (1969) notes, "This conclusion was the result
of the observation that the [*pied niors*] . . . in Algeria could and would
prevent liberal reforms emanating from Paris and that Paris itself might
not be receptive to Muslim demands, particularly if undemocratic forces
governed in France" (41). By World War II, cooperation among the "Muslim Congress" broke apart and the Algerian nationalist movement truly
began as the revolutionaries and liberals would join forces to create the
"Friends of the Manifesto and Liberty" or AML. The AML were supported by the reformist ulama and Messali loyalists of the *Parti du Peuple
Algérien* (PPA), garnering support from the middle classes, but were condemned by assimilationists and communists who were supported by the
working classes (Ruedy 1992, 148).

Consequently, riots broke out among AML and PPA supporters as
they marked Victory in Europe Day. The most noteworthy acts of violence occurred in Sétif and Guelma as news of the violence spread
throughout the countryside, *pied noir* villages were attacked and open
insurrection eventually killed as many as fifteen thousand Muslims by
the time violence was over (Stone 1997, 35). The French government, in
response to the violence, called in ten thousand troops to assist the police
in trying to quell the violence. Bombings of Arab and Kabyle villages
ensued, and after a week, the worst of the insurrection had subsided.

Moreover, by the end of the year, 5,560 Muslims were arrested, including Abbas (Ruedy 1992, 149). Effectively, the Sétif riots are considered by many (Ruedy 1992; Stone 1997; Stora 2000; Horne 2006) to mark
the real beginning of the Algerian nationalist movement as "the pauper-
ized masses of the countryside, the principal victims of the colonial system, had linked up for meaningful action with a nationalist movement
that urban Algerians had created and which had been spreading in the
cities for fifteen years" (Ruedy 1992, 150). Therefore, the nationalists were
more determined than ever to push for separation. From the late 1940s to
1954, they would get their chance.

After the violence in Sétif, the AML was disbanded and after his release from prison Abbas created a new party, the Democratic Union of

the Algerian Manifesto (UDMA), while Messali created the Movement for the Triumph of Democratic Liberties (MTLD). The former called for "a free, secular, and republican Algeria loosely federated with France" while the latter was "committed to unequivocal independence" (Toth 1994, 42). Interestingly, the MTLD was supported by a clandestine organization known as the Organisation speciale (OS) and was initially headed by Hocine Aït Ahmed and later Ahmed Ben Bella. During this period, the French used various strategies to prevent the UDMA and the MTLD from winning elections thereby contributing to increasing tensions (Stone 1997, 36). One such tension occurred between the Berbers led by Ait Ahmed and Messali's MTLD. The Berbers complained the Messali and the MTLD were increasingly using too much Islamic rhetoric instead of being more secular and Marxist (Ruedy 1992, 154).

Therefore, during the spring of 1954, the factionalism described above influenced the creation of a "third force" between the two factions. This third force was the Comite Revolutionnaire d'Unite et d'Action (CRUA) and was created by five former MTLD members: Mohamed Boudiaf, Mohamed Larbi Ben M'Hidi, Moustafa Ben Boulaid, Mourad Didouche and Rabah Bitat with Krim Belkacem, Ben Bella, Mohamed Khider and Aït Ahmed joining during the next two years (Stone 1997, 36). Between March and October 1954 the CRUA created plans for the rebellion against French Rule when it became clear that the MTLD was irretrievably split (Ruedy 1992). In November 1954, the CRUA changed its name to the Front de Liberation Nationale (FLN), the political wing of the Armée de Liberation Nationale (ALN), and launched the revolution leading to Algeria's independence from the French.

The FLN and ALN drew their support from peasants and the urban poor and stated that the goal of the revolution was independence, equality, and a fair distribution of wealth. The War of Independence—or as Algerians call it, the Revolution—was a bloody period in Algerian history with attacks perpetrated throughout Algeria against military installations, police departments, warehouses, communication facilities, and public utilities. The FLN, as the vanguard of the revolution, called for Algerian Muslims in a national struggle for "'the restoration of the Algerian state, sovereign, democratic, and social, within the framework of the principles of Islam'" (Toth 1994, 44). The Algerians' war of independence was not merely a fight between colonizer and the colonized. In fact, one could argue there were multiple conflicts—between the *pied noirs* and Muslims, as well as internecine rivalries between Algerian Muslims.

The FLN leadership recruited broadly throughout Algerian society. According to Quandt (1998), "To keep the FLN together as a broad front, the leaders kept the focus on the one thing they agreed upon—Algeria's independence within an Arab/Islamic framework. But it was nationalism rather than any other ideology that inspired the movement" (19). The FLN operated under collective leadership and consisted of numerous committees, cliques and clans. Externally the FLN was led by Ben Bella, Khider, and Ait Ahmed in Cairo and were assisted nominally by Gamel Abdel Nasser. The external leadership worked to gain foreign support and acquire arms, supplies and money for the war effort. Internally, the FLN established a leadership committee of six led by Mohamed Boudiaf, who established six military regions, known as *wilaya*. Each *wilaya* was headed by a colonel of the ALN and supported by three assistants—political affairs, logistics, and public affairs (Ruedy 1992, 158–59).

The war's first shots were fired on November 1, 1954, and all of northern Algeria was engulfed in violence by the end of 1956. The ALN and its clandestine terrorist groups "engaged in direct attacks against the French army and security forces as well as assassinations, economic sabotage and intimidation of the FLN's opponents within both the Muslim and European opponents" (Stone 1997, 37). The FLN claimed twelve thousand Muslims perished "in an orgy of bloodletting by the armed forces and police, as well as [*pied noir*] gangs" (Toth 1994, 46). By 1956, the ALN "had evolved into a well-disciplined force of some 20,000 armed men with a well-developed terrorist capability" (Stone 1997, 37).

Also, the FLN had consolidated its power co-opting all of the nationalist movements except for one—Messali Hadj. Messali's Mouvement Nationale Algerien (MNA), the successor to the MTLD, was active among Algerian immigrants in France and in the Kabilya engaging in street battles with FLN supporters (Stone 1997, 37). The MNA established a five hundred-person militia to try and counter the FLN; however, because of defeats received at the hands of the FLN and French success in coopting smaller factions, the MNA ceased to be a major threat to the FLN (Ruedy 1992, 146). Effectively, Quandt (1998) argues, "[T]he most famous figure of modern Algerian nationalism at the time of the revolution was shunted aside, treated as a traitor, and his followers were systematically eliminated" (19).

Moreover, the rise in violence around Algeria was not limited to just the FLN. Throughout 1956 and 1957, the FLN was successful in a number of terrorist attacks against French government and *pied noir* interests. The French government under Soustelle's successor, Governor General Robert Lacoste, dissolved the Algerian Assembly and ruled Algeria by decree. The French responded by placing most of northern Algeria under a state of emergency. According to Stone (1997), "Repeated French initiatives to find a compromise solution foundered on the weakness of successive coalition governments in Paris and the strength of resolve of the European colonists, who stubbornly insisted that aid from abroad, particularly Arab nationalist regimes such as that of President Gamal Abdel Nasser of Egypt, was the mainstay of the FLN rebellion" (38). Consequently, the French army divided Algeria into sectors to try and reduce the amount of terrorism, but their efforts at combating the FLN were hindered by the independence of neighboring Tunisia and Morocco, where the FLN was able to maintain sanctuaries to attack into Algeria (Ruedy 1992, 165).

Despite their repeated successes, the FLN was experiencing coordination problems. These problems occurred because, as Ruedy (1992) argues, "FLN efforts on the ground were weakened by interpersonal or intergroup conflicts largely irrelevant to the national struggle; they were hampered by the bewildering turnover provoked by the terrible toll of lives; French counterinsurgency tactics were increasingly effective at isolating the wilayas from each other" (166). To overcome French tactics and improve coordination, the FLN leadership met at Soummam Valley and drafted a forty-page platform that "clarified the objectives of the revolution, formalized the military structures that had been evolving ad hoc, and gave the revolution for the first time a set of overall political institutions (Ruedy 1992, 166). The Soummam conference also established the *Counseil National de la revolution Algerienne* (CNRA), which would become Algeria's first sovereign parliament. The conference reaffirmed the principles of collegial decision-making within the FLN as well as political leadership over the military. In effect, the conference "affirmed the primacy of the internal leadership over the external, a position which was easy to take since none of the external leaders had made it to the Soummam Valley" (Ruedy 1992, 166). Another factor affecting events was the capture of Ben Bella, Ait Ahmed, Hider, Bitat and Boudiaf—five of the nine historic chiefs of the FLN and members of the outside leadership—who were imprisoned in France for the remainder of the war (Ruedy 1992, 38).

At this point, the French felt they were gaining an upper hand in combating the FLN. Accordingly, the internal leadership sought to demonstrate its leadership over the Algerian population by calling for an eight-day general strike and to carry the battle from the countryside to major urban centers through the use of terrorism. The most famous outcome of this policy was the Battle of Algiers in September 1956. As is so accurately depicted in Gino Pontecorvo's stunning film, *The Battle of Algiers* (1967), Saadi Yacef, the commander of the Autonomous Algiers region orchestrated bombings and killings from his hideout in the Casbah section of Algiers aimed at the *pied noir* population of the city. In fact, the attacks occurred until the spring of 1957 claiming a number of innocent civilians (Ruedy 1992, 168). The French responded with a military campaign to isolate the Muslim populations and their neighborhoods.

Both the FLN and the French suffered setbacks from the Battle of Algiers. The French had effectively repressed the FLN's terror campaign within Algiers and "[t]he overwhelming, multifaceted repression further disrupted already fragile communications and command structures" (Ruedy 1992, 169). In part, the French rounded up Algerians by the thousands into settlement camps and secured the borders with neighboring Tunisia and Morocco to cut off communication between leadership who had fled the country and those revolutionaries who were still in the country. The internal leadership was criticized for calling a general strike that failed and launching a campaign of urban terrorism that strayed from the revolutionary aim of appealing to the rural population (Horne 2006, 223–24; Ruedy 1992, 169). The criticism was appearing from a number of different sources within the FLN leadership; namely, loyalists to Ben Bella, led by Ramdane Abane, the leader of the internals, and a rising class of military men known as "the colonels," led by Abdelhafid Boussouf, "who had gradually taken over direction of the war as death, imprisonment, or demonstrated incompetence thinned the ranks of the original revolutionaries" (Ruedy 1992, 170). Abane was firmly opposed to the military dominating a political organization and publicly attacked Boussouf, stating that he and the military were robots. (Horne 2006, 225–26).

The wilayas had become isolated since the Battle of Algiers from the CCE. Consequently, each wilaya developed its own command style and found itself with greater autonomy and power with the lack of directives from the CCE (Horne 2006, 226). The most notable example being Wilaya 5 under Boussouf and his assistant Boumediene, who established a closely-knit, disciplined military machine. As Horne (2006) explains, Boussouf "was held by his subordinates in considerable awe, had imposed a strong stamp of his own personality on Wilaya 5 and would henceforth assume a central role in the FLN leadership" (225).

A meeting of the CNRA was held in Cairo in July 1957, and reversed the Soummam Valley decisions, thereby expanding the CCE (*Comité de coordination et d'exécution*, or executive cabinet) which became dominated by the five wilaya colonels. Abane continued to make disparaging comments against the colonels, stating: "'You are creating a power based on the army. The maquis is one thing, politics is another and it is not conducted either by illiterates or ignoramuses!'" (Horne 2006, 227). The conflict between Abane and the colonels came to a head with the colonels orchestrating Abane's strangulation in Morocco in December 1957 (Horne 2006, 227–30). Therefore, with the death of Abane, the colonels became the undisputed power brokers in the FLN.

By spring 1958, the FLN's leadership quarrels and French counterterrorist measures had left the FLN at a disadvantage at this point in the war. According to Ruedy, "[T]he operational balance of the war more and more favored the colonialists by the spring of 1958. Urban terrorism had been quelled, operational successes in the interior countryside were few and small, and the war on the frontiers had stagnated." It was at this point, however, that "France's interest in a system equitable enough to insure the long-term loyalty of the Algerian Muslims, had, for more than a century, been overridden by that of settlers determined to guarantee their own monopoly of political and economic power" (Ruedy 1992, 170). In other words, French citizens were beginning to question whether it was worth the money, materiel, and lives to support the *pied noirs*, whose overall interests were beginning to diverge from France. Thus, the army and *pied noirs* pressured the French government, specifically French President René Coty to name de Gaulle as prime minister of a government of national unity. On June 1, 1958, de Gaulle's acceptance of an invitation by President Coty to form a government was approved by parliament and de Gaulle was able to rule by decree for six months (Ruedy 1992, 172).

Upon taking office, DeGaulle established the Fifth Republic and proposed that Algeria would be a partner with, rather than an integral part, of the Fifth Republic (Stone 1997, 39). De Gaulle's proposals included "measures for accelerating Algerian integration into France by granting universal adult suffrage, instituting a single electoral college, and assuring that a minimum of two-thirds of Algerian representatives in the Parliament of the Fifth Republic would be Muslims" (Ruedy 1992, 173). In response, the CNRA implemented a three-part offensive to counteract DeGaulle's efforts. First, the revolution was brought to France to pressure the émigré community. Second, Ben Khedda appealed to China for military arms to use "East-West rivalries to Algerian advantage" and finally, a provisional government, the *Gouvernement Provisoire de la République Algérienne*, or GPRA, was organized in Tunis under Ferhat Abbas as president and Ben Bella as vice-president (Ruedy 1992, 173). At this point, the military began to exert its influence as early as 1958, several years prior to independence.

The *pied noir* uprisings, as well as continued violence by the FLN, resulted in de Gaulle opening secret negotiations with the FLN in January 1961 "intended to provide a new mandate to carry through his program of self-determination" (Stone 1997, 39). Despite repeated terrorist attacks by the OAS and guerrilla warfare by the FLN, France and the GPRA met in Evian, France. After a number of meetings in 1961, a cease-fire was agreed to between the France and the FLN known as the Evian Accords. Ninety-one percent of French citizens approved the Evian Accords officially ending 130 years of French rule and offering *pied noirs* equal legal protection with Algerians over a three-year period (Stone 1997, 40). During the spring of 1962, said attacks were a "last desperate attempt to prevent the inevitable by goading the FLN to break the cease-fire", but ultimately failed due to a "combination of an efficient police response and internal divisions within the the OAS" (Stone 1997, 40). The violence, consequently, sent large numbers of Europeans and *pied noirs* fleeing back to France.

On July 1, 1962, Algerians voted nearly unanimously for independence and on July 3, de Gaulle pronounced Algeria an independent country. Nevertheless, eight years of conflict had produced factionalism within the FLN between the interior and exterior leadership that would come to define the development of post-war Algeria. The nationalists who led the revolution against the French were all vying for a share of political power, but without a mechanism for apportioning these claims, conflict between the internal and external leadership would continue into the early years of independent Algeria (Ruedy 1992, 181).

The conflict for power within the FLN involved a number of groups and individuals: The five "historic chiefs" who had been released from detention in France on the day that the Evian Accord was signed; the provisional government (GPRA) under Benyoucef Ben Khedda; moderate Muslim politicians; the military, itself divided between "internals" and "externals"; the commanders of the Wilayas; the trade unions; and leaders of France-based Algerian Muslims (Stone 1997, 43–44). The most important conflict, however, was between the GPRA and the military leaders of Wilayas II, III, and IV. In effect, these personality conflicts were allowing the external ALN to become the most cohesive institution in the country. The ALN's ability to accomplish this was due in no small part to the work of Boumedienne.

Boumedienne, a member of the external ALN, used "ruthless efficiency" to reorganize the ALN beginning in late 1960 (Horne 2006, 412). His priority "was to keep the military apparatus intact, and Boumedienne saw it as his longer-term function to create a well-equipped, disciplined and trustworthy army with which any future Algerian government of the FLN could rule an independent Algeria, against all rivals, in the difficult days that might lie ahead" (Horne 2006, 414).

His first act was to reign in the lawlessness that was occurring in various commands of the external ALN. In Tunisia, because of the boredom of inactivity certain groups of soldiers would mug local Tunisians. Boumedienne rounded up the twenty officers and soldiers and had them executed in front of the troops (Horne 2006, 412). Also, there was an insurrection of one hundred troops in the Moroccan based ALN that was supported by the Moroccan army, which Boumedienne would ultimately put down. According to Horne (2006), "To eradicate permanently this kind of indiscipline, Boumedienne introduced his own tough deputies . . . to weld the whole army closely under his personal control" (412). The ALN General Staff was remodeled along the lines of the French system to include four bureaus, which would include defectors from the French army, to oversee training programs as new weapons from the Communist bloc began to arrive. As part of this training program, Boumedienne included political indoctrination. He also worked to rebuild the interior ALN, especially in Algiers, by ordering them "to maintain a low profile; to refuse combat in the face of continuing French [sweeps]; to break up and dissipate in small groups and, if necessary, take refuge in another Wilaya far from the current offensive" (Horne 2006, 413). Essentially, Boumedienne wanted to remind his fellow countrymen, as well as the international community, that the FLN was still around despite setbacks received at the hands of the French military. With a strengthened ALN, Boumedienne believed that the FLN would be able to rule and counter any rivals that lay ahead in an independent Algeria.

Boumedienne had an ally in this endeavor in Ben Bella. Of all the groups in conflict mentioned, Ben Bella was an "historic chief" of the FLN and the most prominent, mainly due to his arrest during the early years of the war. Consequently, he was able to parlay this advantage through the organization of a political bureau to counter the GPRA. The Political Bureau comprised the five historical chiefs, one wilaya leader, and only one member of the GPRA and was created in Tripoli, Libya to outmaneuver the GPRA (Stone 1997, 44). The GPRA was established after independence in Tizi Ouzou, the capital of Kabylia, which Stone argues was a result of the Kabyle origins of the executive members. Ben Khedda "then attempted to impose his authority over the powerful ALN by dismissing . . . Boumedienne" (Stone 1997, 44). Accordingly, Boumedienne threw his support behind Ben Bella's Tlemcen clan and supported Ben Bella's candidacy over Ben Khedda's. Joining Boumedienne in support of Ben Bella was Boumedienne's Oujda clan, Ferhat Abbas, who was President of the National Assembly, and Mohamed Khider, the Secretary General of the Political Bureau (Ruedy 1992, 198).

The main contention in the struggle for power occurred over the drafting of a constitution, the creation of political institutions, and defining the powers of government, assembly, and party (Ruedy 1992, 198). Ruedy (1992), argues the FLN as a party "separate from the wartime military and bureaucratic apparatus scarcely existed; institutionally, in 1962, it was the five-man Political Bureau" (198). Ben Bella, therefore, ruled by decree and was able to strengthen his power base; in part, his ability to do so was the result of an alliance made with Boumedienne in 1962 (Addi 2014, 429).

Ben Bella would face repeated resistance from internal wilaya commanders of wilayas II, III, and IV. Their opposition concerned the fact that the externals would be charged with transforming the ALN into the *Armée Nationale Populaire* (ANP) "claiming that the plan contravened the spirit of the revolution" (Stone 1997, 44). Stone (1997) notes: "'Internal' military commanders resented Boumedienne's 'Army of the Exterior' for failing to assist them during the war and were anxious to preserve their own authority and privileges that they had established during the previous seven years" (44–45). The Political Bureau attempted repeatedly to negotiate with the internal commanders to no avail. On August 30, 1962, negotiations between the Bureau and commanders broke down and the Bureau ordered the ALN to move on Algiers from Oran. Algeria was on the precipice of civil war. Various wilayas worked to assure their autonomy, especially Wilayas III and IV who maintained their own councils, until the Political Bureau ordered the ALN and the troops of Wilayas I, II, V, and VI to march on Algiers (Stora 2001, 127).

Consequently, with the interior military's defeat, the Political Bureau drew up a new list of candidates for the National Assembly election and Ben Bella ordered the removal of one-third of the candidates (fifty-nine names), including Ben Khedda (Stora 2001, 128). The Political Bureau's list of candidates won a "suspicious" 99 percent of the vote with members of the Tlemcen coalition dividing power among themselves (Stone 1997, 45; Stora 2001, 128). Ben Bella became head of government with Khider becoming secretary general of the political bureau, Boumedienne defense minister and Abbas becoming president of the National Assembly. After the election, Ben Bella, Boumedienne and Khider formed a triumvirate of the army, the party, and government to run Algeria. However, "Ben Bella's ambitions and authoritarian tendencies wee to lead the triumvirate to unravel and provoke increasing discontent among Algerians" (Toth 1994, 57). In short, Ben Bella's establishment of a one-party state and state-controlled economy, known as self-management, engendered opposition and put his government on slippery footing.

Ben Bella believed that the establishment of a presidential regime was the most effective way of ensuring his authority, marginalizing his opponents, and guaranteeing the adoption of self-management. A new constitution was drawn up under FLN supervision and Ben Bella was confirmed as the party's choice to lead the country for a five-year term (Stone 1997, 46). The new constitution gave Ben Bella the powers of chief of state, head of government and supreme commander of the armed forces. His main supporters were the Political Bureau, the 'Tlemcen Group (Boumedienne, Khider and Abbas) and the ANP, particularly the 'Oujda clan'. Ben Bella's coalition was in a fragile state, as he was supported by those with their own ambitions (Stone 1997, 46).

As uprisings were occurring in the early years of the independent Algeria, Boumedienne had no qualms about sending the army to crush when he felt they posed a threat to the state (Toth 1994, 59–60). While the ANP was fighting the insurgents, Ben Bella sought to purge the FLN and the assembly of his opponents. However, when Ben Bella attempted to coopt allies from among some of the same regionalists whom the army had been called out to suppress, tensions increased between Boumedienne and Ben Bella (Stone 1997, 48–49). By late 1964, Ben Bella's regime consisted of himself and a few supporters. According to Stone (1997), "This centralization of power in the hands of such a small group of people and the lack of any viable political base left Ben Bella dangerously exposed, particularly to the single faction over which he had so far been unable to assume control—the general staff" (49).

Accordingly, Ben Bella sought to further consolidate his power by turning his attention toward Boumedienne's Oujda clan. First, Ben Bella appointed a loyalist, Tahar Zbiri as chief of staff of the ANP. Next, in April 1965, Ben Bella issued orders to local police to report directly to him rather than through normal channels in the Ministry of Interior. The minister, Ahmed Medeghri, one of Boumediene's closest associates in the Oujda Group, resigned his portfolio in protest and was replaced by a Politcial Bureau loyalist. Third, Ben Bella sought to remove Abdelaziz

Bouteflika, another Boumedienne confidant, as minister of foreign affairs and was believed to be planning a direct confrontation with Boumedienne to force his ouster (Toth 1994, 60; Stone 1997, 49–50). The final straw "came with leaks that Ben Bella planned to revive Kabyle support for the President against Boumedienne by replacing Bouteflika with the imprisoned Ait Ahmed" (Stone 1997, 50). On June 19, 1965, Boumedienne deposed Ben Bella in a swift and bloodless military *coup d'etat.*

Boumedienne described the 1965 coup as "a 'historic rectification' of the Algerian War of Independence" (Toth 1994, 60). Boumedienne dissolved the National Assembly, suspended the 1963 constitution, disbanded the militia and abolished the Political Bureau which he considered an instrument of Ben Bella's personal rule. Until a new constitution was adopted, political power resided in the Council of the Revolution, "a predominantly military body intended to foster cooperation among various factions in the army and the party" (Toth 1994, 60). The council's original twenty-six members included former internal military leaders, former Political Bureau members, and senior officers of the ANP closely associated with Boumedienne in the coup. Boumedienne was declared President of the council and was charged with forming a new government. According to Ottaway and Ottaway (1970), "The composition of the council suggested that he had finally succeeded in reconciling the wilaya leaders and the officers of the ANP. It also suggested that he had won over two of the most prominent figures in the Ben Bella government, Mahsas and Boumaza, and thus that there might be some continuity in the country's socialist policies, as the council promised" (193). Furthermore, the council was expected to exercise collegial responsibility for overseeing the activities of the new government with a largely civilian Council of Ministers, or cabinet, appointed by Boumedienne. The cabinet was inclusive and shared some functions with the Council of the Revolution—an Islamic leader, technical experts, FLN regulars, as well as others representing a broad range of Algerian political and institutional life (Toth 1994, 60).

Boumedienne was an ardent nationalist, deeply influenced by Islamic values, and he was reportedly one of the few prominent Algerian leaders who expressed himself better in Arabic than in French. Accordingly, the use of French was minimized and the use of Modern Standard Arabic encouraged. Ottaway and Ottaway (1970) argue, "Boumedienne's opposition to Ben Bella's policies was veiled behind a pseudo-religious argument over the compatibility of Islam and Marxist socialism" (179). He seized control of the country not to initiate military rule, but to protect the interests of the army, which he felt were threatened by Ben Bella. Boumedienne's use of religion "assumed great importance during the preparations for the party congress, when the Boumedienne faction objected to the strongly Marxist orientation of the party's new ideological charter, insisting that Islam be declared the country's fundamental doctrine" (Ottaway and Ottaway 1970, 179). However, the dissension between Boumedienne and Ben Bella was not based primarily on ideological differences. Boumedienne "was above all concerned about Ben Bella's rapprochement with the UGTA and the Algerian Communists because he feared that with the help of these new allies the president would eventually oust him" (Ottaway and Ottaway 1970, 180).

Boumedienne's position as head of government and of state was not secure initially, partly because of his lack of a significant power base outside of the armed forces. This situation may have accounted for his deference to collegial rule as a means of reconciling competing factions (Toth 1994, 60). One major program continued by Boumedienne was the Arabization program established under Ben Bella. The purpose of this program was to fully transform a Maghrebi-European society into a fully Arab society. Boumedienne's policies have been called "Arab-Islamic socialism" or "Boumediennism" and are "a synthesis of diverse political, social and cultural influences and ideologies ranging from the teachings of Islam to the nationalisms of the *mudjahidine* [sic] and the Arab east, and the socialism and Marxism of Algerian intellectuals educated in France and later in the Soviet bloc" (Stone 1997, 53).

The policies to garner the most attention were both political and developmental. The first changes made were offered to deliver constitutional government and establish public participation in political life. The 1963 constitution was discarded and work began on a National Charter (a process that would ultimately not be completed until 1976). Boumedienne's vision was "one of political institutions rebuilt through a systematic process of political education at the base supervised from above" (Ruedy 1992, 209). Accordingly, elections were held for the communal assemblies (*assemblees populaires communales-APCs*) in 1967 and the wilaya assemblies (*assemblees populaires des wilayat-APWs*) in 1969. Although their purpose was to implement decisions from above and to provide an avenue for political advancement at the local level, the members of these assemblies were members of and approved by the FLN (Stone 1997, 52).

Second, Boumedienne's Arabization program sought to streamline and homogonize the population to create a state "based on the interplay between the rulers and the ruled, where political education and mobilization were to be channeled from the base upwards" (Stone 1997, 54). However, in practice, Boumedienne's policy created an increasingly influential class of bureaucrats and technocrats. Moreover, due to the haphazard and ineffective implementation of the program, two tiers of educated Algerians developed, one educated in Arabic, the other in French. The result was the predominance of the French-speaking middle class, as industry and commerce continued to operate mostly in French with Arabic speakers denied jobs (Stone 1997, 53–54). Despite state rhetoric, the state "concentrated more on building itself and laying the foundations of a modern industrialized economy than effectively developing the country at large, and the ordinary Algerian was largely denied access to the decision-making process" (Stone 1997, 55).

Additionally, Ruedy (1992) notes, "With the streamlining and homogenization of the government, the growing authority of the technocracy, the bureaucratization of the party, and the harnessing of the labor, student, youth, and women's organizations, Algeria by the 1970s had become increasingly depoliticized" (209). The bureaucrats, technocrats, and military officers who made policy, Ruedy (1992) continues "were functioning in increased isolation from public opinion . . . [taking] decisions of enormous consequence, making vast commitments of human and material resources with little consultation beyond their own tight circles" (209). There was continued criticism of Boumedienne and attempted to eliminate dissension through a practice of collegiality. Their criticisms concerned his policy of self-management and the betrayal of "rigorous socialism."

Some military officers were unsettled by what they saw as a drift away from collegiality. In 1967, there was an attempted coup against Boumedienne led by Tahar Zbiri, but Boumedienne was able to put down the coup by coming to terms with other opposition leaders through cooptation by placing them into nongovernmental posts or into governmental positions without portfolio (Ruedy 1992, 208). Many opponents, at an extreme, were imprisoned and even exiled. Boumedienne's power was consolidated due to the Oujda clan's control of the army.

To this end, the military was experiencing the transformation of the ALN into the professional ANP and this continued throughout the early years of the Boumedienne regime. These early years saw the rise of professionally educated Algerian officers who had received their education in France who were not supported by clans who had taken part in the War of Independence. As a result, by the mid-1970s, "the armed forces had developed into a separate faction that perceived itself as the supreme embodiment of the spirit of the Algerian war of independence and Algerian national identity" (Stone 1997, 54). Consequently, in the 1960s and 1970s, the Algeria under Boumedienne was "a synthesis of nostalgia, revolutionary utopia, exclusive nationalism, and socialist discourse" (Addi 2014, 430).

In December 1978, Boumedienne passed away and was succeeded by Chadli Benjedid. Chadli was regarded as a moderate and was not identified with any particular faction or clan. He did have wide support in the military. In June 1980, he summoned an FLN Party Congress to examine the draft of the five-year development plan of 1980–1984. The First Five Year plan liberalized the economy and broke up unwieldly state corporations. According to Ruedy (1992), "By adopting the theme 'Towards a Better Life,' the planners and the congress signaled a new concern with agriculture, social infrastructure, and light industry, and a relaxation of the austerity theme of the Boumedienne years" (233).

Moreover, while much was made of Chadli's declaration of support for economic liberalization, in reality, Chadli's principal objective was to decentralize the system to be more responsive to capitalism and the needs of society. Corruption had become widespread in state companies, so the sixty-six public corporations were broken down into 474 smaller enterprises; nineteen huge state industries were divided into one hundred and twenty smaller ones and spread throughout the country beyond the industrial hubs of Oran, Algiers, and Constantine (Ruedy 1992, 235). Algeria limited its earnings to the production and sale of oil and gas, because its oil and gas were paid in dollars and Algerian central planners pegged the dinar at a high rate to exert pressure on the price of imports. In short, the first Five Year Plan was considered a disappointment, because Algeria's economic crisis deepened in the mid-1980s, resulting in increased unemployment, a lack of consumer goods, and shortages in cooking oil, semolina, coffee, and tea (Toth 1994). Additionally, women were waiting in lines for food, and young men milled around in frustration unable to find work. To add insult to injury, 1986 saw a huge drop in world oil prices. Dismantling Algeria's state controlled economy seemed to Chadli the only way to improve the economy. Algeria's economic problems produced protests that would come to a head in October 1988.

A series of strikes and walkout by students and workers in Algiers degenerated into rioting by thousands of young men, who destroyed government and FLN property. The violence then spread to Annaba, Blida, Oran and throughout the countryside, necessitating a state of emergency called by the government. More than five hundred people were killed and more than 3,500 were arrested. As Toth notes, "The stringent measures used to put down the riots of 'Black October' engendered a ground swell of outrage" (63). The alienation and anger of the population were fanned by the widespread perception that the government had become corrupt and aloof.

In response, Chadli dismissed senior government officials and drew up a program of political reform, which in essence, was to become a second Five-Year Plan. A new constitution, approved overwhelmingly in February 1989, "dropped the word socialist from the official description of the country; guaranteed freedoms of expression, association, and meeting; and withdrew the guarantees of women's rights that appeared in the 1976 constitution" (Toth 1994, 63). Moreover, the FLN was not mentioned and the army was discussed only in the context of national defense, reflecting a significant downgrading of its political status. Black October "permanently altered the role of the FLN and its relationship to the regime and finally demolished the myth of the military as the honorable guarantor of the revolution" (Stone 1997, 65–66).

Most notably, Chadli's reform of the constitution was the first step to establishing a multi-party democracy in Algeria. Chadli "was particularly anxious to repair his credibility which had been severely dented in the October 1988, riots, and intended his role as 'father of the nation' to be that of a powerful arbiter between its various factions" (Stone 1997, 69). The constitution allowed for the creation of "political associations," but specifically banned those based exclusively on religion, language, region, sex, and race or those advocating violence (Stone 1997, 69). In other words, these associations soon attracted a large following. Addi (2014) discusses the military reticence at accepting these liberal reforms: "[M]ilitary leaders accepted the reforms, hoping that they would ameliorate the economic situation and reinforce the regime" (434).

Opposition to the regime came from Abbassi Madani and Ali Belhadj's *Front Islamique du Salut*, or Islamic Salvation Front (FIS). Islamists in Algeria were gaining influence due to the government's inability to keep its promises regarding economic reforms. Although the constitution prohibited outright religious parties, the FIS was able to form due to the government's choice to interpret the association clause as "allowing organizations 'inspired by Islamic values'" (Stone 1997, 69). Unlike other parties, a national congress did not run the day-to-day operations of the FIS. Instead, the party was run by a Majlis Shura consisting of approximately thirty-five members and headed by a four-man executive body called the National Executive consisting of Abassi, Belhadj, Benazouz Zebda, and Hachemi Sahnouni (Willis 1997, 149). According to Michael Willis (1997), "The precise structure and organization of the FIS remained largely obscure during the first eighteen months of its political life" (149). The FIS established a top-down administrative structure. Executives of the party were established at the wilaya and communal level and were the second and third tier of leadership located just under the National Executive. These three levels dealt with issues of organization, coordination, education, social affairs, planning and programming, and information (Willis 1997, 192).

In local and provincial elections held in June 1990, the FIS handily defeated the FLN in part because most secular parties boycotted the elections. Although, Chadli also encouraged the FIS "in an effort to prevent a victory by (and thus damage his opponents within) the FLN" (Willis 1997, 157). Chadli had underestimated the popular support for the FIS, but was confident that he could prevent the FIS from threatening his power base. In fact, one of the main reasons for this optimism was Chadli's belief that "the FIS would struggle to maintain its level of popular support once it took control of the majority of local authorities it had won . . . [and] prove incapable of fulfilling the frequently ambitious promises it had made during the election campaign and would consequently suffer increasing popular disillusionment" (Willis 1997, 158). The FIS, however, won control over Local Councils in all three urban centers — Algiers, Oran, and Constantine — thereby providing relatively efficient social services by improving cost-effectiveness (Volpi 2003, 49).

The FLN and Chadli were going to do all they could to undermine the FIS. The first attempt by the FLN occurred prior to the parliamentary elections of December 1991. The FLN's response was to adopt a new electoral law that openly aided the FLN. The FLN "thought it would be a good tactical move to redraw the constituencies' boundaries so as to favor their own candidates" (Volpi 2003, 50). The new electoral law increased the number of seats in the assembly from the current 295 to 542. This drew criticism from the smaller democratic opposition parties and the FIS, because the seats were allocated disproportionately to the south of Algeria where the FLN had performed well in the 1990 local elections (Willis 1997, 172). The FIS, in turn, called a general strike, organized demonstrations, and occupied public places. While the protesters initially showed restraint against the police, sporadic gunfire broke out as the FIS spread out throughout four districts in Algiers to demonstrate "its 'strike' could paralyze the capital by asking its supporters to continue occupying all the public places in central Algiers" (Volpi 2003, 50). As violence continued to mount, the police declared that they were unable to cope with the disturbances in Algiers, thus necessitating military intervention.

The ANP would demand the resignation of the FIS leadership. President Chadli approved the intervention of the ANP "to evacuate the 'striking' FIS protesters from the centre of Algiers" (Volpi 2003, 50). As the army rolled into Algiers they were met with continued resistance by protestors and Chadli declared a "state of siege" for a period of three months on June 5, 1991, but he also asked his minister of foreign affairs, Sid Ahmed Ghozali, to form a new government of national reconciliation. Although the FIS seemed satisfied with Ghozali's appointment and his attempts to clean up the electoral law it continued to protest, leading the army to arrest Belhadj, Madani, and hundreds of others (Willis 1997, 179). Interestingly, just prior to their arrests, Belhadj and Madani negotiated concessions from the government in return for calling off the general strike and protest campaign. Consequently, as Madani would state in an interview:

> 'The talks which have taken place between us and the regime have resulted in the agreement on holding early presidential as well as legislative elections within these (next) six months, God willing. Mr. Ghozali has been appointed Prime Minister of a government which will supervise free, legitimate elections devoid of any suspicions of rigging. We tell all workers to go back to work tomorrow' (quoted in Willis 1997, 179–80).

In short, Chadli chose to postpone the elections to allow some time for a cooling-off period. Chadli hoped the extra time would allow the chance for him to raise the appeal of the FLN vis-à- vis the FIS. Although "[t]he comprehensive nature of the regime's crackdown against the FIS which went some way beyond measures needed to end Islamist agitation on the streets and the activities of the party's militant fringes, indicated that there had been a shift in official attitudes towards the FIS" (Willis 1997, 182).

One of the most important institutions of note regarding official attitudes was the ANP. The army viewed the FIS a direct challenge to the Algerian state. As Willis notes, "Largely trained abroad in secular states such as the Soviet Union and France, most of Algeria's senior military figures were essentially hostile to the ideas of Islamism, which were seen as a threat to the foundations of the Algerian state as well as to their [the army's] own positions, should it achieve political power" (Willis 1997, 183). At the time, the chief of the military, General Mustafa Chelloufi, was critical of both the FIS and of the Chadli regime's tolerance of actions leading up to the local elections of 1990. He spoke in *El Djeich*, a journal of the ANP about "the army's intention to 'defend the Constitution' against elements which 'want to exploit democracy,' statements which were rightly taken as implicit warnings to the FIS" (Willis 1997, 183). Moreover, Willis continues, "This mutual hostility persisted even following the replacement of Chelloufi with a figure, Khaled Nezzar, who was generally perceived to be far less fundamentally hostile to Islamism" (Willis 1997, 184). Similar to his predecessor, "he confirmed the army's willingness to 'respond to any organized excesses that might jeopardize the national unity of the country . . . [and] would not hesitate to intervene and to re-establish order and unity so that force remains in the hands of the law'" (Willis 1997, 184).

On December 26, 1991, the parliamentary elections garnered the FIS nearly half of the parliamentary seats in the first round—winning 188 out of 430 seats in a straight majority vote (Volpi 2003, 52). In other words, the party took nearly 44 percent of the total votes cast with no other party winning more than 10 percent of the vote, far ahead of the FLN's fifteen seats (Willis 1997, 231). At this point, Algeria looked as if it would be the first country to elect an Islamic fundamentalist regime. As a fundamentalist regime, the FIS wanted to impose shari'a law on Algerian society. The possibility of an Islamic fundamentalist regime "sent shockwaves through Algerian society," so much so that 40 percent of the electorate, approximately five million people, did not vote (Hermida 1992, 14). Essentially, "[m]ost Algerians were disillusioned after 30 years of [the] FLN's . . . . mixture of Marxist economic doctrine and nationalism [that] had left the country in a mess, with raging inflation, few jobs, and widespread poverty" (Hermida 1992, 14). Protests became widespread from women's groups, intellectuals, trade unions, and smaller parties. Despite the protests, Chadli firmly believed he could keep the FIS in check by relying on a provision in the Algerian constitution which states that the head of state has the right to reform the constitution. In effect, Chadli was considering a government of cohabitation (Willis 1997, 244; Hermida 1992, 14).

While Chadli was willing to consider sharing power with fundamentalists to keep the democratic experiment alive, some members of Chadli's cabinet, fearing a complete FIS takeover, forced the president to dissolve parliament and to resign on January 11, 1992. Leaders of the coup
included Ghozali, and generals Khaled Nezzar (minister of defense) and
Larbi Belkheir (minister of interior). The ANP "was carefully staged to
avoid the appearance of a military takeover" (Hermida 1992, 14). However, as journalist Alfred Hermida (1992) notes, "Prime Minister Ghozali
appeared on television to assure people he was in charge and not the
generals. But with tanks and heavily armored troops surrounding key
government buildings in the capital, Algiers, Ghozali was unconvincing"
(15).

After the ANP declared the elections void, the takeover leaders and
Mohamed Boudiaf formed the High Security Council (HCS) to rule the
country. The HCS is the body which officially issued an edict suspending
the second round of the parliamentary elections (Volpi 2003, 56). On
January 14, 1992, the HCS handed power over to a newly created institution called the *Haut Comite d'Etat*, or HCE. The HCE was an institution
created as the provisional government until new presidential and parliamentary elections could be held and was headed by Boudiaf, the former
leader during the War of Independence; He was assisted by four other
members, most notably, Nezzar, the Defense Minister (Volpi 2003, 57).
Having Boudiaf as leader was done "to give the new regime a semblance
of historical legitimacy. But there is little doubt that . . . Nezzar is the
strongman of the Council" (Hermida 1992, 15). Nevertheless, Nezzar was
able to build a coalition of support in the high command of the ANP
among the generals: "General 'Abd al-Malik Guenaizia, a longtime supporter who, like Nezzar, began his career in the French army; Genearal
Muhammad Lamari, commander of ground forces and leader of the faction of the army most vehemently opposed to the Islamists; General Muhammad Touati, chief of military operations, considered the army's leading intellectual for his analyses in *Al-Jaysh*, the official organ of the ANP;
General Muhammad Mediene, director of the long-geared military internal security bureau; General 'Abbas Gheziel, commander of the gendarmerie; and the head of the navy, Inspector-General 'Abd al-Majid Ta-
right" (Mortimer 1996, 22).

The generals spoke of the need to safeguard national security and
public order, but their real motivation was clear: "Having snatched power from the fundamentalists, the military-backed authorities went on the
offensive to stamp out the movement" (Hermida 1992, 15). As Willis
(1997) notes, "For many senior figures in the military, a FIS government
would spell disaster, economically and politically for the Algeria they
had pledged to defend" (245). In particular, the generals were worried
about Algeria's colossal debt of approximately $25 billion in December
1991, and stood to lose money and investment from foreign oil and gas

companies' exploitation of Algeria's oil and gas resources (Willis 1997, 245). Politically, the ANP was concerned about the possibility of both internal and external conflict. The ethnically distinct areas of Kabylia and Mzab had decisively rejected the FIS candidates in the 1990 and 1991 elections and the military senior leadershp did not want to rule out the possibility that civil war could pit Berbers versus Arabs or, even, the FIS provoking one of Algeria's neighbors (Willis 1997, 246). Most importantly for the military were fears of the survival and integrity the military and the Algerian state. Both senior and junior officers were concerned with the FIS achieving a majority in the National Assembly. Therefore, Willis (1997) argues:

> There was considerable concern amongst the senior figures in the army that once in power the Islamists would waste no time in seeking to use their new political powers to attempt to neutralize their traditional foes, and only truly powerful enemies, the general staff of the military. Such fears were also shared by more junior officers who also saw themselves as the potential targets of the rumored "popular tribunals" and who, having often had a secular and frequently foreign military training were similarly anxious for the survival of a modern and secular state (246).

In short, the ANP was highly suspicious of Chadli and believed he would negotiate with the FIS to prolong his rule in some sort of cohabitation arrangement (Willis 1997, 246). Thus, Nezzar built a coalition around supporters of the military.

In June 1992, Boudiaf was assassinated by one of his bodyguards, a member of the army's Special Forces. According to Volpi (2003), "Although the exact circumstances were never fully brought to light—an isolated act by a supporter of Islamic fundamentalists infiltrating the army, a military plot to eliminate someone with too great political ambitions, and so on—in the public eye Boudiaf appeared to be the victim of the military officers' behind-the-scenes struggles" (63–64). The military elite in the HCE, first and foremost, wanted to contain the threat posed by Islamic guerrillas. This was taken seriously due to members of the army defecting to support the Islamists (Volpi 2003, 64). In response, the military began to impose laws banning the use of religion for political purposes. As part of this policy, two FIS leaders, Madani and Belhadj, were sentenced by military tribunal to twelve years in prison. Moreover, new "anti- terrorist" laws were passed to give more coverage of actions of the security forces. Violence continued to increase across the country culminating in February 1993 with the HCE announcing it would extend the state of emergency for one more year (Volpi 2003, 64–65). In other words, the HCE wanted to postpone the democratic transition until conditions were more favorable toward their position.

Social and political protest reached its zenith from 1993 to 1998, as military repression failed to halt Islamic insurrection against political, economic, and social conditions within Algeria. This climate hastened a reshuffle of government and the military leadership. In addition, the dissolution of the FIS engendered a debate within the Islamist movement of how to counter the state. This will be discussed in more detail below. Suffice it to say, conflict between eradicators and conciliators in the ANP and radicals and moderates inside the FIS, along with the outcome of the civil war, would define the relationship between the military and political elites to this day.

After the civil war, the 1999 presidential election was a hotly contested election with eleven candidates: Bouteflika, Taleb Ibrahimi, Ait Ahmed, Hamrouche, Djaballah, Sifi, Khatib, Ghozali, Boukrouh, Hanoune and Nannah. Of the eleven candidates, Bouteflika was the unofficial candidate of the regime (Volpi 2003, 79). Ghozali, Boukrouh and Hanoune were disqualified for not receiving enough endorsements from elected representatives, while Nannah failed to provide a certificate from the National Association of Mujahidin certifying his participation in the War of Independence (Volpi 2003, 79). As would be uncovered later, Nannah's inability to meet this constitutional requirement for the Presidency was "engineered by the regime to prevent the moderate Islamic leader from joining forces with the rest of the opposition after the election" (Volpi 2003, 79). Subsequently, Bouteflika would receive the support of two-pro regime parties, the FLN and RND.

His main challenger was Ibrahimi, who was a well-known pro-Islamic candidate from a religious family; his father was the president of the Islamic reform movement prior to Algerian independence. Ibrahimi's campaign platform of "national reconciliation" and inclusion of the "ex"-FIS in the political process received support from the executive committee of the FIS abroad; however, on election day, after convening a joint meeting, all the presidential candidates withdrew their names from the ballot (Volpi 2003, 80). Consequently, protests erupted in the Kabylia region and in Algiers and Oran in support of the opposition candidates and the fraudulent election result of Bouteflika winning 70 percent of the vote with independent media reporting a turnout of 20 percent and the regime reporting a 60 percent turnout (Volpi 2003, 80). Bouteflika, with support of the military, worked behind the scenes to build a coalition with the RND, FLN and Islamic parties. However, despite their opposition to Bouteflika, the opposition had very little in common with each other and this led to an inability of projecting a unified front vis-a-vis the military.

In fact, Bouteflika has managed to stay in office now for seventeen years. He continued to receive support from the FLN and the institutional Islamist party MSP-Hamas. What explains this longevity? His longevity can be explained by the support of the military, international support, specifically in the form of economic assistance, and a continued presence of Islamist terrorism. After the 1992 coup, the deteriorating economic situation present since the mid-1980s made the securing of profits from oil and natural gas a top priority for the state and new military rulers (Volpi 2003, 110). If one recalls the earlier discussion of the socialist period of the 1970s, Algeria attempted to break away state-sponsored socialism by re-investing oil profits to ensure autonomous economic development after the rise in oil prices following the 1991 Gulf War.

Today, Algeria has witnessed a status quo ante between the military and politicians. The Algerian government describes the state as a democracy, the governments formed as democratic, the policies implemented as the will of the people, and hold regular local, provincial, and national elections (Hill 2011, 1091). Since the mid-1990s, when Algerians were permitted to vote in elections again, J. N. C. Hill (2011) argues, "[A] range of local, parliamentary, and presidential elections has been staged. Yet on every occasion the parties and candidates who have competed in these have been carefully vetted against a constantly shifting set of critieria. And in many instances the regime manipulated the vote to better ensure that it got the outcomes it wanted" (1092). Manipulation occurred in the 2002, 2007, and 2012 parliamentary elections and the 1999 and 2009 presidential election (Hill 2011, 1092). The election results "are not an index of the popularity of parties; rather, they are a way for the administration to award docile parties and punish unfaithful ones" (Addi 2014, 437).

Due to the presence of Islamist parties in varying incarnations, the Algerian presidency's authority has grown since the mid-1990s. When Zeroual revised the Algerian Constitution in 1996, several powers were transferred from parliament to the presidency: appointment of magistrates, senior military commanders and civilian officials, including the heads of the government, Council of State, security services and Bank of Algeria, as well as passing legislation by degree (Hill 2011, 1093). Under Bouteflika, the constitution was amended to remove term limits of the presidency. Therefore, with power concentrated in the hands of the few, democracy in the Maghreb "occupies a precarious position" since those who hold power seek to "preserve what they can by resisting and undermining that which they think threatens it" (Hill 2011, 1102).

Moreover, the party system was created to serve those in power. The parties will be discussed in more detail below. However, it is important to note that the parties are effectively "state apparatuses that stabilize and legitimize the administration" (Addi 2014, 438). Algeria's multiparty system provided a democratic façade, because military leaders lack trust in politicians and since the military does not want to directly lead the state or establish a dictatorship a multiparty system is established to keep the nationalist narrative of "a populist, antimilitarist, and antifascist liberation movement" alive (Addi 2014, 435).

Next, we move to a discussion of the Algerian military and the various political parties that developed since the civil war who encompass modern Algerian civil–military relations. The regional and international influences on Algerian civil–military relations will also be discussed, since the endurance of authoritarianism in Algeria was heavily influenced by international factors.

## THE MILITARY ESTABLISHMENT

The Algerian military, as mentioned previously, has been an arbiter of Algerian politics. The ALN was a people's army that fought against the French and with independence in 1962 became the ANP. The Algerian Constitution officially declares "The People" as the sovereign based on the revolution. Since independence, Algeria has had four constitutions adopted in 1963, 1976, 1989, and 1996. Although, Algerian scholar Hugh Roberts (2003) argues "The formal constitution is thus at odds with the real constitution of the Algerian state. The People is [*sic*] not sovereign; in reality, the army is. But the army is disinclined to affirm its sovereign status openly" (204). This happened because officers of the ALN played an important role in the early years of the revolution thereby leading to the primacy of the army within the FLN. Put simply, "'politics' . . . was the preserve of the military commanders and accordingly militarist—elitist and commandist—in nature, such that the question of political accountability might not even be raised, much less answered satisfactorily" would be seen as a lesser status than military activities (Roberts 2003, 205).

Additionally, many of the early leaders of the FLN had military backgrounds, thereby legitimizing the revolution and upholding anti-colonial nationalism. According to David S. Sorenson (2007), "For decades, almost every significant policy required military approval, as the military were networked into the ruling structure, a troika of state institutions: military, the party . . . and the bureauacracy" (104). In short, the army's power was exercised through four distinct political frameworks since 1965. The first was under Boumedienne's Council of the Revolution guaranteeing the army would be represented alongside the political Council of Ministers to legitimate the army's backing of Boudmedienne's rule. From 1979 to 1989, the army was required to act within the institutional framework of the FLN with military officers placed on the FLN's Central Committee and Political Bureau to ensure accountability. A third framework was introduced after Chadli introduced multiparty elections. At that point, the army was relegated to a behind-the-scenes role withdrawing its representatives to the Central Committee and Political Bureau. After 1991, the army commanders were now answerable to only themselves and invested in and manipulated the political parties and press "using them as proxies and cat's paws in the factional struggle within the army, thereby creating political chaos" (Roberts 2013, 206).

This factional struggle defined the 1990s, as Algeria was engulfed in civil war, thereby raising the power of the military since the military was battling militants throughout the country (Sorenson 2007, 104). The increased violence, coupled with the election of the FIS, led to the military coup in 1992. The military installed Boudiaf, but with his assassination in June 1992, the military took the opportunity to reexert control. Nevertheless, the multiparty system installed by Chadli was still in place and the military used it to its advantage, since [s]tate power is split between an unaccountable army and an administration that takes its legitimacy from the army" (Addi 2014, 435). Below, we examine Algerian civil–military relations from the mid-1990s to the present to illustrate why Algeria is not a democracy, but instead created a democratic façade where the military is "reluctant to directly lead the state or establish a dictatorship because they emerged from a populist, antimilitarist, and antifascist liberation movement" (Addi 2014, 435).

## CIVIL–MILITARY RELATIONS

Modern Algerian civil–military relations can be traced back to the end of the civil war and the ANP reasserting its influence over the multiparty electoral process. Elections for president and the national assembly are held every five years, but the elected bodies do not hold power, the army does. As Addi (2014) argues, "Institutional reforms were only intended to allow the political participation of a faithful, well-remunerated clientele. The prerogative of the army to designate the president is essential because he is central to decision making" (435). Consequently, conflict abounded not only between the political parties and the military, but also within the military itself. First, an examination of the political parties involved in Algerian politics is in order. Second, a discussion of inter-military conflict between eradicators and conciliators will illuminate military decision-making that leads to the ANP maintaining the bargain with politicians loyal to the military.

Political parties in Algeria are personalistic with two parties consistently "winning" elections since 1997: the FLN and the National Rally for Democracy, or RND. The FLN, as the party which helped Algerians achieve independence from the French, was charged since independence with defending government policies, although, for many years its authority depended upon the charisma of Boumediene. After the October Riots and the introduction of multiparty elections, the FLN was challenged by other parties. (Addi 2014, 443). One such party, the RND, was created in 1997 to support the president in elections and neutralize the FLN. Addi

(2014) states "Since then, the FLN and the RND have competed to defend the regime in return for various perks" (443).

Alternatively, there have been a number of opposition parties that developed, especially since the introduction of multiparty elections. The main opposition group for a number of years, as mentioned above, was the FIS. Within the FIS, there were differing opinions regarding how to deal with the state. The Moderates, headed by Abbassi Madani and Abdelkader Hachani argued that "their political participation in the ruling institutions ought to be dictated by pragmatic considerations, such as its consequences for the Islamicisation [sic] of society" (Volpi 2003, 67). While the Radicals, on the other hand, led by Ali Belhadj and Qamreddine Kerbane, "had pointed out that this political involvement was a means of ensuring that the state repressive apparatus could not be utilized against the Islamic movement" (Volpi 2003, 67). Essentially, the Radicals led by Kerbane and Mohammed Said (after the arrest of Madani and Belhadj) argued that the state would continue to repress them and this justified the development of military capabilities by the FIS. The Moderates "retorted that these tactics were counterproductive and that, besides handing over the moral high ground to the regime, they would endanger the very institutions that the party wanted to utilize for the propagation of Islamic reform" (Volpi 2003, 67). Nevertheless, repression destroyed the organizational capabilities of the FIS by severing links between the party leadership and the base. Consequently, the Islamist movement was left without a party and to fill the void more radical Islamic fundamentalist groups emerged to recruit disgruntled FIS members and sympathizers who had been repressed by police and military brutality (Volpi 2003, 67–68).

The Movement for Society and Peace (MSP) is an Islamist party that succeeded the FIS. The MSP recruits from the urban middle classes, civil servants, and teachers and would denounce projects harming the Islamic character of the regime. However, it participated in all elections and even accepted cabinet posts. Therefore, "[b]ecause its discourse is tolerant of the regime, numerous observers think of it as the third party of the administration" (Addi 2014, 444).

Other parties of note are the Front of the Socialist Forces (FFS), Worker's Party (PT), and Rally for Culture and Democracy (RCD). The FFS, founded in 1963 by Hocine Ait Ahmed, has long been in opposition to the regime since independence. The FFS "suffers from the image of a regional party" in the area surrounding Kabylia (Addi 2014, 444–45). The PT is a party formerly allied with the FFS, which challenged liberal economic reform and social situations. Similar to the PT, the RCD was formed in opposition to the FFS. The RCD's platform involves virulent anti-Islamism and champions "'republican and democratic values'" and recruits from secularist groups (Addi 2014, 445).

In sum, the FLN and RND are the main parties supportive of the regime. The ruling elite used this fact to work with one party or the other depending on whether they view the leadership of either party as hostile (Addi 2014, 436). Moreover, the Islamists and others have been co-opted if necessary to relieve pressure on the government. The reason, Addi (2014) contends, is the intentional design of the party system: "Parties are not autonomous organizations that convy particular ideas; rather, they are state apparatuses that stabilize and legitimize the administration" (438). The ability of the state to accomplish this is a result of the design of the party system and the military's ability to influence the design of the system during the later years of the civil war.

The ANP had its own internal conflict forced upon it during the later years of the civil war. More specifically, factions within the ANP known as the eradicators and conciliators were concerned with how to restore civil order in Algeria. After the death of Boudiaf, General Nezzar declined the role of president of the HCE, instead entrusting it to a civilian, 'Ali Kafi, who along with another civilian, former diplomat Ridha Malik, were charged by Nezzar with the responsibility of rebuilding Algeria's political system. In effect, "[t]he army . . . continued to make policy behind the 'veil' of the HCE after the death of Bodiaf" (Mortimer 1996, 28). On one hand, there were the officers who were aligned with General Lamari, as the leader of the "eradicators," and not willing to share power with the Islamists, instead favoring all-out repression in dealing with political Islam (Roberts 1995, 251). In July 1993, General Lamari became Chief of Staff.

On the other hand, the "conciliators" argued against repression and that a political solution based on a compromise with the Islamists was necessary (Roberts 1995, 251). This faction was led by a retired general named Liamine Zeroual, who was chosen by Nezzar to succeed him as defense minister, because his retirement in 1989 gave him a "clean" record for not being involved in decisions during the last four years (Mortimer 1996, 29). Therefore, Robert Moritmer (1996) argues, "He [Nezzar] was . . . careful to maintain a balance between options within the top military leadership, thereby maintaining his own role as the ultimate arbiter" (29).

Throughout 1993, the HCE's task was to engineer its "demise"— namely, returning the state toward some semblance of an electoral process. According to Mortimer (1996), "[T]he key question was whether or not the FIS should be associated in these talks on Algeria's future political institutions" (30). For the HCE, political parties had to renounce the use of violence, but the FLN contended that requiring the renunciation of violence necessitated the recognition of Islamist parties. In mid-1993, the HCE issued a document entitled "A Platform for Democracy" calling for a national conference. Participation in the conference would hopefully lead to a solution that would work for Islamists, the FLN, and the legal parties or "peaceful opposition" to the regime. As Mortimer (1996) notes, "Most of the legal parties insisted on the inclusion of the FIS in any such conference, arguing that this was the only course that could restore security. Certain parties, like the RCD and Ittahadi, opposed any such gesture of inclusion, as did a segment of the press and the most militantly anti-Islamist associations" (31).

During this period that was marred with increasing violence, one saw precarious conditions within the ALN. Nezzar, who had recently become quite ill, engendered a debate between the eradicators and conciliators regarding his succession. The nomination of an eradicationist prime minister, Ridha Malik, and the return of defense minister Zeroual would ensure a continued struggle over how to deal with the Islamists. In fact, efforts to negotiate with the FIS occurred behind the scenes, with the FIS demanding the release of their leaders for the party to agree to participate in the national conference. According to Mortimer (1996), "Defense Minister Zeroual, at this point, took the further initiative of a secret meeting with the imprisoned politicians in order to see whether they would accept two conditions set by the army for their release: the renunciation of violence, and a declaration of respect for a secular form of government with alternation of power" (32). Both Madani and Bel Hadj demanded their unconditional release, but the army was not willing to accede to their demands.

Therefore, in 1994, the HCE came to an end as the national conference was convened in January. Unfortunately, for the military, "as the non-Islamist opposition had consistently argued that such a conference would be pointless without the participation of the Islamists, not a single political party agreed to attend" (Mortimer 1996, 32). Instead, the military established an institution called the High Security Council (HSC), which appointed Zeroual as Algeria's new president. On balance, the relationship between the conciliators and eradicators shifted toward the conciliators with the accession of Zeroual.

In what became known as the "Zeroual Initiative," President Zeroual attempted once again to reach out to the FIS to forestall a continuing rise in violence. Two of FIS leader Madani's associates were released by Zeroual with the hope that they would take steps to reduce the violence as a good faith effort to work with the regime. With the continued violence engulfing the nation, Zeroual "had little room for maneuver in his own camp because the intensity of the hostilities served the arguments of the hardliners" (Mortimer 1996, 33). Essentially, the army, Islamists, and democrats constrained their own actions resulting in a continuing cycle of violence:

> The army insisted that the first concession come from the opposing camp. On the Islamist side, the political leaders of the FIS could ill afford to give an order that the armed insurgents would ignore; the

defection of a major FIS personality, Muhammad Sa'id, to the GIA illustrated this difficulty. . . . In the third camp, even the advocates of negotiation among the non-Islamist opposition were wary of a military-Islamist deal that would exclude them and snuff out the democratic opening as well (Mortimer 1996, 34).

Zeroual reached out for a second time to the FIS. However, the GIA responded by issuing a statement refusing "'any reconciliation, any truce, and any dialogue with the illegal government'; at the same time, various anti-Islamist groups criticized the government for a 'unilateral concession'" (Mortimer 1996, 34). As Mortimer notes, "In the place of the hoped-for truce, Zeroual found himself confronted by an unprecedented escalation of terrorism: car bombs, another wave of assassinations, and attacks on schools and factories" (Mortimer 1996, 34).

Consequently, the level of violence constricted the chance for a settlement between the regime and the FIS, because neither side was willing to find common ground to begin negotiations often resulting in the extremists "outflank[ing] those who might have been tentatively disposed to negotiation" (Mortimer 1996, 35). The continued violence and the regime and FIS' intransigence occasioned opposition parties to meet in Rome, Italy at the behest of the Sant'Egidio community of Catholic laymen to attempt to reach an agreement on a platform of reconciliation. The Sant'Egidio Platform was designed to serve as the basis for negotiation with the regime and the way forward to return to multi-party elections and included six principles:

1. Respect for human rights, support for contested elections, popular sovereignty, the rule of law, and the constitution of 1989;
2. Rejection of violence as a way of gaining or maintaining power; opposition to dictatorship of any kind; and the return of the army to the barracks;
3. Recognition that the Algerian personality is made up of Arabism, Islam, and "amazighite" (Berber cultural identity) and that both Arabic and Berber are national languages that should be promoted;
4. Before negotiations begin, the FIS leaders should be released and all political parties should resume their activities;
5. Press freedom should be restored; torture should cease, along with extrajudicial killings; and all political prisoners should be released;
6. Attacks on civilians and foreigners should be condemned (Quandt 1998, 70–71).

Zeroual and his regime rejected the platform stating that "it had been worked out under foreign auspices and therefore was unacceptable from the outset" (Quandt 1998, 71). Interestingly, many of the points in the platform "actually mirrored the regime's own language—the support for elections, for 'alternance,' or the change of government by elections, condemnation of violence, respect for the constitution, and so forth" (Quandt 1998, 71).

Despite renouncing the Sant'Egidio Platform, Zeroual still wanted to maintain political momentum generated from the talks. Therefore, he declared that presidential elections would be held in December 1995. Zeroual's attempt to push forward with the election was aimed at making appear publicly that the regime was addressing its crisis of legitimacy (Volpi 2003, 73). Zeroual received support from the moderate Islamic party led by Mahfoud Nannah, Hamas, and the secular, democratic and Berberist party led by Said Sadi, the RCD. However, the FIS, the FFS, GIA and FLN boycotted the elections. Nevertheless, state-sponsored television officially declared Zeroual President-elect with more than 60 percent of the vote and a turnout of 75 percent (Volpi 2003, 74–75). This blatantly fraudulent election result highlighted the opposition's claim that "the participation rate and Zeroual's share of the votes had been artificially increased to show massive popular involvement and to have the president endorsed by more than half of the electorate" (Volpi 2003, 75). Although President Zeroual was able to gain support of Hamas and the RCD, their partnership soon became viewed as "the same authoritarian, nepotistic, and kleptocratic tendencies as their predecessors" (Volpi 2003, 76). With his regime's popularity waning, Zeroual, as is the norm in authoritarian regimes, reformed the political institutions through a rewriting of the constitution.

The draft constitution was a document written after consultation granting large discretionary power to the President. More specifically, he would have emergency powers to name and replace the head of government. Also, there would be presidential term limits of two five-year terms, parliament would be selected using proportional representation instead of previous winner-take-all majority system, and the Constitutional Council would rule on constitutionality of laws (Quandt 1998, 74). Moreover, the constitution gave the president the power to nominate one-third of the Senate and any law voted on by the parliament had to be ratified by three-quarters of the senators to become law (Volpi 2003, 76). Thus, the president's nominees always had a de facto veto over any law passed by parliament. In November 1996, the constitution was put before the people in a referendum and passed with 80 percent of the vote in favor. According to Quandt (1998), "Supposedly more people voted in the referendum than in the presidential election of the previous year— some 80 percent—and of those about 80 percent voted in favor of the new constitution. Suffice it to say that few Algerian commentators believed the figures" (74).

In addition to rewriting the constitution, parliamentary elections were held in 1997. The Zeroual regime was counting on these elections to provide legitimacy and did not want a repeat of 1991 to 1992. Consequently, "[o]ne step toward assuring an outcome acceptable to the regime was the banning of the FIS and obliging Hamas and Nahda to drop the word 'Islam' from their names" (Quandt 1998, 76). The regime also backed its own party, the RND, which was established only three months before the parliamentary elections to counter the influence of the FLN and FFS. As Volpi notes, "The RND was an ill-assorted assemblage of former civil servants and FLN cadres close to the President that was to provide Zeroual with reliable partners in Parliament" (Volpi 2003, 76–77). The results of the election saw the MSP (formerly Hamas) come in second with sixty-nine seats and the FLN came in third with sixty-two seats (Quandt 1998, 77). The RND, MSP, and FLN formed a coalition, but protests erupted and were repressed by security forces.

The blatant rigging of the election and the protests "undermined rather than consolidated the position of the regime. . . . These rigging tactics showed crudely that electoral contests were primarily designed to provide the ruling elite with a façade of political legitimacy and not to elect representative political institutions" (Volpi 2003, 77). After the June 1997 elections, the opposition parties continued to protest the election results. As a result of pressure from his peers (officers within the ANP), Zeroual stepped down and called for an early presidential election in 1999.

During this period prior to the parliamentary and presidential elections, the "eradicator" faction under Lamari began to dominate the debate. One result of this outcome was that between 1995 and 1997, changes were occurring within the military hierarchy, especially for middle-ranking officers. In addition, regional commanders were being replaced by younger officers who had only been in command of army units since the beginning of the civil war. Accordingly, Volpi (2003) notes, "These newcomers had fewer connections with the clans of the war of independence and owed much of their authority to the senior officers nominating them" (85). Moreover, the political, economic, and military autonomy of the clans in each military region was diminished as regional commands were left to languish in favor of more elite forces, particularly the anti-terrorist *gendarmerie*. These elite forces were better trained and better paid than the regular army of conscripts and were equipped with modern military weaponry (Volpi 2003, 85). The distribution of military hardware was used to strengthen certain units and officers as part of specific patronage networks (86). In the ANP, "the chain of command was organized in such a way that local commanders needed a direct authorization from the regional commander or the High Command before ordering any movement of troops" (Volpi 2003, 86).

Interestingly, in 1998, Lamari's control of the political process came into sharp relief. Following Zeroual's announcement calling for new presidential elections, Lamari "vaunted the merits of the new 'Algerian democracy' in a speech intended for the armed forces. After applauding the choices of the President . . . [h]e concluded with a warning that 'accession to power and alternation of power by means of elections must be, from now on, irreversible practices and the foundations on which rest democracy, the state of law and social justice'" (Volpi 2003, 86–87). In short, Lamari was paying lip service to democracy while simultaneously justifying a role for the military in Algerian politics, specifically the control of the state's political institutions.

An example occurred after the 1999 presidential election. To buttress the Bouteflika presidency, the High Command backed an agreement between the FIS-AIS and the government as they did after the 1997 elections (Volpi 2003, 81). The military commander of the AIS, Mezrag wrote a communiqué to Bouteflika stating that he was willing to formalize a truce that was first declared in 1997. Bouteflika responded by "giving a legal framework to this intiative" and two days later, Mezrag answered signaling the intention of the AIS to renounce all military action and place the organization under state control (Volpi 2003, 81). Although a deal with the AIS was worked out, the agreement was not recognized by Hachani, Belhadj Ibrahimi, and Ait Ahmed, who were "concerned by the fact that this agreement did not address the issue of the re-legalization of the Islamic party, the problem of the 'disappeared' and the ending of the state of emergency (in place since 1992)" (Volpi 2003, 82).

Subsequently, Bouteflika decided to release Madani and Belhadj with the condition that they retire from public life and held a referendum called the "law on civil concord" on his agreement with the guerrillas and on the associated general amnesty (Volpi 2003, 82). Thus, with an approval of 98.6 percent and a turnout of 85 percent, the civil war had "ended." The stark reality, however, showed, that short term solutions to political violence strengthened the military establishment *vis-à-vis* the political system and electoral process (Volpi 2003, 82).

Bouteflika would go on to win the 2004, 2009, and 2014 presidential elections. In the parliamentary elections of June 1997, May 2002, May 2007, and May 2012 the FLN and RND would dominate the vote totals and seats won. Algeria, though, is cursed by a major contradiction according to Addi (2014): "It promulgates the right of parties to compete— according to the constitution, '"for . . . access to power [in order to] contribute effectively in this way to the consolidation of democracy.' However, it denies the sovereignty of the electorate by stuffing ballot boxes to favor parties of the administration and distort electoral majorities" (438). Consequently, protests continued to spring up, but were often infiltrated or confronted by the internal espionage and counterespionage service affiliated with the ministry of defense, known as the Département du Renseignement et de la Sécurité (DRS) (Addi 2014, 438). The DRS is the arm of the ministry of the defense that allows the ANP to remain above the fray, allowing the DRS to do its dirty work of monitoring all political actors and those who openly criticize the army's role are repressed.

## REGIONAL AND INTERNATIONAL RELATIONS

The discussion above of electoral politics is not just localized to Algeria, but in fact can be seen in the Maghreb, or North Africa, as a whole. These states confront a youth bulge, an increase in the working age population, chronic unemployment or underemployment, and electoral manipulation. As J. N. C. Hill (2011) notes, "The region's democratic institutions and processes have long been fragile and incomplete" (1090). To justify the restrictions on the democratic process, North African leaders argue that Islamists are a largely homogenous movement and painting them with such a broad brush stroke reduces them to groups with likeminded objectives as Al-Qaeda in the Islamic Maghreb (AQIM), for example. The Global War on Terror, according to J. N. C. Hill (2011), paints a narrative which states, "[I]t is far too dangerous to allow democracy to operate unfettered for it might allow the Islamists to gain power. If that happened, then elections would be abolished, political rights suspended and civil liberties cut" (1090).

Another important aspect that must be considered in combination with the Global War on Terror is Algeria's economy, specifically its reliance on the international community for years. This reliance is due to Algeria's status as a rentier state. By the end of 1992, the Algerian economy "was beginning to feel the strain of the idiosyncratic 'socialist' policies, as well as the costs of the civil conflict" (Volpi 2003, 112). To cope with its increasingly dire financial situation Algeria renegotiated with the IMF an "extended-facilities" loan guaranteeing $1.8 billion per year over a three-year period. In addition, Algeria was able to access $15 billion in debt reschedulings and loans from foreign governments, banks, and international financial organizations (Volpi 2003, 113). In response, Algeria was required to reduce their budget deficit, reduce inflation, cease subsidizing retail goods, and open their market to foreign investment and private enterprise. Unfortunately, in 1995, the Algerian government spent DA 148 billion to pay off the debts of state-owned enterprises before privatization, resulting in a budget deficit of DA 168 billion (Volpi 2003, 113–14). Moreover, Volpi (2003) argues, "For political and geostrategic reasons the United States and the European Union prefer to keep afloat the dubious system of governance devised by Algeria's military rulers through a system of direct and indirect (IMF and Paris Club) aid rather than pressuring for genuine and thorough political and economic reforms" (116).

One area where the Bouteflika regime has benefited is from the rise of oil and natural gas prices between 1999 and 2009. This rise in oil prices has filled the state coffers to the point that its currency reserves are said to be worth around US $150 billion (Addi 2014, 440). Consequently, Algeria's debt has been paid down and decreased from $46 billion to $3.8 billion in 2007 (Addi 2014, 440). Although, as Volpi (2003) notes, "Today more than ever, the fluctuations in the price of oil and gas commodities on the world market and the changing priorities of the international community constitute an endemic cause of instability for the country" (115). Thus, the endurance of authoritarianism in Algeria is partly based off the oil prices siphoned off by the regime.

While the increased oil revenues helped the Algerian government pay down the debt from international financial institutions and undertake infrastructure improvements, the common Algerian has not felt the same benefits. There is a high unemployment rate that remains the highest in North Africa. For example, in 2005, unemployment was 22.5 percent and youth unemployment was 40 percent. Addi (2014) notes, "Thus, to safeguard political legitimacy and the allegiance of much of the population, it continues to manipulate the economy. If the rentier nature of the subsidized economy were terminated . . . the regime would have to change radically" (441). At the moment, this appears unlikely.

In fact, the Arab Spring of January 2011, did not result in the overthrow of the regime despite protests in Algeria's two largest cities, Algiers and Oran. The increased wealth created from oil and natural gas allowed the regime to take steps to mitigate the unrest—namely, salaries of teachers and civil servants were increased and state banks distributed free loans to any young person requesting one (Addi 2014, 438). Nevertheless, the siphoning off of profits by the Bouteflika regime only served to reinforce the population's distrust of government. As a result, popular discontent "fuels the ambition of the Islamic fundamentalists to reform (or topple) the secularist ruling elite and indirectly contributes to the overall instability of the country" (Volpi 2003, 116). For example, over the last couple of years there have been isolated, high-profile attacks by a relatively new movement consisting of the last remaining armed Islamists from the civil war—Al-Qaeda in the Islamic Maghreb (AQIM). The presence of AQIM has served the interests of the United States making Algeria a frontline in the War on Terror since 2001.

Today, the ANP numbers 130,000 active duty soldiers (110,000 in the Army, 6,000 in the Navy, 14,000 in the Air Force), 187,200 paramilitary, and 150,000 reserves in the Army (Military Balance 2016, 320). The ANP has a long history of working with the international community. More specifically, the Soviet Union and the United States sought to influence Algerian politics. Algeria's origin as a postcolonial state allowed Boumediene to champion the nonaligned movement, as well as becoming "the mecca of the national liberation movements of Africa, Asia and Latin America" receiving financial and diplomatic support (Addi 2014, 442). Consequently, Boumediene reached out to the Soviet Union during the 1970s for economic and military support. According to Addi (2014), "His bold position placed the Algerian regime in the anti-Western camp, which led it to increase its economic and military cooperation with the

Soviet Union and strengthen its ties with the socialist countries of Europe and China" (442).

After Boumediene's death in 1978, imperialist rhetoric declined and the regime reached out to the United States and Europe to assist in the development of the oil and natural gas industry. However, between 1992 and 1998, relations with the United States cooled as a result of the cancellation of the election and human rights violations during the civil war (Addi 2014, 442). The 9/11 attacks would influence U.S. policymakers that Algeria's experience in combating Islamist terrorism would be worth tapping into. As such, "the CIA has worked in concert with DRS in order to track the GSPC an organization that lent its allegiance in 2003 to Osama bin Laden and from then on called itself . . . AQIM" (Addi 2014, 445). Moreover, the continued threat of terrorism, conflict in Mali, instability in Libya, and porous eastern and southern borders motivated Algeria to change policy priorities and focus on professionalization and regional cooperation.

## CONCLUSION

A state forged in the throes of violence has continued to come to grips with its identity as it has transitioned from authoritarianism to "democracy." The case study above detailed a strongly egalitarian, nationalist people who, after achieving independence, were swept up in clan politics that grew to define their political system. The ALN, FLN, and FIS each became subsumed in the interclan rivalry and it was these relationships that influenced the course of Algerian politics—from the rivalries within the FLN during the war of independence to the conflicts within the ANP since 1965. Intervention occurred during periods of intense conflict within the military between members of the Military High Command and the generals who would lead the country at various times through its history—Boumedienne, Chadli, Nezzar, Zeroual, and Lamari—as well as during periods of intense conflict with Algerian political elites and Islamists.

Military withdrawal in Algeria, however, has been few and far between. After the 1965 coup, Boumedienne ruled until his death in 1978, whereby the ANP High Command put forward Chadli as a compromise candidate for the presidency. With their man in office, the military withdrew until events, such as Black October, forced Chadli to call for the military's assistance. At this point, the combination of violence, a deteriorating economy, and the emergence of the Islamists forced the ANP back onto the political stage in 1992 after the FIS won the second round of parliamentary elections. Thus, the "democratic experiment" ended and the ANP retained control of government as Algeria continues to come to grips with how to wrestle with contending forces in Algerian society—nationalist, regional, Islamist, democratic and military (Quandt 1998,

162). The ANP will continue to maintain its hold on the levers of power due to history's influence in creating space for "the country's economic and political future" to be influenced by the military (Addi 2014, 446).

# THREE

## Egypt

Since the Arab Spring, Egypt has been at the forefront of discussions surrounding democratic transitions and the endurance of authoritarianism. The concern over the endurance of authoritarianism is a result of the military's involvement in politics. The Egyptian military intervened in politics in 1952 and has subsequently sought to protect their institutional interests. The most recent example occurred on July 3, 2013, with the military's dismissal of President Mohammad Morsi of the Muslim Brotherhood's Freedom and Justice Party.

As Egypt's transition to democracy continues, understanding the role of the military is of increasing importance. The Egyptian case is useful in illustrating the level of conflict and occasional consensus between the military, politicians, and society. In fact, Hazem Kandil (2014) argues, "After a series of wars, conspiracies, coup plots, and socioeconomic transformations, the balance within Egypt's tripartite alliance tilted heavily toward the security apparatus, with the political leadership living contentedly in its shadow, and the military subordinated, if not totally marginalized" (5).

Therefore, this chapter asks what role the military has played in Egypt historically? What does this tell us about the military's involvement during the period of democratic transition since the 2011 Arab Spring? The military, as guardian of the Egyptian state, became a part of what Kandil (2014) called a "power triangle" and reasserted itself after the rule of the Muslim Brotherhood between 2011 and 2013 was deemed detrimental to the security of the Egyptian state. This reassertation was heavily influenced by the importance placed upon foreign economic and military aid from the United States, which has helped the Egyptian military maintain its influence over Egyptian political institutions.

## HISTORY

The origins of the Egyptian military's intervention in politics begins in July 1952 with a group of junior officers, known as the Free Officers, led by Gamal Abdel Nasser. The Free Officers shared a middle-class background and training in the military academy. Their motive was to remove the government of King Farouk, who had been installed by the British. In effect, the Free Officers shared the same concerns as Egypt's other political actors of the era—the Wafd, the Muslim Brotherhood, and factions of the Left—the parliamentary system needed reform, the removal of British influence, and changes to improve the socioeconomic standing of ordinary Egyptians (Cook 2011, 40).

Nasser and the Free Officers developed the Revolutionary Command Council (RCC) to run the country. Nasser appointed members of the officer corps to senior positions in the bureaucracy and public sector to assist the RCC in implementing Nasser's revolution. By March 1954, the Officers were confronted with "a range of internal and external enemies . . . [and] sought both the means to retain their power and to minimize future challenges to their dominance, thereby helping them consolidate their power further" (Cook 2011, 62). After abolishing the Egyptian monarchy, Nasser overhauled the entire political system by emasculating all political parties, tried and imprisoned key politicians, and created a new constitution, which established a new presidential system (Osman 2010 44–45).

The development of Egypt's new institutions was supposed to lay out for Egyptians what was acceptable behavior under the new regime; however, Nasser's revolution was met with repeated criticism from the Left, who saw Nasser and his colleagues as exchanging one imperial relationship with the British for another with the United States (Cook 2011, 52). For example, the United States established political contacts just two days after the coup, the CIA helped the Officers develop their own clandestine intelligence service, and Ambassador James Caffery pressured the Officers to block a Leftist intellectual Rashad al Barawi (who helped the Officers write the Agrarian Reform Law) from joining the cabinet (Cook 2011, 52). The Left's accusations of the Officers as being instruments of imperialism resulted in their arrests. For "[d]emanding the return of constitutional life and social justice was one thing, but openly questioning the Officers' nationalist credentials was quite another because it struck at the very heart of the junta's claims to legitimacy" (Cook 2011, 52).

The other main challenge to Nasser's regime came from the Muslim Brotherhood, founded in 1928 by Hassan al-Banna. The Brotherhood was initially established as a religious outreach association, or *da'wa*, "that aimed to cultivate pious and committed Muslims through preaching, social services, and spreading religious commitment and integrity by example" (Rosefsky Wickham 2011, 92). Furthermore, the Brotherhood was concerned, according to journalist Tarek Osman (2010), "to bridge the gap between traditional religious thinking and the waves of modernity that Egypt witnessed in the first few decades of the twentieth century" (82). Thanks to al-Banna's charisma, the Brotherhood soon became a countrywide political movement heavily involved in Egypt's struggle for independence against the British occupation and as a voice for Egypt's disenfranchised advocating for a religious state and sharia law (Osman 2010, 82).

The Free Officers, however, did not support the Brotherhood's call for sharia. According to Carrie Rosefsky Wickham (2011), "After a member of the Brotherhood attempted to assassinate Nasser in 1954, Nasser had the pretext he needed to try to crush the organization—interning thousands of its members in desert concentration camps and forcing others into exile or underground" (92). Consequently, there were a number of lessons learned by the Brothers. Brotherhood ideologue Sayyid Qutb became radicalized and concluded that the only way to confront the vast coercive power of the modern state was through jihad, while his successor as General Guide, Hasan al-Hudaybi, advocated judiciousness and caution. By 1972, al-Hudaybi's successor, Umar Tilmisani, had "renounced violence as a domestic strategy when President Anwar el-Sadat allowed the group to rejoin the political fold" (Rosefsky Wickham 2011, 92).

In short, the institutions established by Nasser and the Free Officers, challenged by both the left and the right, would be the source of the next sixty years of struggle over the central ideological and organizing principles of Egyptian state and society. The Officers, though, lacked ideological convictions, which resulted in "never-ending political conflict between the defenders of the political system the Free Officers founded and their opponents that produced no small amount of political alienation, economic dislocations and—at times—violence" (Cook 2011, 63).

By the mid-1950s and early 1960s, the Free Officers were able to generate significant economic development and address social ills which the Officers used to gain support from Egyptian society. In part, the Officers also needed to demonstrate Egypt's power and influence abroad. As such, the Officers told the Egyptian people that Nasserism, which incorporated nationalism, socialism, and a strong central government, would make the revolution successful. Nasser took advantage of this and used the Egyptian radio station "Sawt al Arab" (Voice of the Arabs) to broadcast nationalist messages both at home and around the region. In the decade between the nationalization of the Suez Canal and the late 1960s, Egypt became the leader of Arab culture, higher learning and politics, which would be embodied in pan-Arabism.

Nasser's appeals for pan-Arabism would put him in direct conflict with Saudi Arabia and most Arab monarchies, the United States, and Israel. He denounced the Saudis "with their absolute monarchy, Wahhabi-Salafi Islamism, starkly capitalistic ethic, highly conservative social codes and alliance with the West "as the antithesis of pan-Arabism (Osman 2010, 58). The other Arab monarchies received similar scorn for their "reliance on the West, lack of courage and 'disregard for the aspirations of their people'" (Osman 2010, 58). With regards to the United States, Nasser was steadfast in his opposition to U.S. strategic interests in the Middle East. Nasser proclaimed, "[T]he Arabs' oil should be for the Arabs" (Osman 2010, 58). The United States had taken the place of the British as the guarantor of free passage oil through the region, and had supported the Baghdad Pact as part of containment of the Soviet Union. To counter the presence of the United States, Nasser was swayed to side with the Soviet Union and received arms and money to complete the Aswan High Dam. Osman (2010) notes, "Nasser's steadfastness in the face of Western, and especially American, interests in the Middle East made up a significant part of his domestic and regional appeal" (61–62).

Finally, Nasser's pan-Arabism directed highly confrontational rhetoric against Israel. Nasser's position was that all Arabic lands (as Arabs defined them) belonged to the Arabs and that Israel, as a U.S. ally "was an 'arrow directed at the heart of the Arab world'" (Osman 2010, 62). It was toward Israel that Nasser ratcheted up the rhetoric, because many Egyptians were persuaded by his rhetoric, propaganda, and willingness to stand up to Israel and the United States calling Israel "a 'Western military base' at its heart . . . position[ing] Israel, unequivocally, as not only an occupier of Arab Palestine, but as 'the nation's strategic enemy'" (Osman 2010, 62). As a result, beginning with the Suez Crisis in July 1956 (after the nationalization of the Suez Canal) and Nasser's victory over the British, French, and Israeli attempt to overthrow him, Nasser closed the Strait of Tiran to all ships flying Israeli flags, sending Egypt on a path toward war in June 1967.

The Six Day War resulted in the occupation of the Sinai, West Bank, the Syrian Golan Heights and Jerusalem by Israel, and the defeat of Egyptian and Syrian militaries. This defeat was a result of inadequate planning, substandard leadership on the battlefield, and an inability to leverage its superior numbers in hardware (Cook 2011, 99–100). Nasser put responsibility for the defeat on eight hundred officers, including the commander of the armed forces, Field Marshall Abdel Hakim Amer, who at one time, was a close confidant of Nasser's. Amer used his ties with Nasser to build a political and personal fiefdom while the military focused more on day-to-day governance, instead of war fighting (Cook 2011, 100).

More importantly, the defeat upset the Egyptian people who began protesting against the regime. Noteworthy amongst the protestors were a number of students and workers. The regime's prior appeal, based on universal education, guaranteed employment, economic and social development, and geopolitical power, had lost its luster (Cook 2011, 104).

Nasser confronted the protesters with the security forces to maintain order, but the protestors refused to back down. As violence increased, Nasser did what most authoritarian leaders do when confronted with a threat to their authority: he attempted to position himself as a reformer by the retrial of certain air force officers and creation of the March 30 program, a ten-point program for a new constitution (Cook 2011, 104–5). These reforms notwithstanding, protests would continue and in attempt to salvage his reputation he would nearly rebuild the armed forces and initiate and manage a war of attrition against Israel and mend relationships with the Saudis and King Hussein of Jordan before succumbing to a heart attack in 1970 (Osman 2010, 66).

Nasser's successor was Anwar al-Sadat, another member of the military, who served as president from 1970 until his assassination in 1981. As president, Sadat sought to remove himself from Nasser's shadow. On one hand, he was considered a lightweight, owing his rise in Egyptian politics to Nasser, but on the other hand, he was also described as a shrewd operator (Cook 2011, 119). At the time of Nasser's death, Egypt's economy was deteriorating resulting in increasing debt and unemployment. In foreign policy, Egypt's primary foreign policy challenge was the presence of Israel in the Sinai. Sadat believed these challenges were the result of Nasser. Tarek Masoud (2014) argues, "What we do know is that Sadat believed that Egypt had picked the wrong superpower patron. Nasser had reluctantly brought Egypt into the Russian camp, and two wars with Israel had convinced Sadat that this had been a bad move. Russian weapons and expertise were little match for the American materiel that the Jewish state could rely on. And only the United States, not Russia, had the leverage with Israel to bring it to the negotiating table and force it to make concessions" (454–55). Therefore, Sadat reformed political institutions and increased foreign investment, especially from the United States. In 1977, "Sadat legalized political parties, and in 1979 he held Egypt's first multiparty parliamentary elections since the end of the monarchy" creating the desired effects since "Egypt did become an American client, and foreign investment did increase" (Masoud 2014, 455).

Sadat's successor was Hosni Mubarak, a former air force general, who ruled from 1981 until 2011. Mubarak, upon his election, sought to implement limited political liberalization. For instance, according to John Esposito, Tamara Sonn, and John Voll (2016), "he loosened restrictions on freedom of speech and of the press, even allowing critics to critique his administration publicly" (203). Although, the loosening of restrictions was only temporary, since "[p]arliamentary elections—of which there were eventually six during Mubarak's thirty-year rule—were routinely rigged to produce majorities for the ruling party" (Masoud 2014, 455). The National Democratic Party (NDP) would be the beneficiary of these rigged elections in the 1980s and 1990s winning 95 percent of the vote.

Also, in 2005, Mubarak introduced multiparty elections for the presidency, but according to Masoud (2014), "Mubarak's victory with, an improbable 88 percent of the vote, signified to all that the change was more cosmetic than real" (455). In short, "The Mubarak government's fig-leaf or faux democracy was exposed as he employed a heavy-handed brand of 'guided democracy'. . . [i]n elections plagued by fraud and ballot box stuffing" (Esposito, et al, 2016, 206).

A major unintended consequence of this liberalization was the "enabling [of] Islamic movements and organizations to grow, expand their institutions, and become part of mainstream society" (Esposito et al. 2016, 203). The MB championed the interests of the poor and middle class through the establishment of social services. Esposito, Sonn, and Voll (2016) argue that the MB became a mainstream part of Egyptian civil society when Brothers were elected to leadership positions in student unions at universities and in professional associations of lawyers, doctors, engineers, teachers, and journalists (203). Although banned by the government since 1954, the MB would form alliances with recognized parties and run candidates as independents throughout the Mubarak years. Working within the system, the MB "couched their criticisms and demands within the context of a call for greater democratization, political representation, social justice, and respect for human rights" (Esposito, et al. 2016, 204).

Although the MB worked within the system, there were groups, such as Islamic Jihad, who sought to destablize the Egyptian economy, overthrow the Mubarak government, and attack and murder foreign tourists, Coptic Christians, and government officials (Esposito, et al. 2016, 205). Consequently, the government implemented an antiterrorism campaign against the MB and militants. For Mubarak, both the MB and militants were one and the same. Therefore, emergency laws for routinely used for arbitrary arrests and detention without charge for six months, along with trials in state security or military courts (Esposito, et al. 2016, 206).

Subsequently, the state manipulated the 2010 election in favor of the NDP winning 97 percent of the seats to set the stage for a potential succession plan with Mubarak's son Gamal, a businessman, whom had been groomed to potentially replace his father. According to Dina Shehata (2011), "Not only did the country's opposition strongly oppose the succession plan, but many important factions within the state bureaucracy and the military were also skeptical. As 2010 came to a close, the country's ruling edifice was beginning to crack" (143).

Protests (known as the Arab Spring) began on January 25, 2011. Underscoring the protests was the inequality present in Egyptian society. After witnessing the ouster of Tunisian President Zine el Abidine Ben Ali, the blogosphere, Twitterverse, and Facebook groups sprang up in response to the Mubarak regime imprisoning an activist. On National Police Day, youths were scheduled to visit Tahrir Square to protest, but thanks in part to social media, the crowd began to swell within the square. Day after day the protests moved first from the young university students, to shopkeepers, technocrats, attorneys, and teachers. It was not only the poor, but also the youth and middle class Egyptians who were upset at the lack of jobs and economic opportunities in Mubarak's Egypt. Consequently, the protestors formed the Coalition of January 25 Youth and presented a series of demands to the regime: "the resignation of Mubarak, the lifting of the state of emergency, the release of all political prisoners, the dissolution of parliament, the appointment of a government of independent technocrats, the drafting of a new constitution, and the punishment of those responsible for the violence against the protestors" (Shehata 2011, 143).

In an attempt to quell the protests, Mubarak ordered the security services to shut off the Internet, which forced more students and citizens into the streets. Fearing the end was near, Mubarak sent the security services into Tahrir Square to try and disperse the crowds. The protests grew so large that the military was forced to step in, fearing for the stability of the regime. Kandil (2014) argues, "The armed forces facilitated the 2011 uprising because they had become the least privileged partner in Egypt's ruling bloc. Keen on enhancing their institutional autonomy and geopolitical influence, officers welcomed a renegotiation of the existing power arrangement" (245).

The Supreme Council of the Armed Forces (SCAF) forced Mubarak to step down on February 11, 2011, and on February 13, 2011, the constitution and parliament were dissolved. Field Marshall Mohamed Tantawi appointed Vice President Omar Suleiman (a former intelligence officer, and ally of Mubarak) to head the interim government until new elections could be held in September 2011. The elections were later postponed to November 28, 2011–January 11, 2012. The election ushered in the Muslim Brotherhood's Freedom and Justice Party (FJP) after the transitional phase headed by the SCAF.

In late 2011/early 2012, parliamentary elections for both the lower and upper houses of parliament were held. The Brotherhood won 45 percent of the seats in the People's Assembly (the lower house) and 58 percent of the seats in the Shura Council (upper house). The al-Nur Party, won 25 percent in both the lower and upper houses. The largest liberal party, the Wafd, won only 7.5 percent of seats in the lower house and 8 percent in the upper house, while an alliance of liberal parties known as the Egyptian Bloc won 6.7 percent of seats in the lower house and 4.5 percent in the upper house (Rutherford 2013, 43–44).

The presidential elections were held on May 23–24, 2012, with thirteen candidates competing. In the days leading up to the election, there were five candidates in contention: Mohammad Morsi, a senior Muslim Brotherhood leader representing the FJP; Abd al-Monam Abu al-Fatuh, a prominent reformer who used to be a member of the Brotherhood; Hamdin Sabahi, a Nasserist; Amir Moussa, Mubarak's former foreign minister from 1991 to 2001 and secretary general of the Arab League from 2001 to 2011; and Ahmad Shafiq, a former military officer who served as prime minister under Mubarak (Rutherford 2013, 44). Morsi won the election with 24.8 percent of the vote, and Shafiq's 23.7 percent forced a runoff on June 16 and June 17. According to Bruce K. Rutherford (2013), "Morsi was seen as a machine politician who lacked the charisma and political skill needed to unify the country. Shafiq's commitment to the goals of the revolution was in serious doubt . . . [because] he was the figure most associated with the Mubarak regime" (44). As a result of the outcome, the Supreme Constitutional Court (SCC) declared the election law governing the parliamentary elections unconstitutional. In response, the Supreme Council of the Armed Forces (SCAF) dissolved the People's Assembly. This action by the SCAF was met with criticism by the Brotherhood who "asserted that the SCC ruling and the SCAF decision to dissolve the People's Assembly were politically motivated efforts to deny the Brotherhood the political power that it had earned at the ballot box" (Rutherford 2013, 45).

Nevertheless, in the runoff, Morsi beat Shafiq with 52 percent to 48 percent of the vote. The SCAF accepted the results. Rutherford (2013) sums up the significance of the election for Egypt: "For the first time in Egypt's 5,000 year history, the country had an elected national leader . . . [that] promised to be the president of all Egyptians and to build a new Egypt that is 'civil, national, constitutional, and modern'" (45). Morsi, however, would continue to come into conflict with the SCAF, who issued several amendments to the de-facto constitution that increased the SCAF's power at the expense of executive and legislative power. By issuing the amendments, "the SCAF made clear that it planned to play a central role in the development of the political and legal system at least until a new constitution was adopted and a new lower house of parliament was elected" (Rutherford 2013, 45). In short, the military's apprehension is best illustrated by then Defense Minister Tantawi's comment that "'the revolutionaries are our sons and brothers, but probably lack a clear and comprehensive understanding of the situation'" (Kandil 2012, 195).

In August 2012, President Morsi dismissed General Tantawi as Defense Minister, in part, because since the Arab Spring, the military's status has been the subject of a tug of war between Morsi and the Brotherhood, the SCAF, and the military (Fahim and El Sheikh, 8/13/12). In purging Tantawi, President Morsi "leaned on the support of a junior officer corps that blamed the old guard for a litany of problems within the military and for involving the armed forces too deeply in the country's politics." (Fahim and El Sheikh, 8/13/12). Tantawi, as part of the old guard, was insisting on broad political powers, while the new defense minister, Field Marshal Abdul-Fattah al-Sisi was seen as someone who would cooperate and likely except a minimum influence for the Egyptian military in a new Egyptian democracy—a veto over foreign policy issues and control over its economic empire (Fahim and El Sheikh, 8/13/12). Put differently, al-Sisi, as a pious Muslim, was someone whom Morsi felt would be more likely to cooperate with the FJP's political agenda.

Morsi's time in office was deemed to be biased and authoritarian. Morsi was accused of excluding political rivals from his team and declared himself immune to rulings by the courts. In addition, the Brotherhood pushed through an unpopular constitution, but most importantly, the economy was still a glaring concern for many Egyptians. The die had been cast by Morsi and violence spread throughout Egypt culminating in June 30, 2013, demonstrations, which took the name Tamarod (Rebellion), where millions took to the streets on the anniversary of Morsi's election to demand his ouster. In response there were a number of pro-Morsi demonstrations and security forces were called in to break up many of their protests.

Al-Sisi stated that the military would not be silent in the face of increased violence. On July 3, 2013, the Egyptian military deposed Morsi after giving the government forty-eight hours to reach accommodation with various political actors. In essence, the Egyptian military, whose institutional interest is the protection of the Egyptian state, intervened against Morsi, because al-Sisi felt that Morsi and the Muslim Brotherhood were not taking part in a national dialogue. Kandil (2014) notes, "Those who supported . . . the rebellion from the old regime and revolutionary camp had a clear motive: the former were not sure the Brothers were willing to share the spoils of Egypt's patronage state, and the latter resented the Brotherhood's outright hijacking of the 2011 revolt" (254). Referring to mass protests that had occurred throughout the country since November 2012, when religious minorities and secular parties walked out of the constitutional assembly, al-Sisi stated, "I expected if we didn't intervene, it would have turned into a civil war" (Washington Post, 8/3/13).

Field Marshal al-Sisi was born in Cairo on November 19, 1954, graduated from the Egyptian Military Academy in 1977, and served in the infantry, rising in the ranks to later serve as commander of the Northern Military Zone and director of Military Intelligence and Reconnaissance for SCAF (BBC 2013). President Mohammed Morsi appointed General al-Sisi General Commander of the Armed Forces and Defense Minister on August 12, 2012. Al-Sisi is a pious Muslim whom Morsi felt would be more likely to cooperate with him and the Freedom and Justice Party's political agenda.

However, with protests erupting around Egypt, Gen. al-Sisi stated that the military would not be silent in the face of violence. On July 3, 2013, the Egyptian military deposed Morsi after giving the government forty-eight hours to reach accommodation with various political actors. According to a statement issued by the Egyptian military:

> The armed forces repeat the urgency of all the people's demands to be met within 48 hours, and if the demands of the people are not met within that time period, then we will be obliged to fulfill our historical duty towards our country and the great people of Egypt to map out a future plan for the country in accordance to the demands of the Egyptian people and with the contribution of all aspects of the population, especially the youth who have proven themselves time and again, and without exclusion of any political party (Ahram Online, news.rapgenius.com/General-abdel-fattah-el-sisi-announcement-of-military-overthrow-of-egyptian-government-lyrics#note-1939950).

Al-Sisi's coup against Egypt's first elected civilian president was successful not only because of the Egyptian military's position, but through the military's solicitation of support from Egypt's minority and main political parties, respected Al-Azhar University and the Coptic Church (Al-Sharif, 8/14/13). Al-Sisi stated that "there is room for everyone" in Egypt and asked millions of people "to take to the streets to give him a 'mandate' to fight 'violence and terrorism'" (BBC News, 8/18/13).

However, since the July 3 coup, hundreds of Morsi supporters from the Muslim Brotherhood and other anticoup groups were killed by government forces during protests in Cairo. The youth and politically moderate religious groups, although critical of Morsi's performance, were also wary of the hardline, antireligious and anti-Muslim Brotherhood agendas of some of the secular elements in the interim coalition, as well as being worried about the political role of the military and lack of youth inclusion in the new government (Al-Jazeera, 7/24/13).

What do the actions of al-Sisi and the military portend for democracy in Egypt? Al-Sisi is a highly nationalistic officer who one analyst described as "a brilliant officer and . . . the youngest member to occupy a seat in the Supreme Council of Armed Forces" (Al-Sharif, 8/14/13). Throughout 2013 there were many statements in the press about the military not standing by watching the destruction of the country. Most notably, al-Sisi's brother Ahmed stated in an interview with Newsweek, "We come from a family that leads—not one that will be led" (Giglio and Dickey, 8/16/13). Therefore, al-Sisi is a leader who sought to protect the Egyptian state from Islamists who threatened military interests.

From May 26 to 28, 2014, al-Sisi was elected president of Egypt and sworn in on June 8, 2014. Al-Sisi said he was committed to the planned transition and the recent banning of the Muslim Brotherhood was done to potentially accomplish "a military-led resurrection and reformation of the Islamist project that the Brotherhood so abysmally mishandled" (Al Sharif, 8/14/13 quoting Springborg, July 28, 2013). Al-Sisi's retirement from the Egyptian military, declaring his candidacy for president, and the placement of a loyal subordinate, General Sedki Sobhi, as the new defense minister is evidence of a leader wanting to guide the democratic transition.

What is known about al-Sisi's views toward democracy come from a paper he published in 2006 during his time at the United States Army War College in Carlisle, Pennsylvania. For al-Sisi, democracy in the Middle East "is a positive endeavor so long as it builds up the country and sustains the religious base versus devaluing religion and creating instabililty" (Al-Sisi, 4). The Muslim Brotherhood violated this principle by not being more inclusive, threatening stability of the state, thereby necessitating military intervention. This was argued prophetically by al-Sisi in 2006:

> [T]here are security concerns both internal and external to the countries. Many of the nation's police forces and military forces are loyal to the ruling party. If a democracy evolves with different constituencies, there is no guaranty [sic] that the police and military forces will align with the emerging ruling parties. In essence the security forces of a nation need to develop a culture that demonstrates commitment to a nation rather than a ruling party (al-Sisi, 2).

Put simply, al-Sisi is an Islamist, but his professionalism as a military officer motivates his decision-making to put national interest before self-interest. The next section will discuss the power of the military in Egyptian society before examining Egyptian civil–military relations and its regional and international impact.

## THE MILITARY ESTABLISHMENT

The Egyptian military numbers: 438,500 active duty (310,000 Army, 18,500 Navy, 30,000 Air Force, 80,000 Air Defense Command) and 479,000 Reserves (375,000 Army, 14,000 Navy, 20,000 Air Force, 70,000 Air Defense) (Military Balance 2016, 324). Stephen P. Cohen's (1984) work on the Pakistani military is relevant here regarding generational effects. He argues that the beliefs and attitudes of an entire officer corps are derived from four forces: First, are generational differences, as different age groups go through different experiences that influence their worldview. The second force is social class. Third, is the professional education and training and individual (or age group) receives. Fourth, is the promotion policy beyond the rank of major, where political considerations often influence the winnowing process to select the best, qualified candidates (Cohen 1984, 54).

Egypt's military generations are the Nasser Generation from 1952 to 1970, Sadat's American Generation from 1971 to 1981, and Mubarak's American Generation from 1981 to 2011. For our purposes here, the generational classification "is meant to highlight certain major trends, events, and influences that had a particularly powerful impact on one group of officers and in some cases on their superiors and subordinates as well" (Cohen 1984, 55). Each of these generations of military officers learns that the protection of its interests through what has been called the "Deep State" is paramount to the survival of Egypt (Childress, 9/17/13). The "Deep State" was first used to refer to the Turkish military's stepping in and establishing institutions with which it could guide the country. Egypt's "Deep State" includes the military, intelligence services, the police, the judiciary, and state media. Its mission is to "maintain order and stability—the status quo" (Childress, 9/17/13).

Egypt's "Deep State" was made possible by the military's involvement in the economy. More specifically, the military led the early efforts to nationalize the economy beginning in the mid-1950s and have since become one of Egypt's top land and business owners. As journalist Sarah Childress (2013) points out, "Young Egyptian men are required to serve in the military, providing a guaranteed source of free labor to staff the restaurants, hotels and bakeries owned by the military, as well as its factories, where it manufactures bottled water, pasta and other products. The military also owns olive oil, cement, construction and gasoline companies" (Childress, 9/17/13). In fact, these businesses are led by retired generals. Such property "is a 'fringe benefit' in exchange for the military ensuring regime stability and security" (GlobalSecurity.org, 1/29/11).

Therefore, the Egyptian military's position in the economy is a vital national interest. Some estimates put its percentage of Egypt's $189 billion economy at 25 to 40 percent (Childress, 9/17/13). The military insured there would be a lack of civilian oversight over these industries. Consequently, retired officers, in addition to positions with the companies mentioned above, would also be appointed to high-level positions within the state bureaucracy. Hicham Bou Nassif (2012) notes, "The luckiest of these retirees, those placed on boards of directors of state companies, could expect monthly salaries ranging from $16,670 to $83,333—even the low end being an unimaginable bonanza for the average Egyptian" (19). Moreover, Mubarak's acceptance of neo-liberal economic reforms in the 1990s led to the rise of a business class that would end up profiting just as much as the generals. As Kandil (2014) argues, "In character and interests, therefore, this new class was merely an extension of the old: 'the merchants of the seventies were the capitalists of the nineties.' The main difference, however, was that the latter group was no longer satisfied with living in the shadow of power; with so much capital accumulated, it was time to move up in the political world" (207–8).

The first ten years of neoliberalism in Egypt reduced the budget deficit from 15.3 percent to 3 percent of GDP with a 5 percent growth rate (Kandil 2014, 206). The fact that senior-level retirees, mostly generals, and this new business class would receive these economic windfalls while mid-ranking and junior officers were struggling financially led to the belief among these officers that "the regime was stealing Egypt's wealth and that there was a group of thieves around Gamal Mubarak pillaging Egypt" (Nassaf 2012, 20). Kandil (2014) notes that economic liberalization produced a building boom increasing the regime's wealth, coupled with $15.5 billion in savings on interest payments on its foreign debt for agreeing to participate in the 1991 Gulf War (206–7). As a result, private companies were profiting on the backs of Egyptian labor which led the military to believe that a regime led by Gamal Mubarak would threaten the military's position in the economy. This belief stems from the fact that these businessmen joined the NDP and increased their share of parliamentary seats throughout the 1990s and 2000s, thereby increasing their wealth and influence through continued partnerships with global businesses and foreign aid.

Concomitant with the military's position within the Egyptian economy is the influence of the US's yearly $1.3 billion in military aid and $495 million in economic aid (Masoud 2014, 465). Masoud (2014) argues, "U.S. aid accounts for almost half of the economic assistance that Egypt receives from all foreign sources. The rest comes chiefly from international lending institutions, such as the IMF and the World Bank" (465). For Mubarak, the implementation of structural adjustment programs under pressure from the United States and the IMF in the late 1990s was quite successful (as noted above); however, by 2004, further structural reforms involving taxes, trade regulations, privatization, and the floating of the Egyptian pound led to inflation, 6 percent GDP growth by 2010, with increased unemployment and inflation still major concerns (Masoud 2014, 467). Since the revolution, the economy continued to have an important influence on the military (more on this later in the chapter).

A final component of the military establishment affecting civil–military relations is the professionalization of the officer corps. Since 1967, after defeat in the Six-Day War, the Egyptian military was reluctant "to be involved in internal politics or policing in order to avoid the deleterious effects of such duties on military performance in battle" (Nassif 2012, 21). After the revolution, when protestors were in the streets, many wondered if the Egyptian military would intervene on the side of the Mubarak regime or the side of the protestors. According to a retired major general, quoted by Hicham Bou Nassif (2012), "'The mid-ranking and junior officers would not have obeyed orders to shoot on civilians. This is a matter of institutional culture. Egyptian officers are not psychologically prepared to kill civilians They do not receive training in terms of maintaining internal security. . . . The officers receive training to fight against another army, not against civilians'" (21). Therefore, during the revolution in Tahrir Square, the military chose to defend the protestors, since the military is the defender of the Egyptian state.

The next section will highlight the conflict between the military and politicians during Sadat and Mubarak's rule and how this conflict led to the Egyptian military protecting its economic interests and the "Deep State" during 2010–2014.

## CIVIL–MILITARY RELATIONS

In January 1971, Sadat dismissed all of Nasser's men from positions of power. Although the military was not directly running government since defeat in the June 1967 war, Sadat still built a relationship with generals who were considered his men. With his "men" in positions of power, Sadat believed he would be insulated. In fact, Sadat further reduced the military's influence in government "by removing strong military figures who were liable to challenge his policies and by insisting on greater professionalism in the event of renewed conflict with Israel" (Global Security.org, 1/29/11). In effect, Sadat believed these reforms were necessary to remedy the previous two decades of spending. The costs of maintaining a military-dominated state were harming Egypt.

In addition to reaching out to the military, Sadat felt he needed to reach out to the opposition. More specifically, the Brotherhood was allowed to resume some of their activities without being legalized. Accordingly, the Brother's were allowed to re-establish its press, proselytize openly, and gave the Islamists wide latitude to organize on university campuses. Sadat seems to have understood the draw the Brotherhood had within Egyptian society. As Cook (2011) argues, "Even though it was a shadow of itself, the Brothers could claim the legacy of a truly mass movement and thus remained a potential political and social force" to assist Sadat "in the de-Nasserization of politics and society" (124–25).

In sum, Sadat had established full control of the political system, but by 1973, he "remained deeply concerned about potential rivals, economic indicators were mixed with overall growth slowing, and he confronted significant frustration and political opposition over his handling of Israel's occupation of the Sinai and other Arab territories" (Cook 2011, 135). Nasser's fortunes would change after Egypt went to war with Israel in October 1973 to drive the Israelis from the Canal Zone. Egypt's driving of the Israeli Defense Force from the Canal Zone would earn Sadat the moniker "Hero of the Crossing." Although Israel ultimately defeated Egypt, the initial re-capturing of the Suez and Sinai afforded Sadat the opportunity to further pursue his agenda.

Sadat's second set of reforms began with the ouster of the armed forces chief of staff, General el Shazly and the editor of al Ahram, Mohammad Hassanein Heikal, for raising questions about Sadat's potential turn to the United States to mediate between Israel and Egypt after the war despite the fact that the Soviets had provided money and materiel to help rebuild the Egyptian military prior to the war (Cook 2011, 136). Next Sadat issued the "October Paper" to leverage his newfound popularity to chart a new course for Egypt's social and economic development. The most important part of the October Paper was the introduction of the *Infitah* (opening) policy. *Infitah* established a parallel market to open up competition in the Egyptian economy and the military took advantage of this by establishing businesses in defense, manufacturing, industry, and agriculture. According to Cook (2011), "Although the socialist discourse remained, and the state would continue to be the primary economic actor, *Infitah* made it clear that Egypt's future economic development lay with the private sector, foreign investment, and integration of the Egyptian economy with the outside world" (137).

To this end, by 1976, the United States was providing Egypt with almost $1 billion in economic aid (Cook 2011, 141). Also, there was a trade deficit resulting from Nasser's providing of subsidies for basic goods including bread, cooking oil, rice, fuel, sugar, and cigarettes. On the advice of the International Monetary Fund, Sadat proposed a reduction of these subsidies. Consequently, Egyptians took to the streets to protest the proposed subsidy cuts, since the lower-middle, lower classes, and students were most impacted. These protests, known as the "Bread Riots," startled Sadat and when the police were unable to control the protests Sadat asked the military to step in to restore order.

Wary that the military might be blamed by the politicians if something went wrong, field marshal el Gamasy demanded that Sadat rescind the proposed subsidy cuts before he put tanks and troops on the streets. Sadat agreed and the military subsequently restored order. The military leadership noted pointedly "that the army units returned to their barracks as soon as . . . [the emergency] had ended. The efficiency and professionalism the armed forces demonstrated . . . reinforced the public's perception that the army was the ultimate safeguard against militant Islamists or others who might threaten civil authority" (Global Security.org, 1/29/11).

Third, to address the growing unrest within Egyptian society, Sadat opened up the political system allowing multiple parties to run in elections for the National Assembly in 1976. Rosefsky Wickham (2002) notes, "From the beginning, however, admission to the party system was restricted to only a few actors. For example, the Political Parties Law (Law 40 of 1977) excluded parties based on class, religion, or regional affiliation" (65). The purpose of the Political Parties Law was to limit the involvement of the Brotherhood and Nasserists; movements with "the greatest capacity for popular mobilization" (Rosefsky Wickham 2002, 65). As part of the new law, any criticism of the regime "was to be 'constructive' and was not to attack Sadat's major reorientation of Egyptian foreign and economic policy" (Rosefsky Wickham 2002, 65). By 1981, Rosefsky Wickham (2002) continues, "[T]here were only three legal parties: the ruling National Democratic Party, and two 'loyal' opposition parties (center right and center left) headed by politicians close to the regime and lacking ties to a mass base" (65). The outcome of this reform actually had the unintended consequence quite common in many authoritarian regimes undertaking political reform; liberalization created "a political system with a hollow core and a dynamic periphery, in which Islamists barred from contesting power within the formal party system diverted their activity to institutional outlets outside the regime's control" (Rosefsky Wickham 2002, 64).

The liberalization of the political system, promises of economic opening, and an additional emphasis on *sharia* was not enough to prevent the continued deterioration of the domestic security situation. Consequently, more than 1,500 people from various political parties on the left and right were arrested, opposition publications were banned and mosques were placed under the direct supervision of the government (Cook 2011, 153). Moreover, Sadat and his Vice President, Hosni Mubarak, went to U.S. and European capitals several times between January 1980 and October 1981. Sadat requested and received $3 billion of military credits from the United States. As part of the deal, the United States supplied F-15 & F-16 combat aircraft. This began a thirty-year relationship between the United States and Egypt, making Egypt the second largest recipient of U.S. foreign aid behind only Israel.

The increasing reliance on U.S. aid, afforded the United States the opportunity to persuade Sadat to attempt peace with his longtime enemy, Israel. Sadat was assassinated in 1981 at a Military Day parade by an Islamic Jihad assassin for signing the Camp David Accord in 1979 with Israel. Cook (2011) succinctly sums up Egyptian politics at this stage: "At the end of Sadat's reign, the fundamental nature of the political order was more contested than ever" (154).

After Sadat's assassination, Vice-President Hosni Mubarak became president. Cook (2011), describing Mubarak in the early years of his rule, states, "Although he rose through the ranks of the military quickly and was ultimately tapped to become vice president, Mubarak seemed hardly skilled at politics. During the early years of his presidency, Mubarak's reputation as a politician ranged from awkward at best to outright dim-witted at worst" (158). This description notwithstanding, Mubarak was able to consolidate his power by limiting the influence of opposition parties, reinforcing the power of regime loyalists (bourgeoisie, rural notables, and bureaucrats). He also reformed the Political Party Law, which allowed Muslim Brotherhood limited participation in politics. Mubarak's success in consolidating his power can be attributed to his relationship with the military and the economic and military aid received from the IMF and the United States.

When Mubarak took office, there were tensions within the Military high command over their role having been downgraded since 1973. According to Robert Springborg (1989), "Not only had its size and role been reduced, but the debate about additional duties the military might perform as its defense role contracted had produced few tangible results" (97–98). In part, the Egyptian economy was to blame during the 1980s and into the early 1990s. Egypt had a growing population and a GDP of slightly less than $900. There was significant foreign debt and rising unemployment. As Cook (2011) argues, "In order for Egypt to arrest the further deterioration of its economy, a consensus of international financial bureaucrats, U.S. officials, and a somewhat reluctant Egyptian government determined that the country needed a reform program that would bring public debt under control, privatize the state-owned sector, and, overall, make the country attractive to the kind of investment that would produce significant job growth" (159). In 1987, Egypt and the IMF struck a deal to reschedule its debt in exchange for the reforming of price controls, an increase in the interest rate, a loosening of import restrictions; however, the deal fell through after only six months due to Egypt's foot dragging (Cook 2011, 159–60).

Nevertheless, Egypt was still able to count on economic assistance from the United States. Throughout the 1980s and 1990s, the United States continued to provide foreign aid to Egypt in return for Egypt's continued recognition of the Camp David Accords. In return for the aid, Egypt served as an important strategic partner for the United States. Because of this position, Cook (2011) argues, "Mubarak calculated that Washington was not going to let an asset like Egypt sink under the weight of its own economic contradictions" (161). For example, after the Gulf War, Egypt was rewarded for their assistance with U.S. and Arab creditors writing off or cancelling $20 billion of Egypt's debt and Washington convinced the Paris Club to have half of Cairo's debt to Europe forgiven (Cook 2011, 161).

Debt forgiveness allowed Egypt to take out future loans and receive a more favorable interest rate, but more importantly, the military's involvement in Egypt's industrial, military, and agricultural sectors grew under Minister of Defense Abu Ghazala. Despite the government's fiscal austerity, Abu Ghazala purchased modern weaponry from the US during the 1980s and upgraded the living conditions of both officers and enlisted personnel (GlobalSecurity.org, 1/29/11). Robert Springborg (1989) characterizes Abu Ghazala as follows: "He is correspondingly pro-U.S. . . . . He strongly favors the participation of U.S. multinational corporations in the Egyptian economy" (100). While Abu Ghazala tried not to be seen as a rival to Mubarak, Mubarak thought otherwise and removed Abu Ghazala for what some said was a scandal over arms smuggling from the U.S. Others felt that Mubarak considered him too influential (GlobalSecurity.org, 1/29/11).

By the 1990s, the Mubarak regime was once again challenged by the Muslim Brotherhood. In fact, since 1984, the Brotherhood was alternately tolerated and repressed. Rosefsky Wickham (2011) makes an interesting point regarding the Brotherhood's entrance into the political system:

Although the Brotherhood entered the political system in order to change it, it ended up being changed by the system. Leaders who were elected to professional syndicates engaged in sustained dialogue and cooperation with members of their political movements, including secular Arab nationalists. Through such interactions, Islamists and Arabists found common ground in the call for an expansion of public freedoms, democracy, and respect for human rights and the rule of law, all of which, they admitted, their movements had neglected in the past (93).

Moreover, the Brotherhood's repression by the Mubarak regime resulted in self-assessment and the fracturing of the Brotherhood into three different factions. The first is the *da'wa* faction and is ideologically conservative, controls the bureaucratic operations and the allocation of resources. Loyalty for this faction comes from Egyptian youth, particularly in rural areas. Second are the pragmatic conservatives, which seem to be the group's mainstream wing and the faction where members with legislative experience have hailed from. This group "combines religious conservatism with a belief in the value of participation and engagement" (Rosefsky Wickham 2011, 94). The final faction is the reformers who have remained with the Brotherhood. The reformers advocate a progressive interpretation of Islam (Rosefsky Wickham 2011, 95).

In the 1999 and 2005 parliamentary elections the Brotherhood did remarkably well against the regime's party, the NDP, and faced a harsh wave of repression after the 2005 election. The continued repression by the Mubarak regime engendered youth activists to express their grievances through a new generation of protest movements open to anyone (Shehata 2011, 141). As Sadat had done before him, Mubarak allowed limited opposition parties and movements to gain representation in the National Assembly and maintain a limited presence in civil society, as long as the regime's party, the NDP, maintained a two-thirds majority. However over the last five years, "the Mubarak regime began to violate this implicit agreement, by imposing renewed constraints on the ability of political parties and movements to organize and to contest elections" (Shehata, 142).

By 2010, the Mubarak regime's efforts at constraining Egyptian political parties and civil society would be in full view. The parliamentary elections on November 28, 2010, were criticized for extensive irregularities. The NDP won 95 percent of the 221 seats in the first round while the MB failed to win any seats (Esposito, et. al. 2016, 208). As a result, protestors alleged "fraud, ballot box stuffing, vote buying, illegal campaigning at polling stations, and physical exclusion from polling stations by government security forces and other opposition supporters" and with the overthrow of Tunisia's leader Zne al-Abidine Ben Ali on January 14, 2011, the Arab Spring would reach Egypt (Esposito, et al., 2016, 209). Egypt's pro-democracy protestors "were motivated not by the ideologies and slogans of Arab nationalism and socialism or Islamism, but by pragmatic issues. . . . It was broad-based, supported by the secular and religiously minded; young and old; men and women; Muslims and Christians; the poor, middle, and upper classes" (Esposito, et al., 2016, 209–10). Although the protestors would be successful in forcing Mubarak's resignation, the institutions of the Egyptian state—the bureaucracy, military, and judiciary—remained.

On February 9, 2011, the SCAF was created to govern Egypt's transition to democracy. Almost from the outset, the SCAF came into conflict with Islamists, secularists, revolutionary youth, such as the April 6th Movement, and the old guard of the Mubarak regime. There were several indicators, looking back, which indicate that the military had its own interests it wanted to protect. First, was the imposition of an extended emergency law to protect law and order. This led "to military trials of 12,000 people, 5,000 of whom were political prisoners" (Esposito, et al. 2016, 213). Second, the military issued a new timetable for elections; the presidential election was initially to be held in March 2011, but was postponed until after parliamentary elections in September 2011. Finally, the SCAF issued an interim constitution stipulating executive and legislative would reside under its purview. Paulo Gerbaudo (2013) argues, "Forfeiting its promise to guarantee a smooth and rapid transition to democracy, the SCAF repeatedly postponed the transfer of power to civilian authority, using the pretext of instability and engaging in bizarre legal quibbling" (13). Put simply, the military had economic interests it wanted to protect and according to General Mamdouh Shahin, a member of SCAF, "the military should be granted 'some kind of insurance' under Egypt's new new constitution 'so that it is not under the whim of a president,' and . . . not subject to parliamentary scrutiny" (Martini and Taylor 2011, 128).

Accordingly, SCAF's desire to guide the democratic transition would involve the legalization of banned political parties, the implementation of presidential term limits, and strengthened judicial oversight of elections to preserve their power and prevent a single challenger. The SCAF's thinking was summarized by Jeff Martini and Julie Taylor (2011): "Although the move did represent a concession to popular demands, it also diffused political power—something that clearly benefit[ed] the military" (129). This allowed the military to play the various political parties off against one another if necessary and also co-opt the powerful and wealthy, Mubarak's elites, from the NDP who worked in the judicial system, state run media outlets and those in the intelligence and security services to "exploit fears of minority Copts, liberals, secularists, and others who were anxious about life under an Islamist-dominated state" (Esposito, et al. 2016, 214–15).

The MB's victory in the November 2011–January 2012 parliamentary elections with the MB's FJP winning 235 of the 498 seats in the People's

Assembly, or 47 percent, would set the stage for four years of conflict between the MB and the military. In second place was the al-Nour party, a Salafist party. Third place went to the secular, liberal party, al-Wafd, while fourth place went to an alliance of secular parties calling themselves the Egyptian Bloc (Masoud 2014, 459–460). Masoud (2014) notes, "And true to its promise, the SCAF relinquished its legislative authority once the new parliament was seated. But it retained its executive role, and it did not cede to the new legislature the right to appoint the prime minister or any of the cabinet, rendering the parliament relatively toothless" (456). This conflict would carry over to the presidential elections that following June.

Due to the Islamists and Salafists winning 71 percent of the vote, the SCAF issued a declaration/charter in what has been called a "soft coup" to "subvert and delay democratic transitions under the guise of 'protecting' democracy from resurgent Islamist parties that had polled well in the election" (Esposito, et al. 2016, 217). SCAF, subsequently, amended the Egyptian constitution to give itself more sweeping political and military power, control over $1.3 billion in annual military aid from the United States, the ability to wage war without presidential or parliamentary approval, arrest powers, legislative and executive authority to oversee the writing of Egypt's new constitution (Esposito, et al. 2016, 217). SCAF then legitimized the candidacy of General Ahmad Shafiq for the presidential election; he was their preferred candidate. Shafiq ran as the "law and order" candidate and faced off against Morsi, who was the FJP's replacement candidate, after the disqualification of Khayrat al-Shatter, the deputy chairman of the Brotherhood (Esposito 2016, 218–19).

The MB issued a statement on June 18, 2012, denouncing the SCAF's usurpation of power when it dissolved parliament. The MB argued that the SCAF "must respect the will of the people and safeguard the remaining steps in the electoral process, preventing any voter fraud." (Ikhwanweb, June 18, 2012). Morsi used the unhappiness toward the rigging of elections to form an anti-Shafiq coalition and won the presidential election in a runoff on June 16–17, 2012. At this crucial time, why was their support thrown behind Morsi when it was apparent that the state was firmly against the MB? John Esposito, Tamara Sonn, and John Voll (2016) argue, "Many decided to support Morsi not because they supported Morsi or the MB but because they supported the revolution and were against the SCAF's attempted soft coup and the possibility of a return to the pre-revolutionary days of the old guard" (218).

Once Morsi was elected president, he sought to reinstate the power of the parliament, but was blocked by the judiciary, which still was staffed with loyalists to the Mubarak regime. Through a presidential decree Morsi stripped the SCAF of its powers and said legislative and executive authority would flow through his office. This was only the beginning of Morsi attempting to exert his authority over SCAF. First, in August 2012,

Morsi promoted al-Sisi, a devout Muslim from a younger generation of the military than Tantawi, to defense minister, since Tantawi, as spokesperson for the SCAF, represented an old guard that was resistant to change and "had neither an alternative vision for Egypt's future, nor an adequate understanding of its political terrain and socioeconomic complications" (Kandil 2013, 195). Second, Morsi's presidential team was dominated by FJP and al-Nour members and failed to keep a campaign promise to include a youth representative, woman, and Christian as vice presidents (Esposito, et. al. 2016, 220). Third, in late November 2012, Morsi issued constitutional decrees to further increase his power; these included shorting the term of the prosecutor general from a life term to four years, barring judical review of the second chamber of parliament and of his presidential decisions until a constitution was passed (Esposito, et al. 2016, 219–20). In short, Morsi's authoritarian turn, and his attack on the judiciary, which was staffed with Mubarak loyalists, led to conflict between the MB and judiciary and protests in the streets. Morsi supporters believed the Mubarak loyalists were blocking Morsi's initiatives, while the opponents argued that the MB wanted to remove secular judges to increase MB control. Put differently, the judiciary was part of the Deep State and firmly against Islamist policies.

Throughout this period an anti-Morsi coalition would continue to build. According to Espositio, Sonn and Voll (2016), "A broad-based anti-Morsi campaign grew rapidly, supported by elements of the deep state (military, police, judiciary, and bureaucrats), much of the Mubarak-era public media, secularists, April 6 youth, and some Muslim and Coptic religious leaders" and financed by wealthy Egyptians, Saudi Arabia and UAE" (Esposito, et al. 2016, 226). This broad-based coalition developed for two main reasons: secular and religious. The Egyptian public's hostility toward the MB occurred, Kandil (2014) notes, because "[a]s citizens, they were appalled at the Brotherhood's incompetence in government; and as Muslims, they were outraged at how their religion was manipulated to explain away this incompetence" (255). Kandil (2014) continues, "In a word, the people began to realize that Islamists flaunted Islam to excuse their intellectual bankruptcy and lurking authoritarianism. These were not god-fearing underdogs who strove for power to uphold Islam, but another breed of corrupt politicians using religion to justify their taking power" (255).

> By June 30, 2013, protesters once again filled Tahrir Square demanding government reforms and even Morsi's resignation. As the protests grew, five of Morsi's cabinet members resigned and al-Sisi issued a forty-eight-hour ultimatum; Morsi must compromise or the military would intervene (Esposito, et. al. 2016, 227). Morsi naturally rejected calls for his resignation. On July 3, 2013, al-Sisi suspended the constitution and overthrew Morsi. Adly Mansour was appointed as interim president and the military-backed interim government proceeded to

crack down on the MB with arrests and illegal detentions, restoration
of the Emergency Law, and the prohibition of public meetings of more
than ten people without permission (Esposito, et al. 2016, 228–30).

Al-Sisi would schedule the presidential elections for May 26–27, 2014. He
made the claim that his popularity with the Egyptian people would en-
gender a wide turnout; the expectation was for 80 percent of the electorate, some forty million voters (Esposito, et al. 2016, 233). In reality, there
was very low voter turnout. BBC News reported that turnout was about
46 percent and the Islamist, liberal and secular parties boycotted the vote
(BBC News, 5/29/14). Al-Sisi's election re-inforced "a military-guided authoritarian government whose repression, violence and brutality ex-
ceeded that of any government in modern Egyptian history" (Esposito, et
al. 2016, 234). Al-Sisi justified these policies saying Egypt is fighting a war
on terror fighting insurgents in Sinai during the last two years. In an
interview to the Reuters news agency, al-Sisi states, "The Egyptian army
is undertaking major operations in the Sinai so that it is not transformed
into a base of terrorism that will threaten its neighbors and make Egypt
unstable. If Egypt is unstable then the region is unstable. . . . We need
American support to fight terrorism, we need American equipment to
combat terrorism. Not just in Sinai" (Reuters, 5/15/14). Therefore, al-Sisi
uses the war on terror, and fear of Islamist rule, to justify authoritarianism. The next section will examine the influence of the Soviet Union and,
most recently, America in Egypt and the consequences for the region;
namely, facilitating the endurance of authoritarianism.

## REGIONAL AND INTERNATIONAL RELATIONS

As stated previously, Egypt's leaders have long sought international assistance. During Nasser's rule the Soviet Union was the patron, but under
Sadat and Mubarak, the United States had a more prominent influence.
More recently, in the later years of Mubarak, and into the Morsi and al-
Sisi regimes, the military has urged decisions be made with an eye toward protecting U.S. economic and military assistance. While, the military's place in the Deep State was detailed in the "military establishment"
section above, this section will focus on international influence, and more
specifically, how Soviet and U.S. foreign aid were an important part of
the establishment of the Deep State between 1952 and 1981 and the military's calculus in protecting the state instead of the democratic transition
process from 2011 to present.

The Soviet Union influenced the development of the Egyptian state
between the 1950s and 1970s. Arms and military training were provided
after the Free Officer coup so the Free Officers could protect Egyptian
sovereignty and security from the threat of British forces stationed in
Egypt. Moreover, the Soviets assisted Egypt in ending the Suez crisis in

1956 when Soviet Premier Nikolai Bulganin "sent messages to the heads of government of Britain, France and Israel stating the Soviet Union's firm stance with regard to the act of aggression and stressed the USSR's resolve to achieve its ending" (Sinaisky [n.d.], 151). Between 1956 and 1967, Soviet military aid to Egypt was $1.5 billion (Sinaisky [n.d.], 153). After the 1967 Six Day War, Nasser reached out to the Soviets to ask for immediate help in re-arming and rehabilitating the armed forces and developing its economy. In return, the Soviets were provided ports on the Mediterranean (Sinaisky [n.d.], 154). At this point, Soviet and Egyptian cooperation reached the level of strategic partnership.

By 1970, Sadat took office and believed another war with Israel would happen sooner rather than later. As such, Egypt-Soviet cooperation continued to help Egypt prepare for war against Israel. Sergei Sinaisky quotes from Egyptian army chief of staff at the time, General Saad Eddin El-Shazly's, memoirs, "'Without the help of the Soviet Union our battle would have been impossible. . . . No other country or a group of countries simultaneously could and would have supplied Egypt with the arms in the profusion and sophistication needed to combat Israel'" (156). To this end, Soviet military aid to Egypt from 1967 to 1973 was approximately $1.5 billion (Sinaisky [n.d.], 157).

Interestingly, Sadat also reached out to the United States. His goals were to acquire as many Soviet weapons as possible, while simultaneously trying to attract the United States knowing full well that both superpowers were engaged in a Cold War rivalry in the region. According to Sinaisky, "In a bid to interest the U.S. in closer relations with Egypt, he [Sadat] was offering it assurances that once the Israeli troops beg[a]n to withdraw from the Sinai, Soviet specialists would be expelled from Egypt and diplomatic relations with the U.S. restored" (156). Sadat also expressed disappointment with the Soviet Union "which he thought was unable to make Israel, through diplomatic means . . . withdraw from the captured territories, was not prepared to use military muscle for this purpose and was hesitant in supplying Arabs with weapons (Sinaisky [n.d.], 159). As a result, Soviet advisors and military materiel were sent back to the USSR by the end of August 1972 (Siniasky [n.d.], 161).

The United States would take advantage of the Soviet Union's departure shortly after Egypt's loss in the October War of 1973. After the war, Sadat needed to rebuild the Egyptian military, improve Egypt's financial situation, and decided to talk directly with Israel knowing that the United States would approve and would be important for Egypt's future militarily and politically. This turn to the United States was also borne out by the Arab world discrediting Egypt for signing the Camp David Accords. This would place Egypt in financial straits. Subsequently, Galal Amin (2011) notes that the Egyptian economy would pass through two stages: The first from 1975 to 1985, characterized by rapid economic growth, and the second from 1985 to 2006 with the acceptance of neoliberalism economic principles promoted by the West. Egypt's economic weakness from 1975 to 2006 was a result of "very low rate of saving, a persistent balance of trade deficit, and the weak performance of the two main commodity sectors: agriculture and manufacturing" (167–68). Amin (2011) argues that the weak performance of agriculture and manufacturing was a direct result of "the state relaxing its role in those two sectors, an essential part of the model not only encouraged but virtually demanded by Washington" and private sector investment "much higher rates of profit were bound to prevail in the service sectors, such as tourism, commerce, and entertainment, than in the manufacturing and agricultural sectors" (168).

Moreover, the United States and Egypt reestablished diplomatic ties in 1974 and beginning in 1975, U.S. aid would flow in to Egypt. During the Mubarak regime, Mubarak recognized the military necessity of U.S. assistance, and as mentioned earlier, debt was restructured for Egypt joining the coalition in the Persian Gulf War of 1991. In short, U.S. aid "accounts for almost half of the economic assistance that Egypt receives from all foreign sources" along with the rest coming from the IMF and World Bank (Masoud 2014, 465). Since the Arab Spring, Masoud (2014) argues that the country has profligate spending and spent most of its foreign reserves forcing Morsi, in August 2012, to sign a deal with the IMF for $4.8 billion in loans (467).

After the July 2013 coup, the Obama Administration suspended military aid to protest the military's overthrow of the democratically elected Morsi. However, the rise of the Islamic State renewed the United States's need to maintain its relationship with Egypt, despite having suspended aid for eighteen months, to fight terrorism. In March 2015, the United States resumed military aid to Egypt to the tune of $1.3 billion annually along with twelve F-16 fighter jets, replacement kits for 125 Abrams tanks, and twenty Harpoon missiles. A National Security Council spokeswoman said that Egypt remains the second largest recipient of U.S. foreign military aid (Ackerman, 3/31/15).

However, critics of the United States have argued since 2013 that the Obama administration's public support of the revolution, self-determination, and democracy was also buttressed by a support of maintaining stability and the status quo given the United States long economic support of various Egyptian governments. In short, "the message the Obama Administration sent reinforced a widespread belief that when it comes to the Arab world and its aspirations for democratic government, there is a double standard" (Esposito, et al. 2016, 229). The U.S. position, according to Esposito, Sonn, and Voll (2016), "not only reinforced the hand of the Egyptian military but also risked further undermining America's ability to rebuild its credibility and role in the Middle East" (214). Therefore, the military, as part of the Deep State, will continue to use regional instability to maintain military and economic assistance from the United States.

Doing so will create conflict toward the state from civil society and facilitate the endurance of authoritarianism, since the military, bureaucracy, and judiciary have been the stronger state institutions within Egypt since 1952.

## CONCLUSION

At the outset of this chapter, we asked what role the military plays in Egypt. The Egyptian military since 1952 has sought to protect its institutional interests. Over the course of its political development, the Egyptian military's interests became entrenched as part of a Deep State and brought them into conflict with politicians on a regular basis. Nasser, Sadat, Mubarak, SCAF, and al-Sisi were all from the military, while Morsi was from the oft-banned MB. Egypt's Deep State had become entrenched over nearly sixty years of military influence in politics.

Since the Arab Spring, the Egyptian military exerted its influence on the democratic transition process. Generals Tantawi and al-Sisi were officers who were products of their institution; Tantawi as a product of the Soviet-influenced and al-Sisi of the American-influenced Egyptian military. Both sought to protect the interests of the military and, in many instances, continued to face conflict from both politicians and their respective societies for their chosen policies. Both generals wanted to protect professionalism and the military's place in politics, but Egypt as the largest Arab state, is seen as a bellweather for the region. The events of the last few years have shown al-Sisi is using the War on Terror to justify the state's return to authoritarianism and continued influence of the Deep State. The next chapter will take us to Pakistan, a complex, yet fascinating state, facing a similar struggle between its military and Islamist forces.

# FOUR

# Pakistan

The state of Pakistan was founded in 1947 as a state for the Muslim population of India. However, the state has continued to fight numerous ethnic, religious, and linguistic forces as it comes to grip with how to define its identity as the Islamic Republic of Pakistan. The death of Pakistan's founder, Muhammad Ali Jinnah in 1948 set off a chain of events culminating in authoritarianism taking hold throughout the state. This continuous instability between the nation's political elite allowed the state's strongest institutions—the army and the bureaucracy—to usurp power from the elites who were subsumed in ethnic and regional rivalries. Subsequently, the Pakistani state was subject to military rule four times throughout its history: 1958–1969 under General Ayub Khan; 1969–1971 under General Yahya Khan; 1977–1988 under General Muhammad Zia ul-Haq; and 1999–2008 under General Pervez Musharraf.

This chapter examines the domestic and international factors that brought these men in on horseback and what led to Pakistan's brief experiment with "democracy" from 1956 to 1958 under President Iskander Mirza; 1988–1999 under Prime Ministers Benazir Bhutto and Nawaz Sharif; 2008–2013 under President Asif Ali Zadari, and 2013–Present under Prime Minister Nawaz Sharif. Ultimately, the relationship between the dramatis personae that follows highlights a tale that continues to unfold as the nation comes to grips with itself since independence from the yoke of British colonialism.

## HISTORY

From the moment of its inception, Pakistan possessed a strong bureaucracy, legal tradition, military, a powerful uniting figure in Jinnah, and an important strategic position as a bridge between South Asia, Central

Asia, and the Middle East. Pakistan was created as a Muslim Homeland on the Subcontinent, due to the Muslims being the minority in Hindu dominated India (they were only one-fourth the population of India). Interestingly, prior to the British Raj in the eighteenth and nineteenth centuries, Muslims ruled India for more than eight hundred years (Ahmad 2006, 364). Muslims and Hindus were able to live harmoniously during that time in a multicultural and multireligious society.

However, once the British came to power "overt and covert discrimination based on religious identities became a matter of policy" (Ahmad 2006, 364). A coalition was formed between the British and Hindu elites and systematically new agricultural, educational, and economic systems were put into place to discriminate against Muslims. Moreover, the Indian National Congress, representing the Hindu majority, championed secularism, parliamentary democracy, and socialism. As Kurshid Ahmad (2006) notes, "The thrust of this . . . new system was that it produced a new class of people: Indian in race and blood and British in taste and culture" (364). These Indians described by Ahmad became the new civil and military elites in India and were the instruments of colonial divide and rule policy.

From 1906 to 1940, Muslims in India thought they could maintain their distinct ideological culture and political identity after previous years of being able to work together. Unfortunately, it was not to be. Consequently, the political leadership of Muslim India, led by Jinnah, proposed the "Two Nation Theory." This theory "is the principle of plurality of faiths, ideologies, religions, cultures, and identities. 'Two' does not simply mean 'one plus one' — it signifies the fact that there are two major political streams, one based on faith, religion, and divine linkage and another committed to a vision that is exclusively secular and of this world, unrelated to religion and divinely related values" (Ahmad, 366). In other words, the Two Nation Theory was arguing for a Hindu and Muslim nation that should live side by side and coexist, but at the same time justify using Islam to build a state that was different than the western model of secular, democratic nation-state; this was the "Idea of Pakistan" (Cohen 2001).

The "Idea of Pakistan" was first championed by Jinnah, a secular Bombay lawyer and politician. He effectively turned the Two Nation Theory into action by revitalizing the Muslim League in India to pressure the British and the Indian National Congress to accept a state of Pakistan. According to eminent South Asia expert Stephen P. Cohen, "Because he had to weld together disparate elements of the Indian Muslim community, Jinnah's arguments were deliberately vague" (Cohen 2004, 29). Jinnah's use of divisive rhetoric and extralegal procedures prior to independence changed to a vision of a democratic Pakistan that would be tolerant of religious minorities, socially progressive, and constitutionally modern once independence was granted. He continually gave speeches that urged the various ethnic groups to work together. He had to be the glue that held Pakistan together. Although, as Cohen points out, "A few speeches could not erase four decades of emphasis on the differences between Hindus and Muslims and the threat to Muslims from the larger community" (Cohen 2004, 43).

The coups of 1958, 1969, 1977, and 1999 occurred as a result of the conflict between politicians and the military created by a multitude of domestic and international factors. The death of Pakistan's founder Mohammad Ali Jinnah left the political elites without their leader and simmering ethnic and sectarian conflict would break out. The military, as the strongest institution at independence, intervened after ethnic and sectarian violence was engulfing multiple provinces and the politicians were unable to quell this violence. This produced the five-step dance where the military warns "incompetent" politicians that they are encroaching on the military's institutional and elite self-interests, a crisis occurs resulting in the intervention, followed by the military junta introducing constitutional changes to "straighten out" Pakistan (Cohen 2004). This chapter will examine the conflict between the military and politicians along with the implications of Pakistani civil–military relations on South Asia.

Pakistan's independence brought a huge wave of mass migration of Indian Muslims into the new state of Pakistan. Joining the Bengalis (the poorest, but the largest percentage of the population at over half), Punjabis, Sindhis, Baluch, and Pashtuns, were the predominately Urdu speaking migrants, the Mohajirs. The Mohajirs were from North India and most Mohajirs who migrated were from the leadership and professional classes. This group struck up an alliance with the Punjabis, the dominant ethnic group in the bureaucracy and military to form what scholars call "The Establishment" (Cohen 1984; Rizvi 2000; Cohen 2004). Consequently, tensions would consistently boil over vis-à-vis the Punjab-Mohajir Establishment and the Sindis, Baluchs and Pashtuns. Due to the increasing tensions after independence, the Establishment had to construct an ethnolinguistic-nationalist narrative. This narrative before and after 1970 struck the same refrain: a strong central government and limited provincial autonomy (Cohen 2004, 204–5).

In 1948, a year after independence, the development of the Pakistani state would be forever altered. First, Pakistan and India would go to war over the province of Kashmir. According to Cohen, "For many Pakistanis, but especially that first generation, Kashmir's captivity conjured up vivid images of oppression" (Cohen 2004, 52). Second, the state witnessed a leadership crisis when Jinnah passed away and three years later his deputy (and successor) Liaquat Ali Khan was assassinated. Third, the interethnic conflict between Mohajirs, who favored a secular state, and the Muslim Leaguers who favored Islamization, a state-managed economy, and a go-slow policy of land reform continued to grow. Ultimately, Jinnah and Khan attempted to build the political institutions and processes of Pakistan based on justice and fair play, tolerance and consent; however, "they did not appreciate the scale of the task of evolving participatory political institutions in the post-colonial societies, they faltered and adopted authoritarian approaches to political management, increasing their reliance on the state apparatus" (Rizvi 2000, 17). The military was all too willing to use this opportunity to acquire political clout and thus began Pakistan's dance between military rule and "democracy."

Prior to his assassination, Liaquat Ali Khan, was left with the tremendous task of continuing a complicated nation-building endeavor. Liaquat, a Punjabi, was a British-trained lawyer who attempted to get the various ethnicities' interests to coalesce. To accomplish this task, Craig Baxter (1995) notes, "Liaquat used his experience in law to attempt to frame a constitution along the lines of the British Westminster system of parliamentary democracy" (38). However, provincialism and factional politics soon took over. In Punjab, internecine policking resulted in a clash between Sardar Shaukat Hayat Khan and Mumtaz Daultana (Nawaz 2008, 77). Both had joined the Muslim League government, but the government was in the process of fracturing after independence. While the Muslim League's leaders were urban professionals, their political base was mainly in areas that were in India. Punjab was not the only province where the Muslim League was facing problems.

In the Northwest Frontier Province (hereafter NWFP), the Muslim League had established a strong position at partition due to the strength of Chief Minister Khan Adul Qayyum Khan and the commissioner in Peshawar, Iskander Mirza, but clashes soon developed between the Muslim League and separatist leader Khan Abdul Ghaffar Khan. As political analyst Shuja Nawaz (2008) notes, "Apart from this political conflict the autocratic style of Qayyum and his use of condoning of 'jobbery, bribery, and nepotism' that had drawn even the attention of an angry Jinnah, led to a ceaseless battle for control of the province" (77–78). Moreover, in Sindh, there were frequent clashes between a powerful chief minister, Ayub Khuhro, and Governor Ghulam Hussain Hidayatullah. The conflict between Khuhro and Hidayatullah resulted in a judicial inquiry where Khuhro was found guilty of multiple charges of poor administration and misconduct and still was elected president of the Sindh Muslim League.

Consequently, these events throughout each of the provinces led to the creation of the Public and Representative Office Disqualification Act (PRODA) which disqualified a person from politics if they were convicted of misconduct. Categories of political crimes were created and politicians were tried by tribunals appointed by the provincial governor (Talbot 2005, 137). In effect, this Act allowed government to disqualify their political opponents without just cause. Despite the continued factionalism within the provinces, the central government maintained increasing control as Liaquat centralized power and worked to reinvigorate the Muslim League. In addition to the PRODA, Liaquat oversaw three important developments in the history of Pakistan: 1) the passage of the 1949 Objectives Resolution through the Constituent Assembly; 2) the buildup of the Pakistani army, specifically the Pakistanisation of the higher echelons of the officer corps; and 3) the courting of American aid. Each of these developments will be discussed in turn, as they had important influences on Pakistan's path away from democracy and toward authoritarianism.

Pakistan's first Constituent Assembly and its eighty members functioned as Pakistan's legislature. On March 7, 1949, Liaquat moved the Objectives Resolution through the Assembly (Baxter 1995, 40). The principles of democracy, independent judiciary, freedom, equality, tolerance, Islamic social justice, and minority rights were set forth in the Objectives Resolution (Talbot 2005, 139). In other words, the Objectives Resolution, which would become the preamble of the first Pakistani constitution, enshrined Pakistan as Islamic, democratic, and federal. However, the division of executive power between the governor general and the prime minister, the distribution of power between the federal government and the provinces, the electoral balance of power between West and East Pakistan, and the role of Islam were all issues that needed to be worked out (Baxter 1995, 40).

Unfortunately, the next stage of the constitution writing process, the publication of the basic principle's committee's report in October 1950, was mired in controversy "mainly because of Bengali opposition to the denial of their demographic majority" (Talbot 2005, 139). The major point of contention in the early years was the fact that the East Pakistanis had the majority of the population, but representation in government was not proportional to population size. Political control was in West Pakistan and dominated by the West Pakistanis.

The continued factionalism present during these early years allowed the Pakistani armed forces to become a prominent player in the direction of the country. Having recently fought against India after declaring independence, the Pakistani Army "had tasted war in its first few months of independence, seen the civilian decision-making up close, and found it wanting" (Nawaz 2008, 79). At independence, the British split the Indian Army evenly in terms of men and materiel between Pakistan and India. Also, the first commander-in-chiefs of the new Pakistani army were British and during the first few years of independence the army's officer corps was an amalgam of both British and Pakistani officers. Although, shortly after independence, Pakistani officers began to take over more responsibility, since promotions were engineered by senior British officers who "had little patience for the officers who exhibited strong political leanings. . . . [Those] who were promoted in those early days were often accelerated to higher levels, often well before they had the experience or the *gravitas* for command (79). This promotion policy was a direct

result of Liaquat's Pakistanization of the officer corps and would be no-
ticed by a major general named Muhammad Ayub Khan.

Ayub, a Pashtun from the village of Rehana, located fifty miles north
of Rawalpindi, was a member of the Tarin tribe. His upbringing has been
characterized by historian Ian Talbot as "comfortable" and informed his
social and cultural outlook (Talbot 2005, 149). He came from a large family where they made ends meet by working the land well. Ayub would
later draw on this in his land reform program. Moreover, Ayub's father
sent him to Aligarh College where he would "'learn to feel like a Muslim'" (Khan 1967, 5; cited in Talbot 2005, 149). This experience afforded
Ayub an education that shaped his views regarding modernization and
Islam. Consequently, "Ayub made little attempt to hide his detestation of
the mullahs who he declared had, no less than the politicians, been cove-
tous of 'wealth and power and did not stop short of any mischief'" (Talbot 2005, 150).

By the time Ayub was serving in the Pakistani Army, events from
1948 to 1951 reinforced in Ayub a dislike for politicians and the certainty
that Pakistan's survival "was vitally linked with the establishment of a
well-trained, well-equipped, and well-led army" (Talbot 2005, 151). Specifically, Ayub was assigned in January 1948 as the commanding officer
of East Pakistan and he personally witnessed Bengali uprisings against
the central government in West Pakistan. He personally had to send
troops to the Assembly building to prevent students from attacking it
(Talbot 2005, 151). Furthermore, after his return to West Pakistan, Ayub
became a candidate to become the first Pakistani commander-in-chief of
the army. Ayub was not the first choice to be army chief; that went to
General Iftikhar Khan. Iftikhar was previously junior to Ayub, as he was
commissioned a year later, and was reportedly favored by the British to
succeed Gracey. Unfortunately, Iftikhar, his wife and son, and Sher Khan
(another senior general) were killed in a Pak Air aircraft that crashed near
Karachi (Nawaz 2008, 79–80). With the selection process disrupted, Liaquat invited the senior-most officers to a conference in Rawalpindi to
assess them and their thought processes. After Ayub made "a fine pres-
entation," Liaquat "was sold on him [Ayub] as the first Pakistani commander-in-chief, apparently without bringing into account any regional
or other considerations" (Nawaz 2008, 80). Ayub took over his role on
January 17, 1951, and would soon be thrust into the political process. A
vital component behind Ayub's influence in Pakistani politics came from
his cementing a relationship with the United States; a relationship which
began under Liaquat.

For Liaquat, the central tenets of Pakistan's foreign policy were the
integrity of Pakistan, Islamic culture, and economic development. The
United States "was Pakistan's great-power patron of choice, crucial as a
source of weapons and economic aid" (Haqqani 2005, 32). Early on, Liaquat viewed an alliance with the United States just as vital to the consoli-

dation of the Pakistani nation-state as the use of Islam and opposition to India. Former Pakistani Ambassador to the United States, Husain Haqqani argues that since the end of the Kashmir war the Pakistani joint services intelligence was exploring options of how to possibly receive aid from American intelligence to build an "'Islamic barrier against the Soviets'" (Haqqani 2005, 32). To this end, Liaquat was invited to Washington, DC, by President Harry Truman and during his visit declared Pakistan's alignment with the United States, specifically supporting U.S. actions in Korea. As a result, U.S. economic aid flowed to Pakistan; however, Haqqani notes, "Liaquat balanced his generally pro-West policy with a refusal to align Pakistan completely with the United States 'unless Washington guaranteed Pakistan's security against India'" (Haqqani 2005, 33). In fact, to get the United States's attention, he announced a visit to Moscow—which was later cancelled—to counter Indian Prime Minister Nehru's planned visit to the United States (Nawaz 2008, 94). Conditions such as these, put in place by Liaquat, upset the army, which was more concerned with keeping itself well-supplied. Nevertheless, Liaquat, his foreign minister, Sir Zafarula Khan, and Ayub would sit down with the United States to formalize a treaty just prior to Liaquat's assassination in October 1951.

Although Liaquat and Ayub had begun negotiating agreements with the United States, events back in Pakistan were heating up as a group of army officers were dissatisfied and disagreements began mounting between Liaquat and this group of officers. Shortly after taking office as commander-in-chief of the Pakistani Army, Ayub was informed by Liaquat that a group of army officers and bureaucrats were planning a *coup d'etat*, known later as the Rawalpindi Conspiracy, to install a military-style nationalistic government (Nawaz 2008, 83). The coup was planned by Major General Akbar Khan, chief of the general staff, and he and his co-conspirators felt civilians did not have Pakistan's best interests at heart and the British officers in senior positions should be removed in favor of Pakistanis. The fourteen conspirators were arrested, tried in secret, found guilty, and imprisoned. However, four years later the conspirators were released after their sentences were commuted (Nawaz 2008, 83–84).

Meanwhile, Liaquat continued to try and resolve disputes within the Muslim League in the provinces. In particular, he was receiving increasing criticism from Punjabi politicians as a weak, ineffective politician lacking a strong political base. He owed his position in power to Jinnah and was viewed "as an outsider in Pakistan where a battle was brewing between the provincial 'insiders'—those who belonged to the four provinces that formed Pakistan—and the muhajir 'outsiders,' who had migrated from India to the new state" (Nawaz 2008, 85). This prevented Liaquat from concentrating on the production of a constitution for Pakistan and, instead, work on the constitution was delegated to bureaucrats, which allowed them to take a prominent role in the direction of the country along with army. As Nawaz (2008) argues, "Political systems abhor vacuums much like the laws of physics. A weak and dithering central authority gave both the bureaucrats and the Pakistan Army a chance to assert their role in shaping policy nationwide" (84).

Complicating the situation further after Liaquat's assassination was a bureaucratic tug-of-war for power which one author (Nawaz 2008) defined as "The Post-Liaquat Mess." After Liaquat's assassination, Ghulam Mohammad, a Punjabi from the civil service and the former finance minister under Liaquat's administration, was named Governor General replacing Khwaja Nazimuddin, a Bengali, who became prime minister. Mohammad's elevation to governor general meant the ascendancy of the first Pakistani bureaucrat to a position of power (Nawaz 2008, 86). According to Craig Baxter (1995), "Ghulam Mohammad, who relished the trappings of dominance earlier held by Jinnah, asserted his power by declaring martial law in 1953 in Punjab . . . [and a] year later, he imposed governor's rule after the Muslim League defeat in East Bengal" (40). Subsequently, Nazimuddin attempted to limit the powers of Mohammad through amendments to the Government of India Act of 1935, which was still the basic law for Pakistan at the time. This direct confrontation resulted in Nazimuddin asking for the army's assistance. Thus, with the army's assistance of the population during the floods, Major General Muhammad Azam Khan introduced the army as a major force working on behalf of Pakistanis (Nawaz 2008, 87).

By April 1953, Mohammad dismissed Nazimuddin and appointed a "cabinet of talents" headed by Mohammad Ali Bogra, a former Pakistani ambassador to the United States, containing both military and civilian leaders. Former head of the civil service, Chaudhuri Mohammad Ali became finance minister, Ayub Khan became minister of defense and retained his position as commander in chief, while Major General Iskander Mirza (who was governor of East Pakistan during Mohammad's governor's rule) became minister of home affairs. In short, a position in the cabinet would allow the army to take a more direct role.

There was continuing internecine warfare between politicians, bureaucrats, and the military during the next two years with the dissolution of the Constituent Assembly and then the adoption of a new constitution. The politicians "who led the Pakistan movement used the principles and legal precedents of a nonreligious British parliamentary tradition even while they advanced the idea of Muslim nationhood as an axiom. Many of them represented a liberal movement in Islam, in which their personal religion was compatible with Western technology and political institutions" which was in contrast to the traditionalist ulama, "whose position was a legalistic one based on the unity of religion and politics in Islam" (Baxter 1995, 41–42).

The ulama "asserted that the Quran, the sunna, and the sharia provided the general principles for all aspects of life if correctly interpreted and applied" (Baxter 1995, 42). In a sense, the government could not ignore a group who enjoyed influence among the masses in Pakistani society, especially in urban areas among the lower middle class, refugees, and students. Moreover, politicians could not be seen as anti-Islamic, and thus were willing to accommodate the ulama. In particular, a group known as the Jama'at-i-Islami (hereafter JI) has been the most influential Islamist movement in Pakistan. As Baxter (1995) notes, "Unlike the traditional ulama, the Islamist movement was the outcome of modern Islamic idealism. Crucial in the constitutional and political development of Pakistan, it forced politicians to face the question of Islamic identity" (42).

Despite the increased role Islamists would play throughout the country, during the 1950s, Mawdudi's only success was the introduction of Islamic principles into the 1956 constitution, most of which "define[d] ways in which the Islamic way of life and Islamic moral standards could be pursued" (Baxter 1995, 42–43). Nevertheless, the Islamists had entrenched themselves within the internecine warfare taking place between the politicians, bureaucrats, and army. In February 1956, Mirza would become the first president of the Republic of Pakistan. Although, Ayub and the army would seek out a relationship with the United States and with the election of President Dwight D. Eisenhower, the Pakistanis sought to solidify this relationship.

During September and October 1953, Ayub made a visit to Washington, DC, ahead of Pakistan's civilian head of state and foreign minister to offer the Pakistani military's services as "the West's eastern anchor in an Asian alliance structure" (Haqqani 2005, 33). Accordingly, Pakistan signed a Mutual Defense Assistance Agreement with the United States and became a member of the Southeast Asia Treaty Organization (SEATO). The purpose of this alliance was to contain communism as Eisenhower's administration sought to reduce U.S. involvement in military operations undertaken in Korea through the building of military capability of "Northern Tier" states such as Pakistan, Iran, Turkey, and Iraq. Ayub and Mirza saw this alliance with the United States as an opportunity to receive economic assistance for the Pakistani military. In fact, Haqqani (2005) argues, "In their eagerness to seek alliance with the United States, Pakistani officials had exaggerated their commitment to fighting communism and had even pledged that U.S. military aid would not be used against India" and going so far as telling an American official "'Our army can be your army if you want'" (34–35).

The reality, according to Haqqani (2005), was an increase in Ayub's standing with the Pakistani ruling elite and, most importantly, a gateway for the military to remain involved in Pakistan's future development (36). Within a short time, "Ayub Khan had become a powerful figure. Perhaps more than any other Pakistani" (Baxter 1995, 45). This clout earned Ayub an appointment as defense minister in 1953, in addition to his duties as commander-in-chief, and afforded him the ability to veto any policy that was anathema to the interests of the Pakistani military. In effect, he was a behind-the-scenes power broker due to his close friendship with Mirza. It was Mirza who asked the military to assist the bureaucracy in running the state in a "superordinate-subordinate relationship," with the military being subordinate to the bureaucracy (Siddiqa 2007, 70). Between 1954 and 1958, both the bureaucracy and the military increased their influence as the country "went through seven prime ministers and several cabinets during this prolonged period of uncertainty" (Haqqani 2005, 37). The bureaucracy and the army were beset with sectarian and regional divisions, which would influence Ayub as he consolidated his position. After the introduction of the first constitution in 1956, Mirza became a strong president and gave his friend Ayub two extensions as commander-in-chief, ultimately setting Mirza and Ayub on a collision course to determine the true center of power in Pakistani politics.

In 1956, the first constitution introduced a parliamentary system that was weak from the outset. In West Pakistan, Sindh and the Northwest Frontier Province (NWFP) there was increasing discord at the level of political and economic authority given to Punjab, while fear and mistrust was growing vis-à-vis politicians in the Awami League within East Pakistan. Nevertheless, Mirza "continued to try his hand at running the show from his office, disregarding the parliamentary system that he had helped introduce and that had elected him president" (Nawaz 2008, 150). On October 7, 1958, President Mirza suspended the 1956 constitution and implemented martial law with support of the military and bureaucracy. In effect, Mirza's implementation of martial law was used to forestall an electoral defeat in the upcoming 1959 election that analysts in the U.S. State Department argue would have seen Bengali interests win, thereby increasing demand for greater autonomy and public funds for East Pakistan (Nawaz 2008, 157).

Moreover, Mirza saw martial law as the means to rescue the country from its political drift and considered imposing martial law. This put him in direct confrontation with his Chief Martial Law Administrator (CMLA), Ayub, who also articulated a separate vision for the direction martial law was to take. For Ayub, martial law was not to take "'a minute longer than necessary,' but with a caveat that it 'will not be lifted a minute earlier than the purpose for which it has been imposed has been fulfilled'" (Nawaz 2008, 159). To counter the growing influence of the military, Mirza attempted to have four generals in the Martial Law Administration removed and ordered the arrest of Ayub stating that "certain army generals were getting 'too big for their breeches' and that in the interests of national unity they would have to be removed from the scene" (Nawaz 2008, 159). Upon his return from meetings in East Pakistan, Ayub confronted Mirza and Mirza denied having given the order. However, Mirza could not alter the fact that martial law had "shifted the power balance completely in favor of the military, making it untenable for Mirza to remain in charge" (Haqqani 2005, 38).

Mirza's cabinet included three army generals, including Ayub (as CMLA and prime minister), four West Pakistanis and four East Pakistanis. In setting up this cabinet, Mirza did not include anyone with a regional or national constituency. Having this support would be necessary in a confrontation with Ayub (Nawaz 2008, 160). Ayub then met with the other three members of the inner cabinet, Lieutenant Generals Azam, Sheikh, and Burki, and decided that they would ask Mirza to resign and, if he refused, to dismiss him. The generals went to the presidential palace on the morning of October 26, and after some persuasion, Mirza signed a letter of resignation (Nawaz 2008, 161). The next morning, on October 27, 1958, Ayub assumed the presidency.

Ayub Khan ruled as Pakistan's president for eleven years. From the outset he sought to differentiate his regime from previous civilian governments. Ayub's desire was to build national identity based upon Pakistan's economic development, since he believed religion should be a private matter (Nasr 2009, 211). Thus, Ayub worked with his fellow officers to consolidate the position of the military, remove "inefficient and rascally" politicians, and improve stability by altering economic, legal, and constitutional institutions (Baxter 1995, 45).

Between 1958 and 1962, Ayub used martial law to introduce these institutional reforms through the Basic Democracies Order. The Basic Democracies were essentially individual administrative units which were used "to educate a largely illiterate population in the working of government by giving them limited representation and associating them with decision making . . . in local government and rural development" (Baxter 1995, 48). Effectively, in regards to Basic Democracies, Baxter (1995) notes, "They were meant to provide a two-way channel of communication between the Ayub Khan regime and the common people and allow social change to move slowly" (48). Ayub's plan was to allow a semblance of representation but he wanted to maintain control and the bureaucracy was there to assist him.

The Basic Democracies was a multi-tiered system of councils, districts, and commissioners to oversee local development issues. Moreover, Ayub was implementing a guided democracy, but in reality, the Basic Democraces was an electoral college reaffirming Ayub, his policies, and those in society who already held power. According to Talbot (2005), "The Basic Democrats collectively formed the electoral college which affirmed Ayub Khan as President in January 1960 . . . reelected him as President in 1964 . . . and also chose the members of the National and Provincial Assemblies in the partyless elections of 1962, ensur[ing] that a parliament emerged which was dominated by landowners and *biraderi*—clan—leaders" (156).

Ayub promised a return to democracy and the 1962 Constitution brought an end to martial law. Ayub wanted to retain certain aspects of his authority, so the constitution "created a presidential system in which the traditional powers of the chief executive were augmented by control of the legislature, the power to issue ordinances, the right of appeal to referendum, protection from impeachment, control over the budget, and special emergency powers, which included the right to suspend civil rights" (Baxter 1995, 49). As Cohen (2004) argues, "Ayub's 1962 Constitution foresaw a disengagement of the military from politics and a transition to civilian rule by a 'careful tailoring' of Pakistan's political institutions and processes, and a co-option of a section of the political elite" (124). For Ayub, this was a patron-client relationship, not a partnership, with power derived from the proximity to the president.

However, Ayub could not keep a partyless system intact forever. Ayub "viewed the re-emergence of party politics with disquiet" but conditions on the ground forced his hand (Talbot 2005, 158). There were continued rumblings from the provinces. The Bengali and Sindhi elite were dissatisfied with Ayub's economic reforms, especially the One Unit Scheme. As Talbot (2005) notes, "This [alienation] was rooted in part in their [the Sindhi and Bengalis] historic marginalization in what were the preeminent institutions of the state, the Army and the elite cadre of the Civil Service of Pakistan" (161). The civil service, or bureaucracy, of Pakistan became important because of its role in the disbursement of development funds; however, "Bengalis were underrepresented not only at the Central Secretariat level but in the numerous commissions of inquiry which were instituted in such varied fields as land reform, franchise and constitutional recommendations, and the press" (Talbot 2005, 161). In effect, "[t]he Bengali elite's alienation was intensified by the fact that the economic development of the Ayub era largely passed them by . . . as [t]he demand for regional autonomy and for a two-economy policy became linked" (Talbot 2005, 163). Moreover, the Sindhis also felt marginalized from economic development with development funds being directed toward Punjabis, and with the replacement of the local dialect, Sindhi, by Urdu as the official language. In short, "[m]artial law shifted the balance of power in the ruling coalition firmly in the Punjabis' favor" (Talbot 2005, 164).

For Ayub, the development of the economy was of vital importance. His system of guided democracy was justified "not just in terms of cleaning out the Augean stables of the politicians, but also maintained that it could deliver reforms which were essential for the modernization of Pakistan" (Talbot 2005, 164). The Pakistani economy improved during the Ayub regime. According to Talbot (2005), "Large scale manufacturing grew at almost 17 percent and economic growth rates averaged 5.5 percent each year. But development involves more than high rates of economic growth: wealth trickles down slowly if at all, and policy based on the 'social utility of greed' is likely to threaten the fabric of society" (171). In fact, the government's emphasis on growth at the expense of income distribution exacerbated the inequalities in Pakistani society (Talbot 2005, 172).

Development of the Pakistani economy was only one part of Ayub's modernization efforts. As Haqqani (2005) argues, "Ayub Khan was a firm believer in the policy tripod developed within the first few years of Pakistan's creation: he identified India as Pakistan's eternal enemy, Islam as the national unifier, and the United States as the country's provider of arms and finances" (43). In other words, Ayub was combining ideology and economic development to build a Pakistani identity assisted by the United States. Ayub states in a 1960 *Foreign Affairs* article, "'Till the advent of Pakistan, none of us was in fact a Pakistani . . . for the simple reason that there was no territorial entity bearing that name.' Before 1947, 'our nationalism was based more on an idea than on any territorial definition. Till then, ideologically we were Muslims; territorially we happened to be Indians; and parochially we were a conglomeration of at least eleven smaller provincial loyalties'" (Haqqani 2005, 38–39). For Ayub, the state would "exercise the function of religious interpretation and [he] wanted an Islamic ideology that would help him in the 'defense and security and development' and the 'welding' of Pakistan's different races into a unified whole" (Haqqani 2005, 41).

At this point, Ayub Khan was in poor health and his own generals wanted him to leave office. Yahya, as army chief, "had begun to take note of the situation and feared contamination of the armed forces by the issues being raised in the streets" (Nawaz 2008, 243). As one historian described it, "The disorder which had preceded the 1958 coup appeared like Child's play in comparison with the anarchy which now prevailed in some towns and rural areas of East Pakistan" (Talbot 2005, 183). Ayub decided that martial law should be promulgated to stem the violence; however, Yahya refused, insisting that the whole country should be under martial law or none of it (Abbas 2005, 54). On March 25, 1969, Ayub stepped down handing power over to the army's chief of staff, Yahya Khan, so he could see to elections and the transition to democracy. In a sense, the Ayub regime "which had been expected by Western 'neo realists' to demonstrate a superior ability to it is civilian predecessors in initiating 'development,' instead provided empirical support for the contention that Third World military governments are as bound by economic, social and political constraints as are democracies" (Talbot 2005, 184).

Yahya became CMLA on March 25, 1969, and assumed the presidency of Pakistan one week later. As CMLA, he was not alone; he "was the first among equals in a coterie of generals, with whom he ruled by consensus" (Abbas 2005, 56). Essentially, Yahya "relied on his inner circle for guidance and took decisions rapidly—or delegated them to Peerzada, who gradually became his *Eminence Grise* and de facto prime minister, or to Major General Ghulam Umar" (Nawaz 2008, 251).

The military established a hierarchy to parallel and ultimately push out the civil bureaucracy as the army took over more and more of the decision making with military officers and service chiefs having higher rank than civilian counterparts. Thus, Nawaz (2008) argues, "The Pakistan Army of 1969 was different from that of 1958. It had started metamorphosing from a colonial, detached, and politically distant force to an immediate postcolonial army that was involved deeply in the running of its country's government, while retaining the social characteristics of the colonial army" (251–52).

With his regime in place, on November 28, 1969, Yahya called for a return to a constitutional government and announced a plan for elections to be held in October 1970, but a cyclone hit the coast of East Pakistan and postponed the elections until December. Additionally, the One Unit was dissolved and with the issuance of the Legal Framework Order (LFO), the four provinces in West Pakistan were reestablished, Pakistan's official name became the Islamic Republic of Pakistan, and allowed ultimate power to reside in the presidency. Specifically, Yahya retained the power "to accept, amend or reject a constitution presented to him by the assembly" (Nawaz 2008, 254). Yahya determined "that the parity of representation in the National Assembly between the East Wing and the West Wing that had existed under the 1956 and 1962 constitutions would end and that representation would be based on population" (Baxter 1995, 55). Abbas (2005) notes that Yahya conceded that Bengalis in East Pakistan had been treated unfairly, but "this was too little too late; especially when it is considered that in this he was attempting to swim against the tide—a tide swollen no less by the opinion of most of his inner circle" (57).

Put simply, from the early days of the Ayub regime, the "humiliating" attitude of West Pakistan's military, bureaucracy, and political elite toward Bengalis was institutionalized (Abbas 2005, 57). While Yahya was centralizing power under his martial law regime, the East Pakistanis felt "their share in various sectors of the economy such as revenue expenditure, the development budget, and utilization of foreign aid remained most unsatisfactory and unjust" (Abbas 2005, 57–58). Therefore, the Bengali nationalism prevalent in East Pakistan was represented by the Awami League under Mujib ur-Rahman in the 1970 elections through the Awami League's electoral platform known as the Six Points, which delineated responsibilities between West and East Pakistan, giving East Pakistan more autonomy. Nevertheless, both Ayub and then Yahya felt East Pakistan's demands were inspired by India (Nawaz 2008, 258).

The 1970 National Assembly election was held on December 7, and the provincial assemblies held their election two weeks later. The Awami League won a huge landslide victory in East Pakistan taking 161 of 163 seats, thereby gaining a majority of the three hundred directly elected

National Assembly (Nawaz 2008, 262). In West Pakistan, the Pakistani People's Party (PPP) won a large percentage of votes, especially in Punjab and Sindh, but no seats in the East Wing, while the National Awami Party won a plurality in Balochistan and the NWFP (Baxter 1995, 56). Similar results occurred in the provincial election as well. Thus, "[t]he future was in the hands of two political parties, having a mass support base in two different regions, each of whose leaders wanted to be prime minister" (Abbas 2005, 61). As Abbas (2005) argues, "This was the virtual end of Pakistan, but no one in the Western wing could have gathered the wisdom and courage to accept this" (61).

Consequently, over the ensuing months both sides became intransigent. According to Abbas (2005), "The post ballot Mujib was a different man. He went back on every point of understanding he had reached with the president during their months of talks, on the basis of which Yahya had sought to accommodate him" (61). Bhutto refused to participate in discussions over the new constitution leading to a continuation of martial law. As the majority party in West Pakistan, Bhutto felt the PPP should share power with the Awami League. In fact, Bhutto had the support of the Pakistan Army. Gul Hassan, a member of Yahya's inner circle, stated that the army should support Bhutto because he got most of his support from the Punjab, the army's main recruitment center, and he would not do anything to hurt the military (Nawaz 2008, 262). By February 1971, Yahya and his inner circle decided to scrap the cabinet and replace them with "advisors" to smooth the way in dealing with the Awami League (Nawaz 2008, 263).

At the same time, however, an Air India flight was hijacked by two alleged Kashmiri militants who flew the plane to Lahore demanding the release of Muslim militants in Indian Kashmir (Nawaz 2008, 263). It was later determined that Indian intelligence had a hand in the hijacking. As Abbas (2005) notes, "India's part in the faked hijacking and Mujib's reaction to it was interpreted by the military junta as only further confirmation of their belief that he was not entirely his own master and was following a course that had been charted for him by New Delhi" (62). Also, India banned Pakistani International Airlines flights and military flights over India to East Pakistan. Tensions were high and Hassan and other members of Yahya's inner circle—Hamid, Umar, and Peerzada— were already discussing a military solution "in case the politicians did not follow their instructions" (Nawaz 2008, 263). This "solution," known as "Operation Blitz," was issued four days after the elections and authorized the Pakistani Army's Eastern Commander, Lieutenant General Yaqub Ali Khan, to crack down on dissent and restore law and order.

March 23, 1971, was the anniversary of the Lahore Resolution, which was celebrated as Independence Day in West Pakistan. In East Pakistan, Mujib renamed it "Resistance Day" with Bengalis celebrating out in the streets and student militias parading the Bangladesh flag down the streets of Dhaka (Talbot 2005, 207). Consequently, the army command recommended to Yahya that military action was now necessary to suppress this rebellion led by Mujib and the Awami League. At midnight on March 25, "Operation Searchlight," as it became known, commenced. However, the operation commenced without Lieutentant General Yaqub Khan, who resigned a few weeks back citing the efficacy of the operation, the need for more time and more troops, and arguing that a political solution was the only way to prevent a civil war (Nawaz 2008, 266). By the end of April, the army had cleared the urban areas of rebels. According to Talbot (2005), "Yahya later justified [the operation] because of the threats to non-Bengali Muslims, the murders committed by the Awami League and its insults to the Army, the Pakistan flag and the Quaid-e-Azam" (208). The reality, in fact, was the beginning of the third Indo-Pakistani War.

As millions fled to India, the Indian government assisted the Bengali guerrilla forces, known as the Mukti Bahini (liberation forces) in campaigns against the Pakistani Army (Abbas 2005, 64). During the two-week war, Pakistan lost half of its navy, a third of its army and a quarter of its air force (Talbot 2005, 212). Yahya was pressured by the United States to accept the Indian ceasefire terms for geostrategic reasons. The Nixon Administration was committed to Yahya and West Pakistan, as the Yahya regime helped open a diplomatic channel to China. It was from Islamabad that Secretary of State Henry Kissinger set off to meet Chinese leaders in Beijing to pave the way for President Nixon's historic trip. The implications for this new U.S-China relationship and Pakistan's facilitation of it persuaded India to sign a treaty of friendship with the Soviet Union (Abbas 2005, 64). Throughout the war, "the generals in Pakistan had believed that the United States and China would not allow India a free hand in Bangladesh" (Abbas 2005, 66). Abbas (2005) argues, "They [the Pakistani generals] were wrong. The United States knew that East Pakistan had to go and that China was not going to risk a confrontation with the Soviets on the basis of an assurance from the United States" (66). At this point, General A. A. K. Niazi surrendered to the Indian Army in Dhaka on December 16, 1971. With that, East Pakistan became Bangladesh.

Despite their defeat, Yahya and his coterie of generals still hoped to hold onto power. However, "[c]rowds spilled on to the streets of West Pakistan's cities calling for Yahya and his advisors to be tried as traitors" (Talbot 2005, 212). The Pakistani public was not the only one expressing animosity toward the Yahya regime; in fact, a number of junior army officers were as well. In Gujranwala, approximately 150 miles, these junior officers were led by Brigadier F. B. Ali, who "was well known for his integrity, moral courage, and professionalism" (Abbas 2005, 67). Ali sent Colonels Aleem Afridi and Agha Javed Iqbal to meet with Lieutenant General Gul Hassan, the chief of the general staff, on December 19, 1971, requesting that Hassan deliver Ali's ultimatum to Yahya. As Abbas (2005) recounts, "That evening a disgraced and dispirited president of a distraught nation addressed the people of Pakistan and surrendered his office" (68). With the loss of East Pakistan, the Army had suffered a blow to its collective pride and the hostility among the junior officers forced Hassan and air chief Air Marshal Rahim Khan to turn to PPP leader Bhutto to assume the post of President and CMLA on December 20, 1971 (Talbot 2005, 213).

Bhutto was a hugely popular leader with the people of Pakistan. The youngest child of Sir Shahnawaz Bhutto, a Sindhi feudal lord, Bhutto was a graduate of the University of California—Berkeley and also studied law at Christ Church College at Oxford (Abbas 2005, 69). He first became a politician at the age of thirty in Iskander Mirza's cabinet due to his energy, leadership and charisma. As Abbas (2005) notes, "To those around him, he had everything—looks, elegance, wealth, education, family, and office. And those who saw him up close knew him for a sharp mind, an articulate tongue, a sense of humor, and a wit that at times was sardonic. There was also arrogance and a streak of vindictiveness in him that would show itself in times to come" (69).

Over the next six years, Bhutto introduced his own version of Islamic socialism, with a heavy dose of feudalism and autocracy; negotiated with India on the boundary lines in Kashmir and the release of more than ninety thousand prisoners of war from East Pakistan; regained lost Pakistani territory; placed Pakistan in a leadership position of the Third World and the Islamic world; gave Pakistan a new constitution; and put Pakistan on the path to nuclear weapon status. His most visible success, Baxter (1995) notes "was in the international arena, where he employed his diplomatic skills . . . and generally was effective in repairing Pakistan's image in the aftermath of the war" (58). Nevertheless, Bhutto's reign grew increasingly authoritarian as he clashed repeatedly with political opponents, Islamists, and the military, thereby sliding the state further into the unstable civil–military relationship still evident today.

Bhutto, as CMLA, "faced the same dilemmas which had defeated his predecessors, namely how to assert the authority of the elected institutions of the state over the military and bureaucracy, establish a functioning federal system and resolve the role of Islam in constitutional theory and practice" (Talbot 2005, 217). Therefore, to address these dilemmas, Bhutto issued an "interim constitution" granting himself broad powers as president. One of his first acts was to dismiss 1,300 civil servants and to break the power of the twenty or so families who controlled Pakistan's economy during the Ayub era (Baxter 1995, 59). Also, as part of the nationalization effort, Bhutto implemented land and labor reform. In April 1972, Bhutto lifted martial law and convened the National Assembly to reach consensus on three issues: the role of Islam; the sharing of power between the federal government and the provinces; and the division of responsibility between the president and prime minister (Baxter 1995, 59). After a year of debate, the new constitution came into effect in August 1973. Bhutto stepped down as president and became prime minister. To allay fears of the smaller provinces concerning domination by Punjab, the constitution established a bicameral legislature, providing equal provincial representation and a national assembly allocating seats according to population (Baxter 1995, 60).

Bhutto had the opportunity to resolve many of Pakistan's political problems. Unfortunately, Bhutto lost the opportunity because of a series of repressive actions against the political opposition that made it appear he was working to establish a one party state. As Nasr (2009) aptly describes:

> Bhutto proved no democrat; no sooner was he in the prime minister's office than he set out to grab all power, railroading any opponent that stood in his way. . . . Pakistan started to look like many other Third World authoritarian socialist states of the time, where politics was reduced to the cult of personality of the ruler (212).

Nasr's characterization of Bhutto was most visible in Bhutto's conflictual relationship with the military; namely, his repeated intrusion into military interests.

Bhutto's first missteps occurred between him and army chief, Lt. General Gul Hassan Khan around the time of the provincial disturbances in Karachi and NWFP. Bhutto proposed that the army be sent in to Karachi to enforce discipline, but Gul preferred the police be used (Cloughley 2008, 8). Gul "was generally uncooperative" insisting that the police be used, saying "he could not spare troops since they were needed on the borders" (Nawaz 2008, 324). This would be the first of many instances of conflict between Gul and Bhutto: "Bhutto wanted to release National Cadet Corps members (students—PPP supporters) who had deserted and been imprisoned after court martial; Gul refused. Bhutto wanted to go with Gul on his first visit around the army; Gul was firm: 'As of tomorrow,' he said, 'I begin my visits to units, and alone'" (Cloughley 2008, 8). Interestingly, when police were striking in Peshawar, Bhutto again called for military assistance. Without contacting Gul, ex-general Akbar Khan, now Bhutto's national security advisor, ordered deployment of troops and artillery to Peshawar. Once Gul found out he reversed the order and fact, the air force chief, Rahim Khan, refused Khan's order (Cloughley 2008, 9; Abbas 2005, 71). In short, Bhutto and Akbar Khan were circumventing the military's chain of command.

Given his position as CMLA, Bhutto summarily dismissed Gul and Rahim Khan on March 3, 1972, and replaced them with Lt. General Tikka Khan and Air Marshal Zaffar Chaudhury. Tikka Khan, according to Abbas (2005), was not a popular choice for army chief and Bhutto was more concerned with consolidating his rule. Tikka was "the hard and loyal man to whom a superior's order was the final word and never to be questioned" (Cloughley 2008, 11). Additionally, a number of officers were promoted who had fled East Pakistan (Nawaz 2008, 335).

Bhutto's consolidation of power and appointment of Tikka Khan caused disquiet among junior officers who demanded that the generals responsible for the loss of East Pakistan be held accountable (Abbas 2005, 72). More specifically, the junior officers "believed that Bhutto could have averted the surrender of Pakistani armed forces by accepting the Polish resolution in the U.N. Security Council on the eve of the fall of Dhaka, which in their view he artfully avoided" (Abbas 2005, 73). Essentially, Bhutto's regime was viewed similar to Yahya's—one of moral degeneracy and corruption—where the conspirators believed that the military must have a role in safeguarding democracy (Abbas 2005, 74; Nawaz 2008, 336).

Although, as more junior officers were brought into the plot, the group was penetrated by Pakistan's military intelligence, the ISI. Through the ISI, Tikka encouraged Rafi to continue participating in the dissident group. Subsequently, the officers met on March 24, 1973, to discuss the necessity of recruiting senior officers for the coup plot. Major Saeed Akhtar found out through contacts that the army hierarchy was aware of the coup plot and went to Lahore to discuss this with Farouk Adam (Nawaz 2008, 336). Upon hearing that his group had been infiltrated by military intelligence, Farouk stated, "'We are too deep into this to stop now. The way I look at this is, that this is a no-loss situation. If we pull it off, the chances of which are remote, we win. And if we are arrested and are put on trial, the chances of which are bright, we also win, because at the trial we can expose what has happened'" (Abbas 2005, 74). In fact, a week later, all of the co-conspirators were arrested.

Upon their arrest, the officers were held at Attock fort, and Bhutto promised to use "the 'attempted coup' as a means of controlling the army's leadership by playing up the distrust of the senior officers by their younger colleagues" (Nawaz 2008, 337). The officers were tried in a military tribunal in what became known as the Attock Conspiracy Trial. However, Bhutto's efforts at inciting distrust in the army chain of command backfired. During the trial Zia allowed officers to vent their feelings in the courtroom. Rather than turning other officers against the conspirators, the officers were held up as heroes by their younger colleagues (Nawaz 2008, 337). Junior officers were visited by their colleagues throughout the trial at Attock fort and Campbellpur jail (where they were being held) and continued to spread a message of discontent with the civilian leadership throughout the rest of the army (Nawaz 2008, 337). In order to quell the dissent, Bhutto moved the conspirators to cities around the country that did not have cantonments (Abbas 2005, 77). Most importantly, notes Nawaz (2008), "This trial solidified Zia ul-Haq's rise to power. When the time came to replace Tikka Khan in April 1976, Bhutto saw in Zia a potentially quiet and pliable army chief, one who came to Pakistan as a refugee from Indian Punjab and therefore had no ostensible tribal support or another base in the army" (337).

Having dealt with dissent from the military, Bhutto still faced challenges from the provinces—especially, Baluchistan. In March 1972, the Bhutto regime reached deals with the opposition National Awami Party (NAP) and the Jamiat-e-Ulema-e-Islam (JUI) to form coalition governments in Baluchistan and the NWFP. For Bhutto, this deal was meant to buy him some time as he worked to realign his political base (Nawaz 2008, 331–32). The deal, unfortunately, did not last long. Once Bhutto had consolidated power, he fixated on breaking up the hold of these coalitions. The capture of arms in a diplomatic shipment to the Iraqi embassy and the death of his right hand man in the NWFP in February 1975 gave Bhutto the justification he needed to challenge the NAP and Baluch leadership arguing that they had failed to control disturbances in the provinces which was causing insecurity (Nawaz 2008, 333). In short, while Bhutto was able to maintain support in Sindh and Pujab, Balochi's "found their aspirations and traditional nomadic life frustrated by the presence of national boundaries and the extension of central administration over their lands" (Baxter 1995, 61).

Thus, a four-year insurgency began with Bhutto calling in the Pakistani army ostensibly to construct roads, provide water, and electricity to poor Baluchis (Nawaz 2008, 333). In reality, the Pakistani Army, with thirty Cobra helicopters from the Shah of Iran and flown by Iranian pilots, put down the insurgency (Baxter 1995, 61). The significance of these events for Pakistan were twofold: 1) A large number of soldiers and officers became aware that Bhutto was using the army for his own political purposes, and 2) The army was being used to prop up civilian rule (Nawaz 2008, 335). Also, floods and earthquakes hit Punjab, Sindh and NWFP which allowed the army to provide aid and undertake road, well and dam building projects, allowing the army to gradually regain the trust of the population (Cloughley 2008, 21).

On February 28, 1976, General Tikka Khan retired as army chief. Bhutto, in his search for a new chief, looked for a general that he could control. His choice, General Zia ul-Haq, a fifty-two year old commander of II Corps in Multan, "was thought to be a reasonable fellow who, while deeply religious, was apparently not a zealot" (Cloughley 2008, 24). Zia inherited a disenchanted officer corps and Cloughley (2008) argues, "He did not take over a happy team, but that was not his fault, and he tried to place it back on the rails in the best way he knew: with calmness, professional integrity, a genuine religiosity that struck a favorable chord with many of the younger officers and most of the soldiers, and a middle-class pragmatism that was beyond the comprehension of Zulfikar Ali Bhutto" (25). It should also be noted, that while the army was unhappy with Bhutto's moves of centralizing power in his hands, he was able to temporarily maintain support from the army by increasing defense expenditures from Rs 3,725 million in 1971 to 1972 to Rs 8,210 million in 1976 to 1977, to account for an increase in military pay, and expansion of the army to make up for the loss of POWs with India, and the development of a nuclear weapons' program using support from friendly Islamic nations (Nawaz 2008, 339, 343). Moreover, an agreement was reached with the United States to supply arms worth $38.6 million (Cloughley 2008, 26).

In a final step to hold onto power, Bhutto suddenly called national elections in March 1977, hoping to catch the opposition unprepared and give his party total control of the national assembly. When Bhutto and the PPP overwhelmingly won the election, the opposition PNA charged voting irregularities and launched mass protests requiring action by the army to restore law and order. Once martial law was imposed the army came into contact with the people of Pakistan, including Punjabis. The country "was becoming ungovernable and the economy had suffered greatly from the unrest, but it seemed that Bhutto did not realize that time was running out" (Cloughley 2008, 27). The PNA wanted Bhutto's resignation, the formation of an interim government and new elections; however, negotiations became bogged down and violence was worsening throughout Pakistani cities in protest of Bhutto. Nawaz (2008) summarizes Bhutto's predicament: "[B]y estranging the US, [Bhutto] was no longer able to rebuild his military base. Additionally, by using the predominantly Punjabi military, especially in the Punjab, Bhutto was affecting the public's perception of the Pakistan Army as a savior of the country" (352).

Consequently, discussions began between Zia and his military commanders on a response to the escalating violence. The army prepared "Operation Fairplay" in case the violence worsened. Zia, after discussing the deteriorating situation with his military commanders, called a meeting of senior General Headquarters officers and stated, "Both sides in the political struggle . . . had weapons" (Cloughley 2008, 27). Bhutto had been having greater interaction and discussions with senior leadership and this managed to convince the army's leadership "that Bhutto intended to take firm action against the opposition and might even use the armed wing of the PPP for that purpose" (Nawaz 2008, 352). The army, according to Nawaz (2008), "feared that it would be forced to pull the chestnuts out of the fire for Bhutto should his use of force backfire" and Zia "may have been willing to support Bhutto to some extent, but when the discipline and integrity of the army was threatened, Zia decided to overthrow Bhutto (352–53).

General Zia ul-Haq's bloodless coup ushered in the longest period of military rule in Pakistan. As CMLA, Zia suspended the 1973 constitution and the federal and provincial governments were dissolved. The dissolution of government allowed Zia, as in previous martial law governments, to appoint "a combination of the top brass of the Army and the senior bureaucrats [to] rule the country" (Rizvi 2000, 165). During his rule, Zia would rotate like-minded generals and officers into top positions, as well as showering them with favors and creating what Ayesha Siddiqa (2007) terms as "Milbus," or the "business activities or the personal economic stakes of military personnel as a driver of the armed forces' political ambitions" (1). Moreover, Zia was the first ruler of Pakistan who represented the urban lower middle class, a segment of society with conservative values and religiousity (Nawaz 2008, 361).

Zia argued that Pakistan's survival was dependent on building an Islamic state. The Islamization of Pakistan, along with the pervasiveness of the military's role in running the country, would occasion the rise of Islamists in the military and state sponsorship of militant Islamic (largely Sunni) sectarian groups, creating Shi'a backlash and sectarian warfare, as well as international conflict in Afghanistan (Nawaz 2008, 359).

Zia "projected himself as a reluctant ruler who had assumed power because the political leaders had failed to resolve the political crisis" when in reality, "he expanded the goals of the coup from elections to accountability, Islamization of the polity and induction of decency in politics" (Rizvi 2000, 166). Upon taking over, Zia stated he would hold new elections within ninety days; he chose not to ban political parties, but he had to find a way to legitimize his rule. He soon cancelled the elections "because, he said, it was his responsibility first to carry out a program of 'accountability'" (Baxter 1995, 64). In effect, Zia was attempting to give legal cover to his regime. Subsequently, Rizvi (2000) notes, "By an interesting coincidence, it was during these days that the military regime unearthed evidence of Bhutto's involvement in the murder of his political opponents. The military rulers also accused Bhutto of engaging in massive corruption and decided to proceed against him" (167). Bhutto was tried and sentenced to death in 1978 on the charge of conspiring to murder a political opponent. The Supreme Court upheld the sentence and Bhutto was hanged in April 1979.

From November 1979, until August 1983, Zia promised repeatedly to hold elections at an "appropriate" time (Rizvi 2000, 169). The collapse of the Bhutto regime was a shock to the JI and other parties in the Pakistan National Alliance. Nevertheless, the Islamists were still intrigued to discover that Zia held a favorable view toward the Islamist vision of state and society (Nasr 2004, 196). Although Zia was a pious Muslim, he used Islam to serve his own purposes; namely, "to not only shore up state power by ending its war of attrition with Islamism, but also to expand its own powers domestically as well as regionally" (Nasr 2004, 196). Put differently, Zia was justifying military rule and the suppression of democracy in the name of building an Islamic state. According to Nasr (1994), "He had incorporated the demands of the Islamic parities into state ideology, thereby offering the Islamic parties a power-sharing arrangement in which the state would act as a senior partner, but the Islamic forces would gain from state patronage and enjoy a modicum of political activity" (187). The JI used this in their effort to call for early elections.

Between 1977 and 1979, Zia promised the JI that elections would be held and a civilian government would be allowed to form. Subsequently, the JI promoted how it was cooperating with the Zia government and after months of negotiations the PNA returned and was allowed to appoint two-thirds of the cabinet ministers and Zia one-third of the ministers (Nasr 1994, 190–191). This was an important milestone for the JI: "After thirty years of political activity in Pakistan, for the first time in its history the Jama'at had become part of the ruling establishment" (Nasr 1994, 191).

However, JI's time as part of the ruling establishment was short-lived. Continuous reneging on promised elections by Zia influenced the PNA to dissolve the government (Nasr 1994, 191). The JI wanted to distance itself from the Zia regime and felt that the best way to accomplish this task would be to make it known that as Islamists they were against Zia's martial law rule. Moreover, the JI began criticizing many of Zia's policies (Nasr 1994, 191–92). Eventually, Zia agreed to hold municipal elections, but not national assembly elections. The results of the elections saw the JI finish second to the PPP in each of the municipal elections. The JI's political fortunes, which were once so bright, were beginning to dim. Nasr (1994) addresses the reasons for the JI's second place finish: "The Jama'at proved unable to deliver on the claims it had made. Aside from abstract notions about the shape and working of the ideal Islamic state, the party had little to offer in the way of suggestions for managing its machinery" (194). Therefore, the JI was unable to apply Islam to political and economic policies that Zia could use, thereby losing favor in his eyes (Nasr 1994, 194).

Ultimately, during the late 1970s and 1980s, President Zia ul-Haq co-opted the JI for his own purposes and as a result dissension rose within the party over its policies and performance. Ahmad was viewed as a populist leader who was well-liked by the younger members of JI, appealing to both conservatives and liberals. According to Nasr (2001), "As the party's liaison with the Zia regime during the Afghan war, he was favored by the pro-Zia conservative faction, while his populist style and call for the restoration of democracy endeared him to the younger generation who wanted to distance itself from Zia" (55).

Throughout the 1980s, Zia continued to receive protests from his continued cancellation of elections. To try and quell his opposition, Zia chose to hold a referendum asking Pakistanis if they approved of Islamization. Despite receiving objections from a number of military officers in the provinces who felt shame wearing their uniforms in public because the people had associated the army with dictatorship and harsh Islamic justice, Zia held the referendum and offered Pakistanis the choice of "Yes" or "No" on his regime (Nawaz 2008, 379).

The result of the referendum emboldened Zia and in 1985 he ended martial law. National elections were then held absent political parties. All candidates were "independents" and "[c]ontrary to the government's claim that elections held on a nonparty basis would produce a new or better set of political leaders, most of the seats in these elections were bagged by members of landed-fedual class, tribal chiefs and influential religious officials with feudal backgrounds" (Siddiqa 2007, 86–7). As a result, the Pakistani Muslim League (PML) under Mohammad Khan Junejo took over government and Junejo became prime minister. As prime minister, Junejo oversaw a parliament that was, in the words of defense analyst Ayesha Siddqa (2007), "coerced into passing the controversial Eighth Amendment to the 1973 Constitution . . . [which] allowed the president instead of the prime minister to become the supreme commander of the armed forces and to have the power to sack the parliament" (87).

Subsequently, the relationship between Zia and Junejo went from "cordiality and courtesy to coolness" as the prime minister challenged Zia because he did not want to be seen as a puppet (Talbot 2005, 263). Specifically, Junejo refused to accept all of Zia's nominees for cabinet posts, spoke up about reducing perks and privileges for senior military elites; including disapproving of the promotion of two officers to be corps commanders, disapproving over the return of officers to the Army who had served for three or more years in the bureaucracy, and the insistence on removing General Rahman as Director General of the ISI (Nawaz 2008, 380; Talbot 2005, 263; Cloughley 2008, 48). Throughout this time, Nawaz (2008) argues, "[T]he army high command was kept in the dark. The VCOAS [Vice Chief of Army Staff] General Mirza Aslam Beg, was simply told by Zia that he was dismissing Junejo. Beg's views were not sought. . . . Zia had truly become a one-man administration, aided only by his immediate team" (384).

Meanwhile, the JI leadership continued their criticisms of Zia's martial law regime and championed the rule of law, an end to censorship and to hold elections (Nasr 1994, 194). At the same time, a movement called the Movement for Restoration of Democracy (MRD), a multi-party coalition organized by the PPP, sought to reach out to the IJT. Throughout the 1980s the JI would debate whether or not to join the MRD coalition. In fact, a prolonged debate over whether or not to join the MRD would prolong the party's inability to act (Nasr 1994, 196). Consequently, the JI only won ten of the sixty-eight seats it contested in the 1985 election (Nasr 1994, 197). This poor performance in the election, plus the presence of the MRD after 1981, the ban on labor unions, political parties, and student unions by Zia, brought discontent to the rank and file of JI.

The discontent mentioned above was championed by an anti-Zia faction known as the Karachi Group. Established by Ghafur Ahmad, the Karachi Group was interested in returning Pakistan to a populist government. Populism would return to Pakistan, in the Karachi Group's opinion, if the JI broke away from the Zia regime, joined the MRD and established a working relationship with the PPP, the populist movement of Pakistan (Nasr 1994, 198). Simultaneously, the Muhajir Qaumi Mahaz (MQM), was established by former members of the IJT to court, along with the MRD, the secular vote. In response to this jockeying for influence, after the election Zia gave power to the Muslim League, removing the JI, and relegating them to the opposition party (Nasr 1994, 198–99). The JI then began negotiations with the MRD while continuing to denounce Zia's rule. The substance of these negotiations continued to be whether the MRD would consent to a role for Islam within the state (Nasr 1994, 204).

Ultimately the JI did not join the MRD and Zia was killed in a plane crash in 1988 ushering in a new phase in Pakistani politics. The decision of the military elite not to assume power after the death of Zia and leave the constitutional and democratic processes facilitated the holding of party-based elections and the subsequent transfer of power to elected civilian government. According to Rizvi (2000), "The post-Zia Army Chiefs emphasized professionalism and non-involvement of the soldiers in active politics; they supported the democratic process and governance by the civilians. Their decision to stay back was a tactical move based on a realistic assessment of the domestic and international political situations; it did not change the reality of their centrality to the political process" (190).

Accordingly, the military's centrality to the political process expanded under the Zia regime through the proliferation of military officers throughout the bureaucracy and the expansion of Milbus. Ignoring normal rules and quotas, roughly one-fourth of thirty-five to forty senior bureaucratic posts and ambassadorships were filled by senior military officers (Nawaz 2008, 387). In fact, the governors of the Punjab, Sindh, the NWFP, and Balochistan were all former corps commanders, and officers were placed all the way down to the district level to "dog and shadow civilians at all levels of administration" (Nawaz 2008, 387). Furthermore, Zia "took measures to establish the military's financial autonomy and made himself popular among his main constituency, the armed forces, by empowering the senior commanders . . . [with] secret 'regimental' funds" which they had complete control over (Siddiqa 2007, 141). Milbus also included business operations in a variety of different industries; namely, manufacturing, oil and gas, and agri-business (Siddiqa 2007, 141).

After the death of Zia, VCAS Beg consulted with MGO Niaz, General Imranullah Khan, the corp commander of X Corps in Rawalpindi (headquarters of the Pakistan Army), Imtiaz Warraich of the Joint Chief of Staff

Headquarters, General Karamat, and the ISI chief Hamid Gul and concluded that they would not impose martial law and instead follow the
constitution (Nawaz 2008, 396). According to the constitution, the chairman of the Senate, Ghulam Ishaq Khan was next in line to succeed Zia.
Subsequently, Beg was appointed as chief of the army staff as Pakistan
transitioned to a democratically elected government for the first time.

After Zia's death, politics in Pakistan from 1988 to 1999 can be characterized as power struggles between the military and civilian politicians,
Islamist parties, and secular political institutions (Nasr 2004, 197). As
Nasr (2004) notes, "Just as democratic forces sought to recalibrate Pakistan's ideology, moving it away from Islamization to support development and modernization better, the coalition of military forces and Islamic parties sought to resist this trend by ever more tightly weaving Pakistan's foreign policy and regional interests with Islam, and thus continuing to anchor domestic politics in the debate over Islamization" (197). To
this end, the military established a coalition between the Pakistani Muslim League of Nawaz Sharif and the Islamist Parties (JI, JUI and JUP). The
coalition's purpose was to challenge the PPP in the 1988 elections and
give pro-Zia forces a voice in parliament to work against the PPP (Nasr
2004, 197).

The coalition was ultimately successful in preventing the PPP from
consolidating power. Effectively, from 1998 to 1993, Pakistan faced a "crisis of governability," according to Nasr (1994), "Divided parliaments,
facing changing allegiances of party members, economic crises, corruption, and growing acrimony between Nawaz Sharif and Benazir Bhutto
succumbed to paralysis" (198). All of this occurred with the hidden hand
of the military interfering in the democratic process.

Although Ghulam Ishaq Khan was now president; in effect, he was
merely an acting president as Beg, as army chief, along with the president
and prime minister became a troika running Pakistani politics (Nawaz
2008, 411). Beg represented the new Pakistan Army—a mohajir who was
the first army chief commissioned after 1948 and not possessing a military background. While he inherited corps commanders that Zia picked,
they, too, were close to Beg's age and represented a far more professional
force due to a series of rigorous training courses and selection boards
needed before promotion. As part of the training, officers were exposed
to both military and political issues which made senior officers more
prone to take action on political matters (Nawaz 2008, 418). According to
Nawaz (2008), "Beg saw his own role in those early days as that of a
'referee' trying to keep calm on the political playing field and ensuring
that differences between the two leading parties and their leaders were
resolved inside the assembly and not on the streets; otherwise, the army
would be unnecessarily drawn into the squabbles" (416).

After the elections of 1988, Bhutto ran into conflict from the military
almost immediately. Opposition to Bhutto came from within the ISI, Mili-

tary Intelligence, and Sharif (Nawaz 2008, 423). The main areas of disagreement occurred with Bhutto's handling of foreign policy and various domestic matters. According to Esposito, Sonn, and Voll (2016), "Benazir was indeed prodemocracy and not overtly anti-American. But she also continued the policies of her father. She continued to support both Pakistan's nuclear weapons program and Islamist militias as part of her geopolitical strategy, and U.S.-Pakistan relations plummeted" (101). As a result, the United States would cut economic and military aid.

Domestically, in a move she hoped would leave Beg ineffective, Bhutto involved herself in the promotion of general officers. More specifically, she tried to promote an officer loyal to her, Lt. General Ahmed Kamal, to the position of chairman of the Joint Chiefs of Staff Council (Nawaz 2008, 426). A final instance of interference by Bhutto during her first term as prime minister occurred between her and Beg over the state of lawlessness developing in Sindh. The conflict necessitated the PPP government reaching out to the army for help in restoring order to Sindh. Essentially, the PPP got into an argument with Lt. General Nawaz "over a list of 'terrorists' that the PPP wanted picked up. Nawaz refused to do so, stating that the PPP government was trying to 'use' the army to 'crush its political opponents'" (Nawaz 2008, 429).

At a July 21, 1990, meeting of the corps commanders and Beg, the decision was made that Bhutto's government had to go. Beg expressed his discontent with Bhutto to President Ishaq. One month later, Ishaq dismissed Bhutto's government for corruption and misconduct and called for new elections to be held on October 24, 1990 (Nawaz 2008, 430). In sum, Bhutto's first term in office was one of repeated conflict with the army, whom did not want to see her establish her influence on matters of importance to their self-interests.

In October 1990, Sharif was elected with more than two-thirds majority of the National Assembly (Cloughley 2008, 70). A populist and an industrialist who had run the province of Punjab, Sharif's tenure from 1990 to 1993 "saw a continuation of confrontational politics, a crisis in Sindh and claims of corruption which had dogged his predecessor" (Talbot 2005, 315). Thus, Sharif began a series of privatizations to open up Pakistan's highly controlled bureaucrat-run economy, since his family had suffered at the hands of Zulfikar Ali Bhutto's nationalization program. Ultimately, Sharif sought to empower his business interests and his support base who had first brought him to power in the 1990 elections (Nawaz 2008, 437).

However, despite a knowledge of the powers of the prime minister, the presidency, and the chief-of-staff of the Army in the "Troika," Sharif believed that the president and the chief of staff of the army were working against the prime minister; in this case, Sharif himself (Nawaz 2008, 436–37). Moreover, he believed the army wanted to retain three policy areas: Afghanistan, Kashmir, and nuclear policy. This consistently put both Beg and Ishaq in conflict with Sharif. Over the ensuing three years, Sharif and Beg "crossed swords" over Pakistani involvement in the Persian Gulf War and with the selection of a new Army chief (Nawaz 2008, 438).

By 1993, the military's coalition was crumbling and Sharif's PML was losing an increasing percentage of the Islamist vote. Concurrently, the military was keeping an eye on the situation in Afghanistan, where the Taliban was consolidating its hold on power. The military felt that JI's brand of Islamism was becoming ineffectual and saw the Taliban's brand of Islamic extremism would be better suited to controlling Pakistani domestic politics (Nasr 2004, 199). The reasoning behind this decision was strategic going back to the Pashtuns and their arbitrary division by the Durand Line. The Pakistani military has feared a Pashtun nationalist uprising due to the large Pashtun population in Pakistan. Thus, the Pakistani military supported the Taliban, who were Pashtun, and preferred that fighting take place in Afghanistan rather than in Pakistan. After the Soviets pulled out, the mujahedeen leader who came out on top of a struggle for power was Ahmed Shah Masoud, the Tajik, Northern Alliance commander, who was unacceptable to Pakistan's Pashtuns. The Pakistani military wanted the "Islamabad-friendly variety" to rule Afghanistan (Nasr 2009, 217).

Moreover, the military was also concerned with government's poor performance in foreign affairs, specifically regarding the relationship with the United States. In response to Pakistan's nuclear program the United States "suspended military sales, military training programs and economic assistance to Pakistan from October 1, 1990, (one month before Sharif assumed power) by invoking the Pressler Amendment to the Foreign Assistance Act as retaliation" (Rizvi 2000, 212). There was also the issue of the former mujahedeen, mentioned above, who were Afghan war veterans and were threatening U.S. interests through drug trafficking occurring from and through Pakistan as well as their attempts to disrupt governments in the region who were perceived as pro-U.S. Therefore, in 1992, the United States placed Pakistan on the "watch list" of states that sponsor terrorism. For the military, there was an expectation that a diplomatic solution be found to protect Pakistan's image abroad, but more importantly to allow Pakistan to continue to procure weapons from the United States (Rizvi 2000, 213).

At this point, Pakistan's political and economic situation was deteriorating. Economic liberalization, deregulation, and privatization "were marred by stories of favoritism, kick-backs, and corruption" (Rizvi 2000, 213). Moreover, these policies won Sharif support from economic and business elites, but social unrest was beginning to escalate. Thus, the confrontational style between Sharif's IJI and Bhutto's PPP continued unabated, specifically with corruption charges and "misuse of power" cases filed against Bhutto and her husband, Asif Ali Zardari. Consequently, the PPP tried to rally support against Sharif's government through "street agitation, described as the 'Long March,' to force the government to resign" (Rizvi 2000, 213).

President Ishaq would attempt to be the bridge between the government and the military, but this relationship was damaged as a result of the Long March when Sharif's advisers suggested that Sharif go one step further and push out President Ishaq so the PML/IJI could resume control of government. As Rizvi (2000) argues, "This was an imprudent move because, given the internal weaknesses of the ruling IJI, complaints of misuse of state resources and corruption by senior figures in the government, and a virtual breakdown of relationships with the opposition, the government could not afford to alienate the constitutionally powerful president" (213–14). In effect, Sharif listened to his advisers and challenged the president, which ultimately led to his government's dismissal.

Bhutto and the PPP won the October 1993 elections and the PPP candidate, Sardar Farooq Ahmad Khan Leghari, won the presidency. Unlike her first term, Bhutto did not interfere in the internal affairs of the military and generally respected their autonomy (Rizvi 2000, 220). Immediately upon taking office, Bhutto had to deal with foreign policy and work toward rebuilding the relationship with the United States. More specifically, she worked toward re-opening Pakistan's access to U.S. weapons systems, especially the F-16 fighters Pakistan had paid for but were still being held by the United States. (Nawaz 2008, 474). Nevertheless, Bhutto was able to regain U.S. support on her visit to Washington, DC. Her diplomatic efforts resulted in Pakistan being removed from the U.S. State Department's list of state sponsors of terrorism. Her visit also garnered the release of the F-16s and other military equipment blocked by the Pressler Amendment with the United States also agreeing to return the money used to purchase the F-16s by selling the aircraft to other states (Rizvi 2000, 221).

Bhutto's government initially adopted measures for socioeconomic development, projects for health care, the advancement of women and environmental improvements. There were also new projects approved for power generation and infrastructure improvements. However, according to Rizvi (2000), "[I]t was not long before these programs lost their momentum due to defective planning, poor management and resource constraints" from inflation, price hikes, and a devaluation of the Pakistani rupee putting increased pressure on the middle and lower classes (221). Also, ethnic violence intensified in Karachi and Hyderabad throughout 1995 and 1996 between MQM activists and law enforcement. Unable to find a political solution, "the government gave a relatively free hand to the police and Rangers, who used excessive force to control the situation" (Rizvi 2000, 222).

The spiraling violence and deteriorating economic situation was occurring at the same time as charges of corruption were leveled at Bhutto and her husband, Zardari. In the *New York Times* there was an expose done on the Bhutto family fortune and "Leghari says he also 'found to [his] horror' that the PPP government was misstating Pakistan's foreign exchange reserves at that time, some $300 million less than the official figure of some $625 million and the economy was 'bleeding $40–45 million a day'" (Nawaz 2008, 486). Bhutto also created problems by appointing justices to the court, whom were seen as Bhutto loyalists. This irked the judiciary and, according to Rizvi (2000), "Instead of allaying their concerns, the government built pressures on Chief Justice Sajjad Ali Shah (appointed to this post by the Benazir government) to dissade him from taking up an appeal filed against the appointment of new judges" (223). Consequently, the Supreme Court's judgment drastically curtailed the power of the executive to appoint and transfer the judges of the judiciary. Subsequently, a number of Chief Justices of provincial High Courts did not recommend confirmation of previous judicial appointments of Bhutto and Sharif's. In response, Bhutto refused to implement the Supreme Court judgment on judicial appointments. Finally, the Chief Justice turned to President Leghari who tried to persuade Bhutto to endorse the judges recommended by the Chief Justice to no avail; their differences continued to widen (Rizvi 2000, 223).

Against this background and deteriorating situation, the Chief Justice and president began to agree that Bhutto was the problem. In fact, after raising the issue of illicit money-making by senior members of the Bhutto government, including Zardari's involvement in various kickback scandals (his nickname, famously, being 2 percent Ali), Leghari told Karamat he was planning to dismiss Bhutto's government because "'We had reached the point of no return'" (Nawaz 2008, 486).

Bhutto's dismissal on November 5, 1996, "was carried out in coup style" (Rizvi 2000, 224). Essentially, President Leghari appointed a caretaker government until elections could be held February 3, 1997, with the Army taking control of the Prime Minister's house and government offices, arresting Zardari and handing him over to the police, and placing more senior military officers into the bureaucracy and civilian intelligence agency (IB) to minimize its autonomy (Rizvi 2000, 225). President Leghari's reasons for dismissing Bhutto included: 1) Non-implementation of the judgment of the Supreme Court; 2) Attempts to destroy the independence of the judiciary through the accountability law; 3) The bugging of telephones of senior officials and judges, and "extra-judicial" killings; and 4) Imminent economic collapse (Rizvi 2000, 225).

After the 1997 elections and the PML's win of 63 percent of the National Assembly seats, Sharif championed the PML as a "modern democratic party" that would work on issues of development while simultaneously following a mandate of Islamization. In essence, the PML was claiming that it would be the center-right party to speak for Islamist interests in Pakistan. The new government "started with the popular support and goodwill of the military and the President" (Rizvi 2000, 226). Sharif's first order of business was to get rid of the 8th Amendment by putting forward the 13th Amendment, after discussing the move with Karamat and Leghari, which annulled the 8th Amendment and gave the prime minister the power to appoint the heads of the armed services instead of the president (Nawaz 2008, 487).

Next, Sharif introduced a number of socio-economic measures and secured a low-interest $1.6 billion IMF loan. However, according to Rizvi (2000), "[T]hese efforts did not produce the desired results because the government lacked the political will to pursue the policy measures, especially tax collection and recovery of overdue bank loans from the politically influential people" (226). In effect, Sharif was attempting to use the PML's new parliamentary majority to acquire power at the expense of other state institutions. It would be his next move, which would bring to fruition his ultimate fear—another dismissal.

As Sharif attempted his power-grab, he ran into opposition from Karamat who advocated for further army involvement in government (Nawaz 2008, 497). Additionally, Sharif said he felt Karamat had intruded into the affairs of his government by suggesting, in a speech in October 1998 at the Naval Staff College in Lahore, that the formation of a National Security Council (hereafter NSC) would provide stability to the political system (Nawaz 2008, 498).

In fact, the military high command, at this point, was upset by Sharif, especially "the growing alienation in the smaller provinces and polarization along regional lines . . . and the deteriorating economic conditions [that] had started adversely affecting the professional and corporate interests of the military" (Rizvi 2000, 231). Karamat decided to step down three months ahead of retirement rather than withdraw his remarks. Sharif then sought to appoint an Army Chief he thought would be pliable (Nawaz 2008, 499). His choice was General Pervez Musharraf, an Urdu-speaking *mohajir* from Karachi over two senior Pashtuns and Punjabi generals (Rizvi 2000, 232; Musharraf 2006).

After becoming COAS, Musharraf favored the use of Islamist extremist groups "by encouraging increasing radicalization of the Islamist discourse, and [by] supporting extremist forces, the military sought to destabilize the relations between the PML and its constituency, and more generally radicalize Islam to the extent that a viable center-right coalition would not be feasible" (Nasr 2004, 200–201). Thus, the confrontation between the military and the PML exacerbated conditions in Pakistan. For instance, Musharraf pressured Sharif to sign on to war with India, by sending jihadi fighters into Kargil, an Indian held part of Kashmir, which nearly precipitated a nuclear crisis (Nasr 2009, 236).

The U.S. stepped into to negotiate a ceasefire, however time was running out for Sharif. At this point, Pakistan's economy was beset with increased government corruption and growing unhappiness with Sharif's strong-arming of opponents (Nasr 2009, 216). The economic situation derived in part from Sharif's decision to go ahead with nuclear tests following those by India, resulted in embargoes and sanctions (Cloughley 2008, 120). Moreover, Sharif relied heavily on the army to improve administrative efficiency and economic management with several civilian institutions handed over to the Army. As Rizvi (2000) notes, "This may temporarily save the polity from collapsing but it erodes the credibility of the civilian institutions and leaders" (232). By October 1999, Pakistan was heading toward economic and political collapse.

Thus, with his opponents railing against him, Sharif decided to remove Musharraf while he was out of the country and replace him with Lt. General Ziauddin of the ISI, who was loyal to Sharif. Musharraf was on a Pakistani Airlines flight returning from Sri Lanka when his plane was told not to land. At 5 p.m. on October 12, 1999, Lt. General Mohammad Aziz Khan, Lt. General Mahmood Ahmed, and Maj. General Shahid Aziz (Director General of Military Operations) would conduct a counter-coup against Sharif removing him from office (Musharraf 2006, chs. 12 and 13).

In a speech to the nation, Musharraf outlined the rationale behind the army's coup stating, "'The choice before us on 12th October [sic] was between saving the body—that is the nation, at the cost of losing a limb—which is the Constitution, or saving the limb and losing the whole body. The Constitution is but a part of the nation therefore I chose to save the nation and yet took care not to sacrifice the Constitution'" (Nawaz 2008, 528). Sharif was the most powerful prime minister in Pakistan's history, but similar to previous coups, "The inability of politicians to accept probity as a requirement of governance contributed directly to the 1999 takeover, and the country's poor economic situation had been worsened by the Sharif government's terminal corruption" (Cloughley 2008, 120). Therefore, Musharraf took over as "chief executive," a title he chose to befit what he believed at the time would be the temporary nature of his new regime (Musharraf 2006, 144).

The Pakistani military under Musharraf "saw no point in continuing to anchor the military's strategy in a political and ideological position over which it could not have direct control" (Nasr 2004, 201). In essence, Musharraf's most important accomplishment in the eyes of his fellow generals was convincing Washington that Pakistan would remain a reliable ally guarding U.S. interests (Nasr 2009, 221). Although, the events of September 11, 2001, forced Musharraf to go from supporting Islamists to clamping down on extremist *jihadi* groups whom the military had once used in Afghanistan and in Kashmir (Nasr 2004, 202). By allying with the United States in its War on Terror, Musharraf put Pakistan into a precarious political situation.

Domestically, Musharraf was attempting to cloak his regime in legitimacy through a Presidential Referendum and the issuance of the Legal

Framework Order. The referendum on April 30th was used by Musharraf to secure a further five years in office prior to the October 2002 provincial elections. The Legal Framework Order established a National Security Council chaired by the President and restored the president's power to dismiss a prime minister. For Musharraf, these measures were a way of preventing further coups: "'If you want to keep the army out,' he declared, 'you bring them in'" (Talbot 2005, 401). This was Musharraf's "guided democracy," "presuppos[ing] that the army was the savior rather than the cause of Pakistan's political travail" (Talbot 2005, 401).

To further legitimize his rule, Musharraf called elections for October 2002. The main contestants in this election were: the PML, the PPP, the National Alliance, and the MMA, with the major issues being socioeconomic conditions, civilian vs. military rule, and foreign policy. The MMA, or Mutahhidah Majlis Amal, is an alliance formed by the Islamist parties in response to Musharraf's rule, the fall of the Taliban, and with the War on Terror (Nasr 2004, 203). The two largest partners in the alliance are the JUI and the JI with the JUI being the muscle and the JI the brains. Qazi Husayn Ahmad wanted to ensure Islamism remained the purview of Islamist parties. Or, as Nasr (2004) so aptly puts it, "Qazi [Husayn Ahmad] conceived of the MMA as the means to use the tug-of-war between the military, the PML, and the PPP to Islamist parties' advantage" (203). Interestingly, the military supported the MMA, however this alliance "was surreptitious and was characterized by mutual distrust between the two sides" (Nasr 2004, 203).

Due to the increasing distrust of the military, the 2002 elections became the MMA's most successful elections to date. The MMA won 11 percent of the total vote in the National Assembly finishing fourth in the final vote. This caused Musharraf to view the PPP and PML as the real threats to the military's position (Nasr 2004, 205). In provincial elections, the MMA did well in the NWFP (51 of 101 seats) and Baluchistan (14 of 51 seats) and did poorly in Punjab (8 of 297 seats) and Sind (11 out of 130 seats) (Nasr 2004, 205). Essentially, voting became split along ethnic lines. As Nasr (2004) argues, "Pathans voted overwhelmingly for Islamism and the MMA, and the rest of Pakistan shied away from the MMA" (205). In the end, the MMA will continue to be an important presence in Pakistani politics because of a modus vivendi created between the Islamists and the military: "It is through the military's assault on the political process, and as an intended or unintended consequence of the struggle for power between the military and democratic forces, that Islamism has gained ground" (Nasr 2004, 207).

In fact, in 2002, under pressure from the United States, Musharraf agreed to round up extremists and members of Al-Qaeda. However, many of the militants were released a few weeks later in Azad Kasmir—Pakistan's part of Kashmir—or in the FATA region in the Northwest, where they have since associated themselves with the Taliban and Al-

Qaeda (Nasr 2009, 220). By 2004, the Taliban and Al-Qaeda were in the FATA, specifically North and South Waziristan, and were reconstituting themselves This reconstituted group of militants is known as Tehrik-e-Taliban Pakistan (TTP), or "Pakistani Taliban."

The Pakistani Taliban are Pashtun Salafists who are a loose alliance of tribal and ethnic affiliated militant extremist groups who share "a determination to implement a strict Islamic agenda and oppose an international military presence in Afghanistan" (Weinbaum 2009, 75). Their leader was Baitullah Mehsud (killed in a U.S. drone strike in August 2009) and he directed attacks against the Pakistani military conducting operations against these militants with varying degrees of success.

Additionally, there are four other militant *jihadi* groups operating within Pakistan: Sipah-e-Sahaba Pakistan (SSP), Lashkar-e-Jhangvi (LeJ), Jaish-e-Mohammad (JM), and Lashkar-e-Taiba (LeT). The SSP was founded in September 1985, "with the backing of the military authorities, to counter the rise in the influence of Shi'ism [in Pakistan], and apparently had the financial support of Saudi Arabia and Iraq . . . to transform Pakistan into a Sunni Muslim state applying the Shari'a" (Zahab and Roy, 23). LeJ, is a terrorist group that split off from the SSP in 1994, led by Riaz Basra, after disagreements arose over the SSP agenda and have subsequently been implicated in a number of assassinations against Shi'a. Jaish-e-Mohammad is a Punjabi group, led by Masood Azhar, which is the *jihadi* wing of the SSP, and seeks the Islamization of Pakistani society. JM "was one of the first jihadist groups in South Asia to import the technique of suicide missions from the Middle East" (Zahab and Roy, 31).

Finally, LeT is a Wahabi *jihadist* group created during 1989 and 1990 in Afghanistan (Siddiqa 2009, 64). LeT was created, in part, with help from the Pakistani army and ISI, who were looking to control Kashmiri Muslim separatists in Indian controlled Kashmir. LeT's ideology ultimately seeks the establishment of a Muslim caliphate over the subcontinent and has committed a number of attacks on Indian targets in Kashmir since the late 1980s as well as the most recent attack in November 2008, known as the "Mumbai Massacre" (Reidel 2009, 115–16). The LeT "has a wide popularity in Pakistan, especially in the Punjab," which has made it less vulnerable to crackdowns by the Pakistani army (Reidel 2009, 117). Moreover, each of these groups has close links with the Afghan Taliban and Al-Qaeda, as well as with each other. For example, LeT has provided safe haven for Al-Qaeda fighters being driven out of Afghanistan by the United States, as well as Osama Bin Laden having been an early funder of LeT (Riedel 2009, 118).

The Pakistani military's schizophrenic policies of fighting the Pakistani Taliban created a tremendous amount of blowback. The army sought to retain influence across the Tribal areas by using tribal and personal rivalries to divide the Taliban. However, historian Juan Cole (2009) notes, "The FATA tribes began inflicting significant casualties on Pakistani troops who were attempting to bring them under control of the central government" (235). Consequently, attacks and counterattacks went back and forth between the militants and the military. The operations were often short-lived and agreements with local militants to cede local control in exchange for a promise to not attack army personnel and bases, while also refraining from spreading their influence into Pakistan's more populated areas.

However, no enforcement mechanism was established to monitor the deal and the Pakistani government took the militants at their word that they would limit their assistance to the Afghan insurgency. Therefore, according to Weinbaum (2009), "Pakistan's approach to finding a political solution had one basic fallacy: all the agreements were reached from a position of government weakness rather than strength" (76). Weinbaum (2009) goes on to note that part of the Pakistani army's difficulty in its counterinsurgency effort was attributed to the fact that the army is "largely trained and equipped for a conventional ground war in the Punjab . . . but reluctant to remain and provide continuing security or address the complaints that left the area vulnerable to insurgent penetration in the first place" (77).

The inability of the government and army to maintain security in the NWFP emboldened the militants to challenge Musharraf in the cities, especially Islamabad. Thousands of extremists based in Islamabad's Red Mosque sought to impose shari'a law. By May 2007, these self-styled Taliban-like extremists eventually turned violent, attacking video stores and barbershops, and kidnapping a number of Chinese nationalists (Cole 2009, 235). The capture of the Chinese nationalists caused an international incident, as Pakistan is a close ally of Beijing. This forced Musharraf's hand. In July 2007, elite troops of the Pakistani army stormed the Red Mosque complex killing one cleric and numerous extremists. In retaliation, there was a wave of urban suicide bombings targeting police stations and military facilities in the north. Subsequently, tribal leaders who were angered by the massacre at the Red Mosque and the military crackdown, cancelled their truce with Islamabad (Cole 2009, 235). In effect, "The twin urban and rural crises profoundly weakened the Musharraf regime, raising questions about its ability to survive" (Cole 2009, 236).

Musharraf ruled by decree from 2002 to 2007 through "enhanced presidential power via constitutional amendments and ordinances . . . constricting the role of the legislature to that of a decree-stamping institution" (Shafqat 2009, 93). The beginning of the end of Musharraf's regime began in 2007. Nawaz (2008) contends, "Increasingly, Musharraf, who liked to cast himself as aloof from and allergic to politics, seemed to be caught up in the machinations of his political party supporters, as they orchestrated huge rallies and used official resources and connections to produce large gatherings whenever he appeared" (558). Moreover, politically, Musharraf could have allowed a technocratic prime minister to emerge to follow in his footsteps. In reality, Musharraf, who did not have a deputy, kept his Vice Chief and other military officers on a tight leash (Nawaz 2008, 558).

Thus, with domestic political unrest and ethnic tension increasing, Musharraf had to make a number of decisions that would ultimately force him from office. One of the first decisions was whether to relinquish his military uniform by the end of 2007 as required by the 17th Amendment in the Pakistani Constitution (Nawaz 2008, 558). Musharraf wanted to remain both president and army chief and the judiciary would be the last hurdle for him to overcome in his bid to consolidate his power. Accused of being soft on terrorism and of misconduct, Chief Justice of the Pakistan Supreme Court, Iftikhar Muhammad Chaudhry, was dismissed because his challenge to the legality of the Musharraf government and whether the president could serve both as president and army chief (Nasr 2009, 225).

Musharraf's dismissal of the chief justice brought the pro-democracy movement out in force. In particular, thousands of lawyers took to the streets to protest Musharraf's abuse of power. Pakistan had never witnessed this amount of grassroots support for democracy and rejection of dictatorship (Nasr 2009, 226). Emboldened by the public support, the Supreme Court, now headed by Khalilur Rehman Ramday, overturned Musharraf's decision reinstating Chaudhry as chief justice (Nawaz 2008, 560).

Next, in response to the Supreme Court's decision, Musharraf launched a "second coup" on November 3, 2007, to remove the Supreme Court and set aside the constitution. Also, there were restrictions placed on broadcast news media and large numbers of supporters of the various political parties were jailed (Nawaz 2008, 560). Musharraf "remained super-confident and focused on what he saw as his role in Pakistan's history: to restore democracy, with whatever military force he could muster" (Nawaz 2008, 561). At this point, however, according to Cole (2009), Musharraf's "refusal to resign from the military and rule as a civilian president had long been an embarrassment to Washington, which had . . . strongly supported him despite its rhetoric about democratizing the Muslim world" (Cole 2009, 238). The increasing domestic and international pressure would force his hand. New elections were called for January 2008 with the political parties responding by demanding the return of their exiled leaders, Benazir Bhutto and Nawaz Sharif. Musharraf also resigned from the military and installed General Ashfaq Parvez Kayani as army chief and would run for president as a civilian (Nawaz 2008, 561).

Bhutto and Sharif initiated a consultative process, which led to the signing of the Charter of Democracy, an agreement calling for the PPP and PML-N (Pakistani Muslim League-Nawaz) to work together to restore democracy, an independent judiciary, and seek the disengagement of the military from politics (Shafqat 2009, 93). Seeing that the democracy movement was gaining momentum, on October 5, 2007, Musharraf issued the National Reconciliation Order to "exonerate political leaders from charges in cases of corruption and paved the way for the return of these leaders, particularly Bhutto" (Shafqat 2009, 93). The electoral campaign was now underway with Bhutto returning and campaigning in every province.

December 27, 2007, however, became a date that Pakistanis would not soon forget. During campaigning in Rawalpindi, Bhutto was assassinated by members of Baitullah Mahsud's Tehrik-I Taliban (Cole 2009, 238). Her death "roused anger, passion and a wave of sympathy not only for her party, the PPP, but also for other political leaders" (Shafqat 2009, 93). After the assassination, Musharraf sought to postpone the elections for a year, but with the security situation as it was with massive protests and violence, Cole (2009) argues that Washington "appears to have convinced him [Musharraf] behind the scenes that the elections needed to be held" (238). The elections were rescheduled for February 2008 and the PPP won a decisive victory with the PML-N coming in a close second. It would now be up to Zardari as interim head of the PPP (Zardari and Bhutto's son, Bilawal, was appointed leader of the party, but would not be taking over until after completing his studies at Oxford) and Sharif to form a ruling coalition (Cole 2009, 239).

The coalition of PPP and PML-N has "raised expectations that Pakistan may be moving away from a dominant party system to a multi-party system" (Shafqat 2009, 94). The three dominant parties in the ruling coalition, the PPP, PML, and ANP, were joined in their disdain for the rule of Musharraf and each differed on how he should be removed from office. The PML-N was the most vocal about Musharraf's removal and the reinstatement of the judges, while the PPP initially tried to work with Musharraf (Shafqat 2009, 95). According to Saeed Shafqat (2009), "The PPP also wished to dilute the issue of the restoration of the judges, which strained the coalition as the PML-N's expectation was the judges would be restored by May 12, 2008. When that did not happen, the PML-N's cabinet ministers submitted their resignation to the prime minister, and the party subsequently withdrew from the coalition" (95). The PML-N became the opposition party in the National Assembly and in August 2008, Musharraf resigned. One month later, Zardari became president of Pakistan.

President Zardari's rule was tenuous. Despite $11 billion in American aid during Musharraf's tenure, Pakistan remained a poor country (Cole 2009, 240). The country faced political wrangling during the early years of renewed civilian rule, along with suicide bombings and counterterrorism operations in the NWFP (Nasr 2009, 229). These events notwithstanding, the military under Gen. Kayani chose to remain behind-the-scenes. He ordered serving officers to withdraw from civilian positions and acted as an arbiter to help end the political stand-off between Sharif and Zardari in 2009 (BBC News, 6/17/09). As Shafqat (2009) notes, "The present army chief seems earnest to disengage the military from its hegemonic position" (106).

Pakistani politicians, therefore, have walked a tightrope in recent years dealing with a faltering economy, widespread poverty, corruption, and Islamic militancy within the Tribal areas. Therefore, from 2009 to 2013, Pakistan's civil–military relationship could be characterized as one of conflict; albeit, conflict through proxies, as the military under General Kayani used the judiciary to improve its standing vis-à-vis politicians. According to C. Christine Fair (2014), "Kayani has been very much a part of Pakistan's political machinery even while cultivating meticulously the impression at home and abroad that he is a professional officer waiting for the civilian leaders to lead" (580). Frederic Grare (2013) argues that Kayani used the judiciary as a "'sword of Damocles' against the Asif Ali Zardari government to render it more vulnerable to army pressures. Although he was unable to coerce the President into stepping down, Kayani nevertheless succeeded in pressuring Zardari to forgo the use of considerable parts of his powers" (589).

Throughout Zadari's rule, there was mass discontent and conflict within Pakistani civil society. In December 2012, this discontent bubbled to the surface. Tahirul Qadri, a Canadian religious cleric of Pakistani origin called for electoral reforms to battle corruption, specifically to prevent corrupt candidates from running in upcoming elections the following year. According to Grare (2013), "With apparently unlimited access to resources of unknown origin, the cleric sustained his campaign with numerous television advertisements and extensive organized rallies. He then launched a 'Long March' from Lahore to Islamabad and staged a sit-in in front of Parliament House, calling for the immediate dissolution of the parliament, the provincial assemblies and the Election Commission of Pakistan" (989). Eventually, the Supreme Court declared Qadri's demands unconstitutional.

Nevertheless, the Qadri episode is emblematic of the battles between the military and politicians between 2009 and 2013. On one hand, Qadri's efforts could be seen as the military seeking to indefinitely postpone the elections. On the other hand, the Qadri episode may have been the military's attempt at a bloodless coup (Grare 2013, 990). Grare (2013) argues, "Whatever the reasons behind the Qadri campaign, it demonstrates that the military is not voluntarily disengaging from politics. The security establishment may no longer take a direct role in partisan games, but it is still playing politics by proxy" (990). In other words, the security establishment has allies in the judiciary but also with other politicians or political parties to check the power of the mainstream parties, the PPP and PML-N, and protect their interests.

The 2013 elections saw the PML-N win 186 seats in the National Assembly, and secure a majority. Sharif once again became prime minister. According to Rana Banerji (2014), a Distinguished Fellow at the Institute of Peace and Conflict Studies, a South Asian think tank in New Dehli, India, "In a sense, the 2013 electoral verdict was pleasing for conservative forces in the Pakistani Establishment, both within the military and civilian bureaucracy as left of center or centrist parties like the PPP, ANP, and MQM(A) could neither canvass forcefully, nor did well except in Sindh" (January 10). The military under Kayani took a public position that it was open to free and fair elections, but Banerji (2014) argues that Kayani:

> indicated that the Army would not be averse to intervene in difficult internal situations like in FATA and Balochistan if asked to do so by the political leadership. He supported talks with the Tehrik-e-Taliban Pakistan (TTP) but cautioned that these would have to be within the ambit of the Constitution. Issues like laying down of arms and a ceasefire could be discussed by the civilians but no agreement could be concluded without taking the military on board (January 10).

Put differently, Kayani "was deliberately creating doubts about their [politicians'] capacity and in a larger sense, the very efficacy of democracy as a system" (Banjeri, 1/10/14).

Kayani inherited a demoralized army. He restored Pakistani's confidence in the army and while proclaiming his democratic credentials, he "likens coups to temporary bypasses that are created when a bridge collapses on democracy's highway. After the bridge is repaired, he says, then there's no longer any need for the detour" (Fair 2011, 579).

Pakistani democracy since the May 2013 election experienced a number of challenges for Sharif. First, Sharif appointed General Raheel Sharif to be the new Army Chief of Staff over two senior generals in November 2013. Second, there was growing discontent among the population over the faltering economy, widespread poverty, growing militancy, and the inability of the government to deliver on basic services such as a steady electric supply (BBC News, 8/14/14). Consequently, Imran Khan and Qadri have sought to challenge Sharif. On August 14, 2014, each led protest marches from Lahore to Islamabad. The marches culminated in rallies on August 15, 2014, at the east end of Islamabad away from the city center (BBC News, 8/14/14). Both Khan and Qadri are calling for investigations into government corruption and new elections.

Today, the Pakistani civil–military relationship is one based on a history of the military creating a nationalist narrative. According to C. Christine Fair (2014), "Pakistan's civilian institutions are unable to constrain the army in part because of their own weaknesses but also because they ultimately embrace or at least tacitly accept this narrative" (574). The Pakistani army has built itself as the guardian of the nation; therefore, this narrative is one of Pakistani nationalism, which allowed the army to

expand its influence throughout the state by acquiring economic interests, coopting bureaucrats and political elites, and securing strategic part-
nerships with the U.S. (Fair 2014, 574). The next section will discuss the
generational effect and nationalist narrative of the military before turning
to a discussion of Pakistani civil–military relations and the regional and
international influence.

## THE MILITARY ESTABLISHMENT

To understand why the Pakistani military intervened in politics it is essential to understand how the military's identity was formed. As Cohen
argues, "Armies are total institutions that mold the beliefs of their members for life" (Cohen 2004, 98). Young Pakistanis wishing to serve the
military must first be selected to the Pakistani Military Academy (PMA)
and then as officers they attend the Staff College at Quetta, and for generals (aka brigadiers), the National Defense College in Islamabad. This education, in addition to their social and class background, ethnicity, ideology, and corporate identity to the army itself, all shape the worldview of
the young Pakistani officer. According to Cohen (1984), there are four
generations of Pakistani officers that have influenced Pakistani politics:
the British Generation, the American Generation, the Pakistani Generation — 1972–1982, and the Next Generation.

The British Generation is important because it established the educational and training facilities of the new Pakistani Army and developed a
professional army modeled after the British. The American Generation
were set apart from the other generations because of the training they
received from the American military in doctrine, nuclear planning and
the revision of the army structure to include an American-equipped armored division in addition to extra infantry divisions. Also, this generation distorted their perception of themselves in relation to India since
they had had no war-time experience against their Indian counterparts.

The Pakistani Generation was considered the most "Pakistani" since
"they were more representative of the wider society in class origin, had
less exposure to American professional influence, and believed the United States had let Pakistan down" (Cohen 2004, 106). These officers joined
after Pakistan lost the second war with India over Bangladesh. This period (1965 to 1971) saw military honor and professionalism slip away, as
the military was challenged repeatedly by civilians; namely, Zulfikar Ali
Bhutto, who ridiculed senior military leadership for losing the war (Cohen 2004, 106). Bhutto implemented reforms with the help of his Army
Chief of Staff General Muhammad Zia ul-Haq. Zia's long tenure as Chief
of Staff and later President was influential among the officer corps because of Zia's willingness to Islamize the officer corps in pursuit of building the nation.

Finally, the Next Generation comes from the middle class and joined the army to improve its standard of living, "because the army is seen as a path to social mobility, [but] . . . in Pakistan's case, the army is also seen as a path to social and political power" (Cohen 2004, 109). In short, the Pakistani army views itself as the nation's savior. Accordingly, this generation has seen fit to manipulate civilian politicians, manage civilian institutions, and invest in a military economy to ensure its hold on power (Siddiqa 2007).

Today, the Pakistani military numbers 643,800. The breakdown of active duty forces is as follows: 550,000 Army, 23,800 Navy, 70,000 Air Force and 282,000 Paramilitary (Military Balance 2016, 279). Since 2008, the Army's primary mission has been counterinsurgency and counterterrorism. Given that the military has long sought a say in Pakistan's foreign policy, "Pakistan's feudal-tribal-military industrial complex has manipulated both popular opinion, by focusing on external threats, and religious sentiment, providing priviliges for those religious organizations willing to overlook violations of the Objectives Resolution" (Esposito, Sonn, and Voll, 79–80). In other words, since the founding of Pakistan, the military has influenced the state arguing security in the South Asia region takes priority over domestic development.

In fact, Fair (2014) argues the Pakistani military's strategic culture is heavily influenced by foreign policy; namely, revisionism regarding its place in South Asia. Pakistan seeks to acquire Kashmir and resist India's rise in South Asia. To do so, the military focused on three important components of its strategic culture: Islam, strategic depth, and security through alliances (Fair 2014, 13–33). As mentioned above, Pakistan was established as a state for Indian Muslims. Consequently, at independence, the Objectives Resolution codified that Islam would be the ideology of the state to tamp down ethnic sectarianism within Pakistan (Fair 2014, 69). Subsequent politicians, such as Z. Bhutto and B. Bhutto, and Sharif, and military leaders, such as A. Khan, Y. Khan, Zia, and Musharraf, all embraced Islam when it suited them and their government's politically.

The next important aspect of Pakistan's strategic culture is the Pakistani military's belief in the need to influence politics in Afghanistan for the purposes of having strategic depth to fight a future war in India. Fair (2014) cites Lt. Col. Israr Ahmad Ghumman from his 1990 article in the 1990 *Pakistan Army Journal* where "[h]e ties Pakistan's domestic stability to these external forces, not that 'the delicate internal balance of Pakistan due to law and order, Pakhtoonistan and refugee problems, have the potential of being exploited by external factors through subversion, terrorism and insurgency. . . . The dissident elements and miscreants can be exploited by Russia, India and Afghanistan in their nefarious designs" (117). In other words, the Pakistani military believes India and Afghanistan are out to undermine Pakistan. Consequently, the Pakistanis have supported ulema parties, such as Jamaat-e-Islaami and Jamiat-ulema-Islami to promote Pakistani interests. Fair (2014) argues, "Pakistan's continued investment in these proxies ostensibly stems from the army's desire to restrict the ability of India to operate in Afghanistan. However, while Pakistani military personnel are wont to accuse India of any number of nefarious activities, ranging from support for Baloch insurgents and terrorists in FATA to bombing targets deep within Pakistan, they also deny that Pakistan seeks strategic depth" (133–34).

The final aspect of strategic culture important for Pakistan is its alliances with the international community, especially the United States and China. Although, alliances with North Korea and Saudi Arabia have also been used to bolster Pakistan's security. Pakistan, since its independence, relies on aid, military assistence, access to conventional and nuclear weapons, and training for its armed forces (Fair 2014, 174). As Fair (2014) astutely observes, Pakistani defense writers have said the United States "is a perfidious ally, necessary evil that Pakistan's weaknesses force it to endure, [while] China appears as an all-weather friend, one that has not imposed onerous conditions on its support for Pakistan" (175). The influence of these states was engendered by Pakistan's geopolitical positioning but also by the international political order of the day, the Cold War and post-9/11 liberal international order.

Below, this chapter examines how this focus on foreign policy neglected domestic policy and increased factionalism and dependence on foreign aid, resulting in military intervention and undermining democracy.

## CIVIL–MILITARY RELATIONS

Pakistan's civil–military relationship is defined as one where the military viewed itself as guiding democracy to best represent its interests. Military rule occurred from 1958 to 1969, 1969 to 1971, 1977 to 1988, and 1999 to 2008. Throughout these periods of military rule, the military's interests were driven by security and economic need, "[y]et Pakistan was created to specifically be a democracy, and the military has allowed civilian governments to rule intermittently, so long as they protected the interests of the military" (Esposito, et al. 2016, 83). This section will examine how the military dominates this relationship before turning in the next section to the importance foreign aid has played in solidifying the military's position within the state.

First, Pakistan's place in South Asia as a Muslim state has greatly influenced the military's desire to influence politics. As mentioned above, Islam and the Two Nation Theory are influential in forming the basis for the military's worldview. Christine Fair (2014) argues, "Pakistan's generals step in when they believe that the civilian order has failed disastrously and that their service to save the nation is required by virtue of their duty to the nation and because they believe that Pakistan's citizenry welcome the intervention" (28). After the intervention, most military elites want to remove the military from direct day-to-day governance. To do so, before elections are held, the military works with intelligence agencies to co-opt Islamist parties, such as the JI, who receive a certain percentage of the vote to counter the mainstream political parties, in this case the PML and PPP, and the constitution is rewritten to place extraordinary powers into the presidency and allow the military to rule from behind the scenes.

Second, the military intervened to ensure its financial interests are maintained. This is done both from the military's involvement in the civilian economy and through the billions of dollars in foreign aid Pakistan receives yearly. For example, Ayesha Siddiqa, in *Military Inc.: Inside Pakistan's Military Economy* (2007) details extensively the military's involvement in the civilian economy through land holdings, as well as welfare foundations running private businesses, insurance companies, and heavy industry. The amount of aid Pakistan receives according to Esposito, Soll and Voll (2016) is quite extensive: "Since 2012, Pakistan has received over $26 billion in total US aid . . . [while] also receiv[ing] significant aid from international organizations such as the IMF and from other countries, including England, China, Saudi Arabia, and the United Arab Emirates (83).

Therefore, throughout Pakistan's history, politics and the civil–military relationship is driven by foreign policy to the detriment of domestic political development. Below, an examination of periods of military rule along with the democratic interregnum highlights the effect regional security and international aid had on Pakistani civil–military decision-making.

## REGIONAL AND INTERNATIONAL RELATIONS

For Pakistan, independence created the conditions benefiting the military over the civil. The death of Jinnah early on in the state's existence pushed both sides to try and one up each other to push their interests above the others. In other words, both sides were attempting to define the nationalist narrative as part of the Two Nation Theory that was fundamental to the creation of the Pakistani state. This nationalist narrative, Haqqani (2013) says, fueled paranoia about global conspiracies to destroy Pakistan (23). The state's leadership was faced with a quandary which would confront it throughout its history: "Pakistan actively sought to become a Western ally, on the one hand, and embraced anti-Western Islamist vocabulary, on the other. Economic and military necessity forced Pakistan to seek an international patron in the United States, whereas an inadequately defined Islamic nationalism made shunning the idea of being that patron's client equally necessary" (23). Therefore, the behavior of political and military actors in Pakistan must be examined in light of international influence predominating South Asia since the end of World War II.

The 1950s were the early years of the Cold War, where the United States and the Soviet Union engaged in geopolitical chess around the globe. Both the United States and the Soviet Union were attempting to prevent the other from persuading states joining their "side." In the early years of Pakistan's independence, Liaquat was friendly to the Soviet Union and Iran, but also extended a hand of friendship to the United States. Liaquat used Pakistan's strategic location to both the Middle East and Southeast Asia to acquire economic and military assistance from the US. According to Haqqani (2013), "His argument was simple: if Americans helped with Pakistan's existential challenges, Pakistan could help protect American strategic interests in both Southeast Asia and the Middle East" (50). Subsequently, Pakistan would join the Southeast Asia Treaty Organization (SEATO) in 1954 and the Central Treaty Organization (CENTO), also known as the Baghdad Pact, in 1955. The United States "persuaded Pakistan to join SEATO, in return for $250 million in aid 'so they could quadruple the size of their army'" (Esposito, et al. 2016, 85). By joining these security alliances, Haqqani (2013) notes that between 1954 and 1959, $425 million in U.S. aid was given to the Pakistani military in addition to $855 million in economic aid over the same period (83). Fair (2014) argues, "Americans generally understood that, despite Pakistan's professed rejection of communism, its participation in these arrangements was driven primarily by its fear of India and secondarily by its desire for access to U.S. military equipment, training, and doctrine, all of which had an important impact on Pakistan's military posture and military capabilities" (181).

By the early 1960s, the combination of a new American president, John F. Kennedy, and geopolitical events involving India, China, and the Soviet Union would strain the U.S.-Pakistani relationship. U.S. foreign policy in South Asia sought to ensure the containment of communism with Pakistan's inclusion in SEATO and CENTO. Ayub permitted the United States to station U-2 spy planes in Peshawar for use in missions over the Soviet Union. Moreover, U.S. policymakers "did not wish to see any cracks emerging in their wall of treaty partners around the communist world's two major countries, the Soviet Union and China" and sought to become allies with India "as a potential counterweight to the Chinese giant to the north . . . even while India solidified its military and economic ties with the Soviet Union"(Nawaz 2008, 195).

In October 1962, China attacked India "reacting to India's imprudent 'forward policy,' that is, establishing military posts behind Chinese positions in the mountains" (Abbas 2005, 40–41). Although the Kennedy Administration had promised to consult Ayub on any assistance it was to provide to India, this did not occur, and the United States immediately provided military aid to India. The United States asked Pakistan "'to make a positive gesture of sympathy and restraint'" toward India regarding Kashmir (Abbas 2005, 40). Ayub stated that he had no intention of taking advantage of India at this point, but was angered at not being consulted. His response engendered a response from President Kennedy that qualified U.S. support for India by stating, "'Our help to India in no way diminishes or qualifies our commitment to Pakistan and we [the United States] have made it clear to both countries'" (Nawaz 2008, 199). Consequently, Ayub sought to distance Pakistan from its relationship with the United States.

During the Sino-Indian conflict, Ayub's foreign minister, Zulfikar Ali Bhutto, convinced Ayub to turn to China for support. The Sino-Pakistani alliance included: a border agreement in 1963, highway construction connecting the two countries through the Karakoram Pass, trade agreements, economic and military aid (Baxter 1995, 52). According to scholar and former Pakistani government official, Hassan Abbas (2005), "For Pakistan, the mortal threat to its security lay in India, which the United States saw as a country to be salvaged and indemnified against the Chinese threat, while Pakistan saw in China an insurance against India" (40). Nevertheless, Ayub still wanted "to keep the spigot open" on U.S. aid and despite the strain in the U.S.-Pakistani relationship, Pakistan received $143 million as part of a U.S. military assistance program (Nawaz 2008, 199–200). In Pakistan, U.S. aid to India was seen as helping the Indians prepare for war in Kashmir. Therefore, Ayub believed the Sino-Indian conflict offered Pakistan the opportunity to settle the issue of Kashmir militarily, because the conflict highlighted India's relative military weakness at the time (Nawaz 2008, 200).

Ayub was concerned with increasing his legacy, as the general whom would return all of Kashmir to Pakistan (Nasr 2009, 211). Consequently, overestimating Pakistan's military capability, Ayub led his forces to war with India in 1965. This Indo-Pakistani war started as a series of border clashes along undemarcated territory at the Rann of Kutch in the southeast and along the ceasefire line in Kashmir. According to Baxter (1995), "The Rann of Kutch conflict was resolved by mutual consent and British sponsorship and arbitration, but the Kashmir conflict proved more dangerous and widespread" (52). The Pakistan Army, in the hopes of supporting an uprising by Kashmiris against India, trained guerillas to help foment local dissent, but "[n]o such uprising took place, and by August India had retaken Pakistani-held positions in the north while Pakistan attacked in the Chamb sector in southwestern Kashmir" (Baxter 2005, 52–53). In fact, Nasr (2009) argues, "Underestimating India's military capability, or perhaps overestimating Pakistan's . . . the overconfident Pakistani army soon found itself scrambling to stop the Indians from taking Lahore, the country's second largest city and the capital of the Punjab,

Pakistan's most populous province" (211). Pakistan's military counter-punched into the heart of Indian Punjab, but neither state was capable of sustaining a prolonged military campaign due to military supplies being cut off by the United States and Britain. Thus, with victory in Kashmir dwindling, "Ayub Khan had overreached and was now humiliated" (Nasr 2009, 211).

On January 10, 1966, Ayub and India's prime minister, Lal Bahadur Shastri, signed the Tashkent Accord ending the 1965 Indo-Pakistani War. Although the conflict ceased between these two bitter rivals, domestic conflict was heating up within Pakistan. As Nawaz (2008) notes, "Once the euphoria produced by the official propaganda during the war had died down in Pakistan, people realized that Ayub Khan and the military leadership had failed the nation militarily . . . Pakistan, which had been led to believe it had won the war, was feeling particularly let down and was looking for answers" (239–40). Discontent grew, not only within the Ayub regime, but in the streets as well. Bhutto distanced himself from Ayub over the next year and eventually left government in 1967 and formed the Pakistan Peoples' Party (PPP).

Through his election slogan of "*Roti, Kapra, aur Makan*"(bread, clothing, and housing), Bhutto appealed "to the dispossessed masses, particularly in the western wing of the country . . . [and] promised to break the powerful business interest groups whose domination of the economic scene had been in the news" (Nawaz 2008, 242).

Within the army, a split emerged between the generals and younger officers. Nawaz (2008) argues, "Although the lower ranks and younger officers showed remarkable courage, both in Pakistan and India, general-ship was not of the highest caliber and the war was marked by indecision and timidity" (240). Accordingly, Musa retired as commander-in-chief of the army and was replaced by General Yahya Khan, a protégé of Ayub. Yahya then began to strengthen his position by promoting his own loyalists and sending his number one challenger for commander-in-chief, General Akhtar Malik, to Ankara, Turkey. As Abbas (2005) notes, "This was a major step of promoting the interests of personal loyalty over those of competence and professionalism" (52).

By 1968, to try and regain support from the population for Ayub, the government sponsored a celebration called "The Decade of Development." Instead of being a celebration, in reality, the festivities highlighted the growing income inequality of the urban poor, a result of rapid economic growth and the 1965 War (Baxter 1995, 54). Pakistanis were angry and frustrated and a robust democracy movement sprang up bringing together secular and religious parties to call for free elections and the return of civilian rule (Nasr 2009, 211). Protests occurred throughout East and West Pakistan and "Ayub reacted by alternating conciliation and repression" which spread disorder. As Baxter notes, "The army moved into Karachi, Lahore, Peshawar, Dhaka, and Khulna to restore order. In rural areas of East Pakistan, a curfew was ineffective; local officials sensed government control ebbing and began retreating from the incipient peasant revolt" (Baxter 1995, 54). By the end of the year, Air Marshal Asghar Khan, the respected former Commander-in-Chief of the Pakistan Air Force, and Justice Murshed, of the East Pakistan judiciary came out against Ayub (Abbas 2005, 54). Nevertheless, Ayub invited the politicians to come talk with him in Rawalpindi, promised a new constitution, and said he would not stand for reelection in 1970 (Baxter 1995, 54).

The 1970 elections brought the PPP, and its leader Bhutto, to power. While initially insisting that Pakistan be a part of the Non-Aligned movement, "Bhutto's PPP would continue Pakistan's militarization at the expense of socioeconomic development, and it collaborated with both East and West to achieve its goals" (Esposito, et al. 2016, 87). Bhutto's geopolitical view was an "'unending danger of Indian aggressive tendencies fostered by Moscow,'" which would require the United States and China to support Pakistan (Haqqani 2013, 185). Haqqani (2013) cites a memorandum from the secretary of state. William P. Rogers, about Pakistani plans and American concerns. In short, the memo states that Bhutto had already cemented a relationship with China and needed to further solidify one with the United States. Bhutto "considered the prospects of U.S. military support as fairly good because of U.S. concerns over Soviet policy toward India and [America's] developing relations with China" (187–88).

The Nixon Administration's view of the subcontinent, however, was done purely through a Cold War lens (Haqqani 2013, 188). Although it should be noted that the United States and Soviet Union were moving towards détente. As a result, the United States withheld military aid from Pakistan and India, since both had used previously acquired military aid against each other. According to Haqqani (2013), "The U.S. refusal to resume military supplies was intended to force a policy reappraisal in Islamabad; instead it invigorated Pakistan's search for economic and military assistance from other sources" (204). For example, Saudi Arabia gave a $100 million interest free loan in addition to providing contributions to various charities and the building of mosques (Haqqani 2013, 205).

Additionally, Bhutto continued the relationship with China to further develop Pakistan's nuclear weapons capability. The need for a Pakistani nuclear capability would take on increasing urgency for Pakistan with India's detonating its first nuclear bomb in 1974. Fair (2014) cites military officers writing in the *Pakistani Army Journal* who, since the 1960s, have treated China as a far more favorable partner than the United States (196). An article in 1971 by Maj. Muhammad Aslam Zuberi discusses India's nuclear aspirations and advocates for Pakistan to acquire a minimal deterrent in collaboration with China (Fair 2014, 197). Zuberi "concludes that a nuclear guarantee from China or some other form of nuclear assistance from China is the safest course for Pakistan" (Fair 2014, 197). Fair (2014) cites another *Pakistani Army Journal* piece from 1995, which states that the United States is "'determined to assign an important role to India, ostensibly with the aim of neutralising the strength of Chinese and also decimating all the power potential of Pakistan'" which means "'Pakistan has had no choice but to seek a nuclear weapons capability, relying on all available sources to help'" (197).

Another regional development of importance for South Asia, but also the U.S.-Pakistani relationship, occurred in 1979 with the Soviet invasion of Afghanistan. At that time, Pakistan was ruled for two years by the military dictatorship of Zia. The 1979 invasion of Afghanistan by the Soviet Union, and subsequent U.S. support, would firmly embolden Zia vis-à-vis Pakistani domestic politics. As Haqqani (2005) argues, "Once international attention was focused on the developments in Afghanistan, Zia ul-Haq had virtually no external or internal compulsions for returning Pakistan to democracy" (140). For Pakistan, its Afghan policy "emphasized its Islamic ideology with the hope of blunting the challenge of ethnic nationalism supported by Afghanistan, tied Afghan aspirations for a Pastunistan to an Indian plan to break up Pakistan, and sought U.S. assistance in pursuing an agenda of regional influence" (Haqqani 2005, 159). In other words, Pakistan was looking for strategic depth in its confrontation with India and the Soviet invasion allowed the United States to work with Zia as part of its containment policy. In his Pulitzer Prize winning account of U.S. involvement in Afghanistan prior to 9/11, *Ghost Wars*, journalist Steve Coll (2004) notes:

> He [Zia] feared that Kabul's communists would stir up Pashtun independence activists along the disputed Afghanistan-Pakistan border. Pashtuns comprised Afghanistan's dominant ethnic group, but there were more Pashtuns living inside Pakistan than inside Afghanistan. . . . A war fought on Islamic principles could also help Zia shore up a political base at home and deflect appeals to Pashtun nationalism (62).

Thus, covert assistance from the CIA to the ISI began under the Carter Presidency and was ratcheted up once President Reagan took office.

The Carter Administration offered an initial $400 million in economic and military assistance to Pakistan, which Zia "described . . . as 'peanuts'" (Haqqani 2005, 187). Zia, the pious officer that he was, encouraged the financing and construction of hundreds of madrassas along the Afghan-Pakistani border as "a kind of Islamic ideological picket fence between communist Afghanistan and Pakistan" (Coll 2004, 61). While the Carter Administration was concerned about Pakistan's human rights record and its nuclear program, in the Reagan Administration, Zia found an ideological ally who would grant him the respect and legitimacy he desired "as the military ruler of a frontline state in the struggle against Soviet expansion" (Haqqani 2005, 187). Under Reagan, the U.S. assistance package to Pakistan was extensive—$3.2 billion in economic and military aid over a five-year period, followed by an additional $4.02 billion in aid in 1986, with the United States also rescheduling and writing off portions of Pakistan's debt (Haqqani 2005, 188).

As part of the relationship with the United States, "Zia sought and obtained political control over the CIA's weapons and money. He insisted that every gun and dollar allocated for the mujahedin pass through Pakistani hands" (Coll 2004, 63). To this end, Zia appointed a personal friend and close confidant, General Akhtar Abdul Rahman, the Pakistani intelligence chief and head of the ISI, to lead Pakistan's efforts against the Soviets (Haqqani 2005, 184). According to Coll (2004), "No American—CIA or otherwise—would be permitted to cross the border into Afghanistan. Movements of weapons within Pakistan and distributions to Afghan commanders would be handled strictly by ISI officers. All training of mujahedin would be carried out solely by ISI in camps along the Afghan frontiers" (Coll 2004, 63). Zia's ability to dictate the foregoing speaks volumes regarding the perceptions the Zia regime and the Americans had toward the Afghan imbroligio.

For Zia, Afghanistan was the turning point in Pakistan's quest for an Islamic identity at home and leadership of the Islamic world. Haqqani (2005) argues, "By codifying Islamic principles in the country's constitution and legal system, Zia ul-Haq was paving the way for the day when 'the lower rungs of society are mobilized in favor of greater Islamization.'" (193). Put simply, Zia hoped support for the Afghan jihad would spur an Islamic revolutionary movement which Pakistan could lead, thereby "replacing artificial alliances such as the Baghdad Pact" (Haqqani 2005, 193).

Alternatively, for the United States, Afghanistan was "just the largest in a series of covert wars—others were being fought in Nicaragua and Angola—that were meant to punish the Soviet Union and inflict a heavy cost in men, money, and prestige" (Haqqani 2005, 193). By 1988, the U.S.-assisted mujahedeen defeated the Soviets, and in victory's wake, there was a much larger ISI, which would continue to build its relationship with Islamists and become a greater factor in Pakistani domestic and foreign policy. As Haqqani (2005) notes:

> Pakistan still wanted U.S. economic and security assistance as it had since its inception, but its military leaders were more convinced than ever that they needed to chart their own course and that the only practical basis for Pakistan's relations with the United States would be for both sides to use each other. Pakistan's military leadership believed the Americans would have to learn to live with Pakistan saying one thing and doing another. Pakistan would not settle for anything less than the major role it sought as a leader in its region and the Muslim world (197).

Pakistan's support of the U.S. fight against communism was important, but with the Soviet withdrawal, Pakistan still had to confront mounting ethnic tension, sectarian strife, and civil disorder.

After Zia's death and a return to electoral democracy, Islamists would continue to influence politics. Since moving to Pakistan in 1947, the JI was active in Pakistani politics through national, municipal and provincial elections. The JI has been an opposition party challenging the military-led governments and also used by civilians, Sharif and Bhutto, to prevent other political parties from gaining seats in parliamentary elections. Although the JI participated in politics, the extent to which Islamization could occur was always regulated by the state. According to Nasr (1997), the state followed two approaches in regulating Islam vis-à-vis politics: "The first was directed at incorporating Islam into the state's discourse on sociopolitical change while simultaneously limiting the role of Islamic parities—the self-styled advocates of Islamization—in the political process. . . . The second incorporated Islamic politics into the state's discourse by including Islamic parties in the political process and even in the running of the state, all with the aim of establishing control over them" (142). The first approach characterizes the Ayub Khan and Zulfiqar Ali Bhutto regimes during the period of 1958 to 1977, while the second approach characterizes the Zia regime from 1977 to 1988, the "democratic period" from 1988 to 1999 under Benazir Bhutto and Nawaz Sharif, and the "armored democracy" from 1999 to 2008 of Musharraf. (Nasr 1997 and Shah 2013).

Benazir "continued to support both Pakistan's nuclear weapons program and Islamist militias as part of her geopolitical stratetgy, and U.S.-Pakistan relations plummeted" (Esposito, et al. 2016, 101). The United States was especially concerned with nuclear proliferation. In 1985, the U.S. Congress passed the Pressler Amendment which established conditions on U.S. economic and military aid. Annual verification was done to ensure Pakistan did not have a nuclear weapons program and "[l]acking such verification, military and economic aid would be cut off" (Esposito, et al. 2016, 101). Under President George H. W. Bush, U.S. aid to Pakistan was cut off and Benazir was dismissed in favor of Sharif and the PML. Sharif would ally Pakistan with China, continue Zia's privatization of the economy, and Islamization of society. The Pakistani government, according to Haqqani (2013), "continued to lie to the United States as well as the Pakistani people. To the Americans, Pakistani officials insisted that there had been no change in Pakistan's nuclear status, whereas the Pakistani public was told that the Americans were discriminating against Pakistan by preventing access to technology available to India" (282–83).

The second terms of Benazir and Sharif would see sharply contrasted persectives toward the United States and South Asia. Benazir sought economic growth for Pakistan, including military aid and cash (Haqqani 2013, 287). Haqqani (2013) notes that relations with the United States "came to a standstill when the ISI decided to end the Afghan civil war bu supporting the Taliban" (287–88). Pakistan's support for the Taliban came down to the concept of strategic depth for security purposes. The Taliban were supporters of terrorism, "but as long as they refused an Indian presence, they helped assure Pakistan's national security" (Haqqani 2013, 292). Sharif's second term included economic and trade agreements with India. However, the dispute over Kashmir would create what Haqqani (2013) says was "a South Asian version of the Cuban Missile Crisis" (302). Musharraf sent Pakistani troops to occupy mountainous terrain in Kashmir hoping to force India to negotiate a settlement to the Kashmir issue. However, India quickly retook the territory. Nevertheless, the international community demanded Pakistan's withdrawal. Haqqani (2013) states, "The Americans were concerned about reports that Pakistan's generals might use nuclear weapons to reverse defeat in conventional fighting" (302). President Bill Clinton would intervene in the crisis and pressure the Pakistanis to withdraw their troops. This withdrawal was resented by the Pakistani military and would lead to confrontation between Sharif and the military when Sharif sought to appoint loyalists in the military chain of command and to replace Musharraf as Chief of Staff of the Army. The result of this interference in military affairs was the 1999 coup bringing Musharraf to power.

Under the Clinton administration, the U.S.-Pakistani relationship was a tenuous one, but the Pakistanis "welcomed the inauguration of George W. Bush as president of the United States . . . [since] during his campaign, Bush had spoken little about South Asia" (Haqqani 2013, 308). The events of 9/11, however, would have a tremendous impact on U.S.-Pakistani relations. The United States received Pakistan's assistance with intelligence and logistic support as part of the U.S. invasion of Afghanistan to go after Al-Qaeda and the Taliban. In return, the United States lifted the sanctions imposed by the Pressler, Glenn, and Symington Amendments against Pakistan. This created a pattern over the ensuing decade, whereby "[t]he United States provided large amounts of economic and military aid including fresh batch of F-16 aircraft, some frigates for the navy, and updated equipment for the army" (Haqqani 2013, 312). In return, Pakistan would hand over Al-Qaeda and "also received reimbursement for what it spent to fight terrorism . . . between 2002 and 2012 [which] amounted to $25 billion" (Haqqani 2013, 312). Although, while cooperating with the United States, Musharraf "continued a policy of support for Islamist militants in efforts to assure a Pakistan-friendly government in post-Taliban Afghanistan, as well as in efforts to keep India from establishing permanent control in Kashmir" (Esposito, et al. 2016, 105).

Since 9/11, there has been a rise in Islamic militancy not only in Afghanistan, but in Pakistan as well. Militant groups in Pakistan who were opposed to the United States's presence in Afghanistan also fought against the Pakistani government. These militants were based along the

Pakistani border in the Tribal areas, now known as KhyberPaktunwa, the Swat Valley, and in Quetta. According to Esposito, Sonn and Voll (2016), "[I]t was Pakistan's support for the U.S.-led campaign in Afghanistan that gave rise to the Pakistani Taliban which, in turn, brought the U.S.-led 'Global War on Terrorism' (GWOT) into Pakistan, with the introduction of drone strikes in June 2004. . . . [T]he drone strikes predictably exacerbated anti-American sentiment in Pakistan overall and further radicalized its militants" (106–7).

Increased militancy would lead in December 2007 to the assassination of Benazir Bhutto. An important consequence of the assassination was Pakistan's return to democracy. From 2008 to present day, the PPP and PML alternated running the state. Both Zadari and Sharif continued to cooperate with the GWOT. The Pakistani military has undertaken counterinsurgency missions against Haqqani Network militants in the Tribal areas. The continued assistance of Pakistan in the GWOT earned Pakistan significant amounts of U.S. foreign aid. For example, in 2010 and 2011 the United States gave Pakistan $1.2 billion per year. Due to increased criticism from the Obama Administration over the Pakistani military's ineffectiveness in counterterrorism against the Haqqani Network (some in the United States believe the Haqqanis are supported by the Pakistani military and ISI), the last few years saw the yearly amount of U.S. foreign aid decreased to $300 million (Naviwala 9/4/15). These funds are known as Coalition Support Funds and total $13 billion since 9/11, but this past year Congress threatened to withhold $300 million unless conditions were met regarding Pakistan's counterterrorism efforts (Naviwala 9/14/15).

The Pakistani government's response was to seek out support to the tune of $46 billion in development aid from China (Naviwala 9/14/15). In addition, China has strengthened its ties with Pakistan through the development of a China-Pakistan economic corridor. However, as Nadia Naviwala (2016) notes, "[U]ntil the corridor is a reality, Pakistan will have to find a way to boost trade in actual goods and private sector services if it want to decrease dependence on foreign aid payments . . . and move away from a transactional foreign policy (9/14/15). In essence, Pakistan is forming other alliances in the event of further cuts in U.S. foreign aid.

However, the Defense Authorization Act for 2016 authorizes $900 million for Coalition Support Funds. There are requirements that the Department of Defense withhold $300 million if Pakistan does not "demonstrate meaningful action" against the Haqqani Network as well as promoting "stability in Afghanistan and encourage reconciliation talks between the Taliban and the government of Afghanistan" (Naviwala, 9/14/15). As these negotiations play out over the next year, Pakistan will continue to be an important strategic partner in South Asia for the United States. Pakistani leadership, both civil and military, are aware of this position and "'in important negotiations, Pakistan usually tries to create a sense of obligation on the part of the United States, or to nurture and intensify the fear that failure to honor Pakistan's requests will lead to disastrous consequences for U.S. interests'" (Schaffer and Schaffer 2011, 3; quoted in Fair 2014, 199). In other words, Pakistan has used the international context of the Cold War and the War on Terror to extract the resources it needs from the United States and "Pakistan's general 'institutional culture of avoiding blame or self-criticism shows up at the negotiating tables as a strong tendency to blame the army's problems on the United States, and to try to make their American counterparts feel guilty about Pakistan's difficulties'" (Schaffer and Schaffer 2011, 65; quoted in Fair 2014, 199–200).

## CONCLUSION

Pakistan's civil–military relationship can be defined as a relationship lacking in trust. Since the founding of Pakistan, ethnic and sectarian tensions have been centrifugal forces pulling the political and military elites further and further apart regarding Pakistani identity. Consequently, the military, the state's strongest institution, took advantage of these tensions, especially those tensions between political elites, to intervene in 1958 to ensure the survival of the Pakistani state. Once in power, however, military elite self-interests grew along with their disdain for politicians, whom they felt were corrupt. After 1958, military rule has dominated Pakistan's history with further interventions in 1969, 1977, and 1999.

Furthermore, in the few times when the military has withdrawn from politics, political elites have taken this as carte blanche to attempt any number of reforms. Often, the PPP and PML will be in conflict with one another or with the military and cause the military to view politicians' actions as encroaching on their interests and halt the brief periods of democracy that occurred from 1956–1958, 1988–1999, and 2008–Present. What makes the Pakistani case even more unsettling is the ongoing fight against Islamist extremists and Pakistan's on-going relationship with the United States. While Pakistani-U.S. strategic interests were not always similar, Pakistan has always been of geo-strategic importance for U.S. policymakers. The Pakistanis knew this and exploited this fact, often saying one thing for domestic consumption and another for those in Washington. Thus, Pakistani civil–military relations are still a work in-progress; namely, both sides working to build trust in institutions to limit the military's role in politics.

One example of a civil–military relationship where trust in state institutions has occurred is Turkey. Chapter five, the final case study, examines civil–military relations in Turkey to highlight the domestic and international factors that contributed to military involvement in politics and the factors contributing to Turkey being held up as an example of how democracy can function in the Middle East.

# FIVE

# Turkey

The Ottoman Empire's collapse left remnants of the Ottoman army to move forward and forge a national identity for Turks in Anatolia. The culmination of these efforts resulted in the establishment of the Republic of Turkey in 1923. Led by a hero of World War I, Mustafa Kemal, later known as Atatürk, Turkey developed as a modern nation-state. Kemalism was a top-down modernization effort designed to forge a new identity of what it meant to be a Turk. As one of the strongest institutions of the former Ottoman Empire, the Turkish Armed Forces became the guardian of Turkish identity.

In 1960, 1971, 1980, and 1997 the Turkish Armed Forces "rescued" the Turkish nation from politicians who were deemed to be harming Ataturk's vision. After the founding of the Turkish state, Ataturk ruled under a single party, the Republican People's Party, until his death in 1938. Turkey was then led by Ataturk's deputy, and later Turkey's prime minister, Ismet Inönü, who continued Atatürk's vision and installed multi-party elections in 1945, resulting in the election of the Democrat Party in 1950. Subsequently, from 1950 to 1960, discontent and violence increased throughout Turkish society. The military took notice and intervened for the first time in 1960 and ruled the country for three years, withdrawing in 1963. At this point, Turkey saw a rise in social movements on the left and the right—Kurdish separatists who latched on to communism and political Islam. Both movements were seen as a threat to Kemalism and led to the military interventions of 1971 and 1980. Under General Kenan Evran, the Turkish military and society would confront the ideological forces of secularism, communism, and Islamism, as well as economic turmoil and systemic corruption which led to the rise of the Refah (or Welfare) Party. Refah's election resulted in the 1997 "coup by memorandum."

After negotiations to ensure the protection of Kemalism, parliamentary elections were held in 2002 with a new party, the Justice and Development Party (or AKP), being swept into power. Since then, the military, initially threatened by this moderate Islamist party, challenged the AKP, but recently has sought to stay behind-the-scenes and let the politicians govern. The progression in this civil–military relationship is the subject of this chapter, as we examine the domestic and international influences that affected the conflicts between the Turkish Armed Forces, politicians, and society.

## HISTORY

From 1919 to 1922, Turkish nationalists would fight a war of independence against the Allies, as well as Greece. Atatürk "gather[ed] like-minded officers about him and weaved independent groups that had sprung up to protest Allied occupation into the basis of a nationalist movement . . . against the Greeks in Smyrna, the French in the south and the Armenians in the east" (MacMillan 2001, 434). While the terms of a peace treaty between the Ottoman Empire and the Allies was presented at San Remo, it was never implemented. Atatürk was sent to eastern Anatolia as inspector general to supervise the Ottoman demobilization but, in reality, he was being kept away from Istanbul for speaking against the Allied occupation (Glazer 1996, 33). Atatürk organized cadres of a nationalist army, which fought against the Greek army. Also, a telegram from Atatürk was sent to a number of civilian and military authorities throughout the country detailing the nationalists' program and calling for a conference to assert the rights of the Turkish nation.

In July 1919, the nationalists met in Erzurum, in eastern Turkey, and met in a congress "voic[ing] their loyalty to the sultan-caliph, [but] they also pledged to maintain the integrity of the Turkish nation" (Glazer 1996, 33). The most important achievement of the congress was the drafting of the National Pact which stated "the renunciation of claims to the Arab provinces, the principle of the absolute integrity of all remaining Ottoman territory inhabited by a Turkish Muslim majority, a guarantee of minority rights, the retention of Istanbul and the straits, and rejection of any restriction on the political, judicial, and financial rights of the nation" (Glazer 1996, 33; Lewis 2002, 248).

From 1920 to 1922, the nationalists battled the Greeks in their War of Independence. Initially the Turks were outmatched in numbers and materiel and were badly defeated. However, in January 1922, "a Turkish force under Colonel Ismet halted the Greeks in a valley near Inönü. In a second, more important battle, fought in Inönü on March 31–April 1 . . . Ismet again repelled the invaders" (Lewis 2002, 253). Ismet would later take the town of this victory as his surname and became Ismet Inönü. The

Greeks did not give up and clashed with the Turks on the Sakarya river. It was here that "a great battle took place, and the Turkish forces, under the personal command of Mustafa Kemal, won a decisive victory" (Lewis 2002, 253).

Atatürk quickly worked to consolidate the Turks' position. He moved west beginning in August 1922, and drove the Greeks out of Izmir and eastern Thrace. This campaign "threatened to put the Turks in direct confrontation with Allied contingents defending access to the straits and holding Istanbul, where they were protecting the Ottoman government" (Glazer 1996, 35). By October 1922, an armistice was signed between the nationalists and the British, who were the only remaining Allied force in Anatolia. This armistice led to a peace conference in Lausanne in November 1922, and over the next eight months, negotiations ensued, which resulted in the dissolution of the Ottoman Empire and the creation of the Turkish Republic. According to Lewis (2002), "Turkey, alone among the defeated powers of the First World War, succeeded in rising from her own ruins and, rejecting the dictated peace imposed on her by the victors, secured the acceptance of her own terms. For the Treaty of Lausaunne was substantially an international recognition of the demands formulated in the Turkish National Pact" (254–55).

On October 29, 1923, the Grand National Assembly proclaimed the Republic of Turkey and Atatürk became the first president of the republic and Ankara its capital (Glazer 1996, 36). At this point, Atatürk sought to modernize Turkey by initiating a series of political, social, and economic reforms. Additionally, he chose to make peace with the Greeks, demilitarized the Straits, renounced foreign ambitions and all pan-Turkish, pan-Ottoman, or pan-Islamic ideologies (Lewis 2002, 255). Atatürk urged his fellow citizens to "look and act like Europeans" (Glazer 1996, 36). Accordingly, a secular legal code was established along European lines introducing laws that affected women, marriage, and family relations. The ideological foundation of these reforms became Kemalism.

The six basic principles of Kemalism were set forth in the Republican People Party's 1931 party program: republicanism, secularism, nationalism, populism, statism, and revolutionism (reformism) (Zürcher 1997, 189). Republicanism stated "'sovereignty is vested in the nation' and not in a single ruler" (Zürcher 1997, 189). Secularism and nationalism were not new phenomenon, as they were distinctive characteristics of the Young Turk ideology since prior to World War I. During the 1930s, however, secularism and nationalism "were carried to extremes, secularism being interpreted not only as a separation of state and religion, but as the removal of religion from public life and the establishment of a complete state control over remaining religious institutions" (Zürcher 1997, 189). In effect, hypernationalism was used as *the* instrument to build a national identity, which would take the place of religion (Zürcher 1997, 189). Populism meant the furtherance of national solidarity by putting the interests of the nation ahead of any group or class, which entailed "a denial of class interests (according to Kemalism, Turkey did not have classes in the European sense) and a prohibition of political activity based on class (and thus of all socialist or communist activity)" (Zürcher 1997, 189). Statism "emphasized the central role reserved to the state in directing the nation's economic activities" to justify state planning of Turkey's mixed economy and large-scale investment in state-owned enterprises undertaken by Ataturk to prevent undue foreign influence on the Turkish economy (Glazer 1996, 38). Finally, Revolutionism or Reformism was a means to codify "a commitment to ongoing change and support for the Kemalist reform program" (Zürcher 1997, 190).

These six principles were incorporated into the Turkish constitution in 1937 and as the basis of Kemalism would be taught in schools, disseminated throughout the state via the media, and be the governing ideology of the army (Zürcher 1997, 190). The defeat of the Ottomans gave the army its stature as defender of the nation. According to Hale (1991), the army was in an ambiguous position: "On the one hand, Ataturk was determined to keep the army out of the political system, to make sure that the army itself was not divided by politics, and that ambitious officers could not challenge his leadership. On the other hand, he continued to look to the army as the ultimate guardian of his achievements" (ix). Put differently, the Turkish army's *raison d'être* is to preserve the integrity of Turkey and its secular and democratic order.

The military, as protector of the secular and democratic order, was also joined in support of the order by urban, educated elites, the business community, the mainstream press, and the judiciary. Opposition to this order would come from the Democrat Party (DP), led by Adnan Menderes, from 1950 to 1960 resulting in the DP government being overthrown on May 27, 1960, and its leaders arrested in a military coup led by a group of middle-ranking officers who had opposed the Democrat regime. The officers' junta was known as the National Unity Committee (NUC) and was led by General Cemal Gürsel. The NUC would rule Turkey from 1960 to 1961 and was beset with divisions between older officers who favored an elected civilian government and younger radicals more interested in a long-term authoritarian reformist regime (Hale 1991, x).

At this point, a constitution created Turkey's Second Republic underpinned by the principles of Kemalism. A number of reforms were undertaken. In particular, the TGNA was divided into a bicameral body with the same powers as elaborated in the 1924 constitution with multipartyism institutionalized (Cook 2007, 98). Further, the judiciary was tasked with overseeing elections through a body called the Supreme Election Board. Most importantly, according to Cook (2007), "the constitution of 1961 established a Constitutional Court with the power of judicial review—a critical check in the balance of power between the different branches of government" (98). As discussed above, the Menderes government was moving Turkey away from the Kemalist principles as established by Atatürk and the CHP. Thus, the 1961 Constitution was "intended to limit the potential power of any political formation that might, like the Democrats, endeavor to alter the way in which state resources were distributed and/or offer a seemingly viable counter-narrative to Kemalism" (Cook 2007, 101). Ultimately, the constitution was approved by 60 percent of the Turkish electorate (Glazer 1996, 43). Scholars (Hale 1994; Zurcher 1997) have identified the creation of the Constituent Assembly and the 1961 Constitution as the beginning of the military's effort to return political power to civilians.

Beginning in February 1968 on a university campus in Ankara and continuing off and on throughout 1968, 1969, and 1970, the civil unrest and clashes between armed militants of the left and the right continued unabated with bombings, robberies, and kidnappings. According to Glazer (1996), "Unrest was fueled in part by economic distress, perceptions of social inequalities, and the slowness of reform, but protest was increasingly directed at Turkey's military and economic ties to the West" (49). After the 1969 elections, the presence of the extreme parties resulted in Demirel's government losing its parliamentary majority. Effectively, by 1970, there was a crisis of governance; namely, complaints were made that the country was ungovernable due to the 1961 Constitution and the RPP accused the Demirel government "of reneging on the principles of social justice and reform enshrined in the same constitution" (Birand 1987, 12).

Consequently, the military issued a memorandum forcing the resignation of the Demirel government. The 1971 "coup by memorandum" came together due to three elements: First, senior, conservative generals believed Demirel had lost grip on power and his government was unable to deal with violence and the rise in political terrorism so law and order had to be restored; Second, officers appeared to be unwilling to "carry the can" for perceived government misdeeds; Third, a new group of reformist officers believed that progress was not possible within a liberal democratic system of government and advocated an "egalitarian, more independent and more 'modern'" authoritarian regime (Hale 1994, 185–86).

The subsequent 1973 election saw the CHP win 33 percent of the votes and the JP win 29.8 percent (Aksin 2007, 274). This outcome meant that in order to govern the CHP had to form coalitions; in this case, with the far right Islamist party, the National Salvation Party (MSP), after drawn out negotiations. Led by Necmettin Erbakan, the MSP's platform sought the restoration of Islamic law and practice in Turkey with improved relations with Muslim states. Also, this coalition has been described as "a marriage of convenience which . . . had some common basis in a distrust of European and American influence" (Zürcher 1997, 274).

In sum, the paralysis described above can be explained by uncoopera-tiveness within the major parties resulting from differences in ideology and personal rivalry between the leaders, which resulted in the inability of government to address Turkey's two overwhelming problems of the 1970s: political violence and economic crisis (Zürcher 1997, 276). The ris-ing tide of violence and economic crisis would bring Turkey almost to the point of total collapse necessitating the third intervention of the Turkish military into politics on September 12, 1980.

By 1980, the renewed surge of politically inspired violence threatened to drag Turkey down into a Lebanese-style collapse of the state. During the first seven months of 1980, "over 1,250 people were killed by political-ly inspired desperadoes of either right or left. The economy was in chaos, with triple-digit inflation, a huge foreign trade deficit, and a rampant black market in essential commodities" (Hale 1991, xi). The civilian politi-cal elite had failed to heed repeated warnings by the military to drop their mutual rivalries by forming a national unity government. Therefore, the MSP and other political political parties were closed down. Under General Kenan Evren, the army established a five-man junta, which re-stored law and order and successfully tackled the country's economic problems by bringing down inflation and the foreign trade deficit. (Hale 1991, xi).

General Evren and the chiefs of staff of the army, navy, air force, and gendarmerie formed the National Security Council (NSC) to be the exec-utive and legislative authority, enacting 268 laws and abolishing the government and legislature (Aksin 2007, 280). Since one of the main tasks of the generals was to "save democracy," all political parties were banned, with all four leaders of the main political parties except Turkes (who evaded arrest for two days) arrested, and mayors and municipal councils were all dismissed (Zürcher 1997, 293). Under the Law on Con-stitutional Order, all executive and legislative power was vested in the NSC and General Evren was officially declared head of state on Septem-ber 14, 1980. To assist the NSC in running the country, a twenty-seven-member cabinet composed of retired officers and bureaucrats, led by retired admiral Bulent Ulusu, offered advice to the NSC and executed decisions. One member of the cabinet, Turgut Özal, was retained as dep-uty prime minister to continue with his responsibility for fixing the econ-omy (Hale 1994, 248). In addition, regional and local commanders were used under martial law and given wide-ranging powers, to include deci-sion-making over education policy, the press, chambers of commerce and trade unions (Zürcher 1997, 293).

The NSC was, in effect, preparing the country for elections in 1983, which ushered in the Third Turkish Republic from 1983 to 1997. The November 1983 election saw the ANAP win 45.2 percent of the votes, which gave the party 212 seats in the TGNA and an overall majority (Hale 1994, 269). Özal's ANAP was a "somewhat eclectic" party "drawing its membership and policies from the three main strands of the right and center-right of Turkish politics—that is, the liberal conservatives . . . the Islamicists [*sic*] . . . and the ultra-nationalists together with others who had no background in party politics" (Hale 1994, 277). From the outset, the ANAP relied on Özal's personality to keep the broad ideological currents under the ANAP banner. Özal emphasized his ability to deliver benefits for the population and worked to establish a modus operandi with President Evren (Evin 1994, 26).

At this point, Evren took responsibility over "all matters relating to internal and external security, as well as foreign affairs and higher education—matters about which the military commanders were highly sensitive," while Özal conceded these policy areas and, in return, was given control over the economy (Evin 1994, 26–27). To explain his decision, President Evren often deflected questions about the economy by stating, "'the economy is the government's problem'" (Evin 1994, 27). Although there seemed to be cooperation between the President and Özal government, Zürcher (1997) contends that Özal was determined to re-establish civilian politics over the military (298). The military, however, was returning to the barracks on its own terms. Specifically, Evin (1994) notes, "Beginning in 1984, martial law was gradually lifted, province by province, but the military presence in public life remained strong. Those indicted under martial law continued to be prosecuted in military courts, and the trials, which were reported in the press, increased public awareness of military authority" (27).

In the 1980s and early 1990s, Islamists would begin to make a comeback in Turkish electoral politics. Before the March 1984 municipal election, the ANAP was facing growing criticism from opposition parties that were excluded from the 1983 election. Consequently, the ANAP-controlled TGNA voted to allow these opposition parties to participate in the 1984 municipal election. The Social Democratic Party (SDP) led by Professor Erdal Inonu, the son of the late Ismet Inönü, the True Path Party (DYP), led by political cronies of Demirel, and the Refah Party, a reincarnation of Erbakan's NSP, were allowed to participate, essentially, to divide the votes of the opposition parties and thereby improve ANAP's majority in the assembly (Zürcher 1997, 298). Accordingly, the ANAP won 41.5 percent, followed by the SDP with 23.5 percent and the DYP with 13.5 percent and the Welfare (*Refah*) Party with 4.5 percent (Zürcher 1997, 298). Thus, the elections created conditions whereby the opposition parties had lost their legitimacy. As a result, in November 1985, the PP merged with the SDP and the NDP voted to dissolve itself (Glazer 1996, 63). Furthermore, in national elections for local government officials on September 28, 1986, ANAP received 32 percent of the votes, the DYP won 23.7 percent, and the new Social Democratic Populist Party (Sosyal Demokrat Halkçi Parti—SHP) won 22.7 percent of the votes (Glazer 1996, 63). At this point, pressure was building against the army to restore the pre-1980 political leaders, whom the army had tried to exclude from the system.

Following a national referendum on September 6, 1987, these leaders regained their political rights. Demirel became head of True Path Party (DYP); Bulent Ecevit refused to cooperate with Inönü and formed the Democratic Left Party (DSP); Necmettin Erbakan assumed leadership of the Welfare Party (Refah); Alpsan Turkes resumed control of his party which after an interval reverted to the name of MHP. The result of the above moved Özal to announce early national elections for November 1987.

Özal's campaign focused on the government's economic achievements. In particular, Turkey's economy grew with "GNP running at an average of 6.6 percent per year between 1984 and 1987" (Hale 1994, 280). This success rested on policies implemented by Özal during the Demirel government—opening the economy to foreign markets, the application of market principles internally and reducing the role of the state sector— however, he was unable to control public expenditure and inflation (Hale 1994, 280). Nevertheless, the November 1987 elections saw the ANAP get 36 percent, the SDPP 25 percent, and the DYP 19 percent of the vote (Aksin 2007, 288). The next four years would see a number of domestic and international events impact on civil–military relations in Turkey: concessions to Islamists, ethnic conflict, economics, European Community (EC) application, the Gulf War, and the dissolution of the Soviet Union.

From 1987 to 1991, within Özal's ANAP, there was dissension over the role of Islam in politics. The government made a number of concessions toward fundamentalists, including the expansion of religious education, Friday prayer for civil servants, and permission to wear the headscarf in university classes (Hale 1994, 281). The headscarf issue would become the "hot-button" issue in the debate on secularism that would continue into the 1990s and 2000s with the electoral wins of Refah and the Justice and Development Party.

The Refah Party's coalition government with the DYP, after their 1995 electoral victory, would not last long, since the military intervened on February 28, 1997, in what has been depicted as a "post-modern coup" (Eder 2014, 836). Erbakan and the Welfare party were outlawed from political activity. The Virtue Party was created from former Welfare Party members, but would later split into the Felicity Party (Saadet Partisi) following Erbakan's legacy and the AKP led by Recep Tayyip Erdogan. The AKP would win national elections in 2002, 2007, and 2011. The AKP, as a proponent of pluralism, wanted to move beyond Ataturk's state-defined social values "allowing society to open up to a range of values other than those of Kemalism—including more cultural rights for the country's Kurdish minority" (Nasr 2009, 242). Therefore, since 2002, the AKP engaged the General Staff "in a shadow play of symbols and oblique rhetoric" allowing the AKP to test the extent the General Staff would defend Kemalism, while the General Staff aimed to avoid overt intervention into the political sphere (Jenkins 2006, 186).

## THE MILITARY ESTABLISHMENT

The Turkish military's role in society came from its role in the war of independence as the first institution to mobilize the population against foreign occupation. From its inception, the Turkish military was faced with challenges that included: a lack of a democratic culture, the strong influence of Islam and a Kurdish minority opposed to assimilation. Consequently, as Aylin Güney (2002) argues, "At the end of the independence war the new state was left with the generals, lieutenants, and other army officers, on one side, and a highly illiterate, leaderless, devastated and extremely poor society on the other" (162). Thus, this section will discuss the military officers' important role in the process of transforming Ottoman identity to Turkish identity (Güney 2002, 163).

An officer in the Turkish Armed Forces takes an oath upon entering the military academy swearing they "'will eagerly sacrifice my life for my country' and are told that: 'A land is a country if there is someone dying for its sake'" (Jenkins 2001, 31). Moreover, officers are told they are joining an elite group within society. In essence, Kemalism is an ideology whereby officers are sworn to protect Turkey against both internal and external enemies of the state. Beginning at the military academies, "the social isolation of the academies and the inculcation of a sense of being distinct from society at large inevitably combine to produce an increasing identification with their fellow cadets and the armed forces as an institution" (Jenkins 2001, 31). Gareth Jenkins (2001) argues, "Turkish officers are expected to be model citizens . . . and are encouraged to regard Atatürk as having an almost physical presence in their lives" (31–32). Accordingly, future officers study Atatürk's speeches containing directives on a number of different areas, from the importance of the Turkish state, to the functioning of the economy and democracy. Therefore, as Turkish journalist Mehmet Ali Birand (1991) notes, "[Kemalism] is not a static ideology but one that undergoes a 'dynamic' development according to the conditions of the time. Hence it is not inflexible like other ideologies, but keeps changing in the light of previous experience and progressing towards the 'ideal.' This is emphasized as the 'Dynamic Ideal'" (58). The "Dynamic Ideal" is the driving force in Turkish civil–military relations.

From the beginning of the twentieth century, the army has been the guarantor of the state and the academies place considerable emphasis on the foundation of the Turkish Republic (Birand 1991; Jenkins 2001). Officers "are taught that the Ottoman Empire was eroded by a combination of foreign avarice and a paucity of patriots prepared to defend the home-land" (Jenkins 2001, 32). Atatürk's military battles, both his struggles and his victories—Gallipoli, the War of Liberation, and the crushing of Isla-mist and Kurdish revolts in 1920—are used to depict Ataturk as "'the bright sun which tore apart the dark clouds' and 'a soldier turned reform-er who demonstrated his genius by sustaining . . . a brand new republic on Turkish soil, its borders drawn in blood'" (Jenkins 2001, 33). Jenkins (2001) argues "Indeed, cadets are explicitly taught that, although circum-stances and methods may change, the external and internal threats to the country—threats which they are legally as well as morally obliged to repulse—are fundamentally the same as in Ataturk's lifetime" (33). Therefore, in an ethnically and ideologically heterogeneous state such as Turkey, the army must continually be wary of societal conflicts, which could destroy the army as an institution.

The teaching of history, as just described, allows the army to control the indoctrination process and create an elite-*making* institution (Aydinli 2009, 586). Professor Ersel Aydinli (2009) defines the Turkish army's elite-making process as follows:

> It recruits cadets largely from rural Anatolian towns, but with its care-fully crafted and closed institutions, turns these Anatolian kids into a unique new societal elite—a group neither completely inside nor out-side of society. In many cases, while the immediate relatives of this new elite carry socially common ethnic and religious identities, the officers themselves become stripped of these identities through the mil-itary's own "eliticization" process and absorb the institutional identity. Interestingly, they still feel a part of society and believe that they are the true representatives of the society (586).

This "eliticization" process drew the army into conflict with society, espe-cially politicians. Consequently, the Turkish army created mechanisms to maintain its identity as the defender of what it meant to be Turkish but also keep itself insulated from what it viewed as society's weaknesses and potential from fragmentation (Aydinli 2009, 586).

For the army, politicians "are contemptuous" (Jenkins 2001, 33). Due to the professionalization process of the Military Academy, officers' problem with politicians results from "dissatisfaction and annoyance with the lack of discipline and organization in civilian society" (Birand 1991, 75). Thus, for a Turkish officer, Birand (1991) argues, "He loses the little tolerance he has when he observes such deficiencies compounded by the question of political responsibility. Because of the difference in education background, his conception of 'the state' is very different from that of the civilian. He has a far greater respect for the state and cannot accept the politician's failure to conform to the rules taught at the Mili-tary Academy" (75). While in the Academy, the officer is taught how democracy "should" function, but discovers once he leaves the barracks that his actual experience with democracy changes as he finds out "that it takes a long time for society to absorb certain issues, that it is natural for political parties to struggle for power, that it is inevitable for social classes to engage in conflict for a share of the national cake" (Birand 1991, 77). Birand (1991) states that the general conviction of the Armed Forces can be summed up as follows: "what we do, the politicians undo" (75).

Nevertheless, despite their disdain for politicians, the military prefers to not become involved in the day to day governing of the country. Traditionally, it has taken action "only when it believed that the machinery of government was unable to cope with critical problems or when it feared a deviation from Kemalist principles" (Jenkins 2001, 34). Coups were always seen as temporary measures, because "the Turkish military has learned from experience that, although it can successfully topple a government, none of its interventions to date have been able to install an administration or system capable of ensuring domestic stability or good governance" (Jenkins 2001, 34).

In fact, despite four military interventions, Turkish civil–military relations is defined by broad social support for the military and the view of the military as ultimate guarantor of the nation (Aydinli 2009, 585). After experiencing its first taste of multiparty politics, in 1960, there was a growing fear that politicians were becoming totalitarian in pursuing their agenda. Backed by public mass demonstrations of academics, bureaucratic elites, and student leaders, the military stepped in and overthrew Prime Minister Menderes. Moreover, with the country in the midst of a civil war between pro-communist groups and right-wing nationalists, "there was an understanding of popular acceptance for a military takeover to restore order, later verified by societal approval of the militaristic Constitution and of the long-standing ban on former politicians from participating in politics that was instituted in 1980" (Aydinli 2009, 585). The "post-modern" coup of 1997 where Erbakan's Islamist government was ousted was influenced by a call from NGOs and civil society groups advocating for state intervention against the government. Most recently, in 2007, "the government's call to place Abdullah Gül, an Islamist sympathizer, in the Turkish presidency was met with broad protests across Turkey, in which slogans such as 'We have the army' were among the most flaunted" (Aydinli 2009, 586). In sum, over the last fifty years the Turkish military has implemented two full-blooded coups (1960 and 1980) and twice (1971 and 1997) put pressure on politicians from behind the scenes (Jenkins 2001, 35). What explains this evolution in the military's relationship with society?

Put simply, there are two factors explaining the new dynamic in the military's relationship with society: 1) The role of the West, specifically the European Union; and 2) The Paradigmatic Divide of the "Pashas" (Cook 2007; Aydinli 2009). In the five years between 1997 and 2002, the EU offered Turkey an invitation to become an applicant for succession.

Political scientist Steven Cook (2007) notes, "While the European Union has often been duplicitous in its relations with Turkey . . . the requirements for EU membership offer great hope for the consolidation of liberal democracy in Anatolia. The combination of material and political benefits associated with EU membership created a vast constituency in support of the reforms Europe demands" (130).

Consequently, the relationship between the Islamists and the military was affected by Turkey's EU candidacy. The Islamists, who have railed against the West since they first became active politically in 1969, saw membership in the EU as critical component of Turkish political development (Cook 2007, 131). As Cook (2007) states, "[T]he promised benefits of EU membership encouraged Gül, Erdogan, and their followers in AK to discard the anti-Western shibboleths of the past and portray themselves as the Islamic analogue to Europe's Christian Democrats" (131). Effectively, becoming a member of the EU would force the state to deal with the religion issue and move toward a system that guarantees freedom of religion; namely, by having to do away with its *laïcité* system, which governs the state's role in religious affairs and places restrictions on various aspects of religious practice (Cook 2007, 131).

Naturally, this placed the Islamists in direct conflict with the military, specifically the General Staff. As part of the Copenhagen criteria for joining the EU, the Turkish military would need to reform its civil–military relationship whereby military officers would defer to politicians and resemble the civil–military relationship inherent in western, liberal democracies. Consequently, Cook (2007) argues:

> [T]he military establisment found itself in a decidedly awkward position. If the officers had opted to oppose the EU reform program, it would have exposed their devotion to central Kemalist tenets such as modernization and democracy as a fraud and confirmed what the Islamists had been saying for the better part of the previous decade, that they were the appropriate stewards of a democratic, modern, and secular Turkey (131–32).

Ultimately, the military consented to certain aspects of the EU reforms, because if the Islamists became the agents of modernization in Turkey, "[t]he result would be a significant diminution of the prestige of the officer corps, which would simultaneously enhance that of the civilian leadership, rendering it more difficult for the officers to act autonomously, influence the political arena, or defend the political order" (Cook 2007, 132). Therefore, since 2002, a divide has begun to emerge between the officer corps of the Turkish army.

Today, there are two groups of "Pashas" in Turkey. Pasha is an honorific title given to all Turkish army officers who reach the rank of General. The first group "is a traditional conservative majority group that views the Turkish military as the ultimate guard of the status quo—the

Republican regime, its territorial integrity, and its political parameters as established at the beginning of the Republic" (Aydinli 2009, 587). The origins of this group derive from the army's institutional strength at the end of the Ottoman Empire. Today, the conservatives within the military establishment "emphasize Turkish society's ideological and social fragmentation, and argue that revolutionary and risky moves—foregoing the watchful eye of the guardian army—would be disastrous" (Aydinli 2009, 589). In other words, the army is guarding the state more from challenges within rather than without.

In upholding Kemalism, conservative Turkish army generals would prefer to see a similar transformation occur in society along the lines of what they went through in becoming an officer—make Turkey increasingly secular and Western while also advancing the country economically and educationally (Aydinli 2009, 589). Consequently, when the military sees that secularization and modernization are not occurring in large numbers or quickly enough, they conclude that there is a need for more time for that transformation to take place at the national level. For general officers, Aydinli (2009) notes, "Such conservativeness naturally grows because their transformation takes place quickly in a carefully isolated vacuum, but society's transformation takes place very slowly in an open field, exposed to all kinds of winds and influences both local and international" (589).

The second group is a smaller, progressive group interested in guarding the modernization of the nation so that it protects the status quo (Aydinli 2009, 587). Turkey's integration with transnational organizations, global markets, and the EU, as well as its membership in NATO have greatly influenced the proponents of this view within the officer corps. The progressive's position is closely associated with Hilmi Özkök, the Turkish Chief of Staff between 2002 and 2006. The progressives agree with the conservatives on the need for Turkey to be a modern, Westernized, Europeanized country. Where they differ is in their degree of cautiousness. The conservatives in the army are more risk-averse and remain cautious about politicians' ability to deal with Turkey's problems, while progressives feel Turkey is ready for the completion of modernization and feel the army should support politicians in the democratic process (Aydinli 2009, 589). The remainder of this chapter will highlight the domestic and international factors influencing the role of the military in Turkish politics. Today's divide between conservative and progressive officers is an outcome of the trust Turkish society has for the army's role as guardian of the state.

Turkey is currently situated at the crossroads of Europe and the Middle East. Accordingly, its active duty military has 510,600 forces and 378,700 reserves training regularly with the armed forces of its NATO partners (Military Balance 2016, 147). Moreover, the relationship with the

EU has influenced its reform efforts over the years. The implications of this relationship will be discussed below.

## CIVIL–MILITARY RELATIONS

At this point, a distinction must be made between two distinct aspects of the Turkish population. On the one hand, there is the "the mass of the population" (peasants, the industrial workers) and, on the other hand, there is the Kemalist regime (the officers and bureaucrats, the Muslim traders in the towns and the landowners in the countryside) (Zürcher 1997, 215). Peasants and industrial workers made up approximately 80 percent of the population and were unhappy that there had not been any improvement in their standard of living, while large landowners (who had been an essential element of the Young Turk coalition since World War I), were alienated by two government policies: the Tax on Agricultural Produce and a land distribution bill entitled "Law on giving land to the farmer." According to Zürcher (1997), "Discontent among the mass of the population was not new and in itself would probably not have led to political change" (Zürcher 1997, 216). What was important, however, was the loss of support for Inönü's government that was building within the Young Turk coalition that gave birth to the Kemalist movement (Zürcher 1997, 216). Aware of this discontent, Inönü remembered Atatürk's experiment with the Free Party in 1930, and allowed the formation of another political party because under Kemalism the government-favored democracy and never accepted dictatorship (Hale 1994, 88).

Inönü's speech opened the door for four dissident members of the CHP—Celal Bayar, Adnan Menderes, Fuat Köprülü, and Refik Koraltan—to demand the withdrawal of government restrictions on the economy and the right to establish an opposition party (Hale 1994, 88). Bayar and Menderes were the two leaders out of the party's founders to distinguish themselves. On January 7, 1946, these four dissidents established the Democrat Party (DP) as the first serious challenger to the CHP. The DP represented a diverse range of people who resented the CHP's monopoly of power—"farmers who felt neglected by the regime's concentration on industrialization, businessmen who hoped to end the dominant role of the state in industry, urban workers and clerks who had suffered severely from wartime inflation, and some religious conservatives who wished to soften the official emphasis on secularism" (Hale 1994, 89).

Concurrently, the move to multi-party democracy was also influenced by the international community. Throughout the 1920s and 1930s, Turkey and the Soviet Union had a close relationship; however, the signing of a nonaggression pact (the Ribbentrop-Molotov pact) and Turkish neutrality during World War II soured the relationship (Zürcher 1997, 217).

During 1945 and 1946, Turkey became the target of Stalin's ambitions over territory, specifically the Straits (separating Anatolia from Eastern Europe) and Turkey's eastern frontiers (Hale 1994, 90). In particular, President Harry Truman took notice of Stalin's foreign policy efforts in Eastern Europe and the United States encouraged Turkey to stand up to the Soviets; this reaction forced the Soviets to drop their demands (Zürcher 1997, 218). The United States reevaluated the strategic importance of Turkey and on March 12, 1947, President Truman issued the Truman Doctrine, which stated that the United States "should and would help defend 'free nations' whose existence was threatened by foreign pressure or by militant minorities inside their borders" (Zürcher 1997, 218). Shortly thereafter, in June 1947, the Marshall Plan provided financial support to Europe to assist the European recovery effort, sustain export markets for U.S. businesses, and eliminate poverty (Zürcher 1997, 218). In other words, American political, economic, and military support was contingent upon Turkey's conformity to political and economic ideals of democracy and free enterprise.

The first general election in the new multi-party system occurred in July 1946. Nevertheless, tension was building between the DP and CHP. The CHP knew of the discontent that the population had for the CHP one-party rule and subsequently moved up the election to July 1946 from its original date in 1947. In the end, the CHP won the election with 395 seats to the DP's sixty-two seats (Glazer 1996, 41). Inönü selected Recep Peker as prime minister. The DP were understandably upset over the outcome of the election and sought to mobilize public opinion in its favor.

By 1947, the CHP and DP conflict came to a head. New complaints were introduced in the assembly almost on a daily basis. The DP and CHP each accused the other of being soft on communism (Zürcher 1997, 223). The main point of contention between both sides was the election law, which was one of a number of laws that the DP felt was undemocratic. The DP saw itself as the rightful party to continue what Ataturk had begun. Through the Freedom Pact, DP members of parliament were authorized to leave and boycott the national assembly if the government would not withdraw undemocratic laws (223). Not until Inönü stepped in and issued the Twelfth of July Declaration were DP and the multiparty electoral process legitimized. As a result, Peker was forced to resign and was replaced by a more liberal cabinet of Hasan Saka (Zürcher 1997, 224). Therefore, with the path now cleared for multiparty politics, the elections held in May 1950 resulted in a landslide win for the Democrat Party.

At this point, it's important to ask: Why did the military not intervene in the dispute between the CHP and DP? Hale (1994) argues, "While many officers were evidently worried by the demise of the single-party state, with which they had grown up, there were others who were determined to see that liberalization was not abandoned" (91–92). In the summer of 1946 there were two groups of officers who formed, one led by Colonel Seyfi Kurtbek and the other by Major Cemal Yildirim. Both groups were fearful that the 1950 elections would be rigged against the Democrats and said they would force the regime to hold new elections. In fact, Yildirim's group, needing a serving general to give his group of officers credibility and authority within the army, reached out to General Fahri Belen, the Army Corps Commander in Gallipoli. Belen met with Bayar to assure him that if the government were to rig the elections then the army would oppose it (Hale 1994, 92). In fact, these juntas were not in positions of influence within the army to influence the political debate at the time, because shortly after the election both resigned from the army to run as Democrat Party candidates. Their loyalty to the Democrats was subsequently rewarded; Belen was appointed Minister of Public Works and Kurtbek became Minister of Transport (Hale 1994, 92). Moreover, one officer who was in a position of influence was the Chief of the General Staff, General Abdürrahman Gürman, who told the DP leaders that the army would respect the election results.

Once the DP was sworn in, on June 6, 1950, the Chief of the General Staff, the commanders of the army, navy, and air force, and a number of other generals were all purged. The purge sought to prevent the possibility of a future coup by anti-Democrat officers and keep the Ataturk tradition of the army being loyal to the civilian regime alive (Hale 1994, 93). To this end, the CHP began legislative changes between 1946 and 1950 to the electoral law to disenfranchise all officers, soldiers and cadets. The status of the chief of the general staff was also changed in 1949 making the chief of staff responsible to the Ministry of Defense rather than the prime minister with the defense minister able to advise the prime minister on the selection of the chief of staff. With Inönü in charge, this new legislation "probably made little practical difference to the army's political situation," since the military chiefs and middle-ranking officers' loyalty was to Inönü (Hale 1994, 93–94). However, after the Democrat victory, there was a feeling among the commanders that their status had been downgraded, which created a general malaise within the army (Hale 1994, 93–94).

The DP era "began in a spirit of optimism and with great expectations" as President Bayar and Prime Minister Menderes focused all their efforts on economic development (Aksin 2007, 253). Menderes's economic policy attempted to reduce the influence of the state and instead encouraged private enterprise and foreign investment in industrial development. The prices of raw material and agricultural produce rose with an increase in arable land. Through funds from the United States an extensive motorway system was created opening up markets like never before; national income increased by 40 percent (Aksin 2007, 253; Hale 1994, 94). Moreover, Turkey's participation in the Korean War boosted the military's self-esteem. In February 1952, Turkey joined NATO and younger officers "began to travel more widely, to become familiar with new technology and to contrast the equipment and methodologies used by foreign militaries with those used by their own forces . . ." (Jenkins 2001, 35). Once in power, the DP's popularity was rising. Although, similar to democracies everywhere, electoral promises soon met with the realities of governance.

Opposition to the DP gained momentum in 1954 as economic indicators turned against the government with a decline in economic growth and an increase in inflation and balance-of-payments deficit (Hale 1994, 94). Menderes reaction to the growing discontent was political repression. The DP's "earlier democratic rhetoric of the 'unconditional sovereignty of the nation'—as enshrined in the 1924 Constitution—gave way to a *de facto* 'authoritarianism of the majority' which was periodically confirmed in dubiously conducted elections" (Birand 1987, 10). In effect, Professor Sina Aksin (2007) argues, "[T]here was a sense of unease and vexation emanating from the DP and more specifically from Menderes and Bayar. Possibly they felt their position was insecure, although the 1954 elections resulted in an even greater victory for the DP than those held in 1950. For this reason, some historians have concluded that Bayar and Menderes suffered from 'İnönü phobia' (i.e., fear of İnönü's prestige") (254).

Consequently, the DP implemented a number of laws to counter the influence of the CHP. First, as the 1954 elections approached, journalists came under the purview of a law imposing heavy penalties for openly criticizing the government, which included imprisonment. Second, in 1955, the DP invoked the National Protection law "instituting police and judicial measures, price controls and rationing"; effectively, this meant that government officials who had served twenty-five years could be relieved of their duties "'when necessary'" and sent into retirement (Aksin 2007, 255). Third, academic freedom was restricted. Each of these laws were taken against groups in society who the DP felt were loyal to İnönü and the CHP. Consequently, many of the DP's early supporters left the coalition and became estranged from the party because of its authoritarian policies toward the press, universities, and the judiciary (Zürcher 1997, 241).

At this point, Turkey was also faced with the issue of Cyprus. Greece had been suing for control of Cyprus, a British colony, and Turkey also made its own claim. According to Aksin (2007), "Turkey had initially laid claim to the whole of Cyprus (with the slogan 'Cyprus is Turkish and will stay Turkish'), but after reassessment it was decided that this was unrealistic and a new demand arose for the island to be partitioned between Greece and Turkey (the new slogan being 'Partition or death!" (256–57). Subsequently, the Greek Cypriots staged demonstrations and conducted terrorist acts on Cyprus and in Istanbul Turks attacked thousands of Greek houses, businesses, churches and cemeteries were attacked, pillaged and destroyed. In fact, it would be discovered later that the DP had utilized these disturbances for its own gain. Menderes and his foreign minister, Fatin Rüştü Zorlu, organized student demonstrations in Istanbul which would be pro-government, but the demonstrations got out of hand with the demonstrators protesting against Greek businesses and forced the government to implement martial law (Zürcher 1997, 242).

By the 1957 elections, the DP was confronting increased opposition among "city-dwellers and the more educated," a worsening economic crisis, and "sometimes resorted to an appeal to religious sentiments, describing the Republicans as communists and unbelievers and boasting about the number of mosques an religious schools opened under the Democrats" (Zürcher 1997, 243). Dissent was so great within the DP that the liberal wing of the party was protesting the press law against journalists. Consequently, the liberal wing, under the leadership of Fevzi Lûtfi Karaosmanoglu, broke away from the DP and formed the *Hürriyet Partisi* (Freedom Party). According to Zürcher (1997), "The Freedom Party seems to have had the support of big business, which by now wanted a more sophisticated economic policy with a degree of planning which Menderes would not provide" (242). The DP won the 1957 election, but lost seats to the opposition—the CHP, the Republican National Party, and the Freedom party. Nevertheless, criticism continued unabated against the Menderes government.

In 1958, the DP government was forced to accept the conditions set forth by the International Monetary Fund (IMF) and the World Bank. Specifically, measures were implemented to increase the value of the Turkish lira vis-à-vis the U.S. dollar, as well as expanding the sphere of state-owned enterprises, and ending the National Protection measures (Aksin 2007, 257). Ultimately, the acceptance of the IMF stabilization program led to $359 million in aid sent to Turkey (Zürcher 1997, 251). In the fall of 1958, the DP adopted a new series of repressive measures. The DP government "seemed to have come to a point where it could no longer bear the idea of opposition leaders circulating freely throughout the country" (Askin 2007, 261).

The spring of 1960 witnessed tensions between the DP and the opposition, particularly the CHP, reach its zenith. The DP accused the CHP of "'plotting armed insurgence against the government' and certain organs of the press supporting these plots by publishing false and distorted news reports" (Aksin 2007, 262). Consequently, the DP formed the Investigation Commission, consisting of fifteen members, all of whom were from the DP, and the TGNA granted the Commission extraordinary power to "suppress any published material, to close down printing offices and periodicals, to take precautions and make decisions concerning all political activities for the furtherance of the investigation and, in order for it to realize this aim, to make use of all the agencies of the state" (Aksin 2007, 263). There were a number of newspapers that defied the prohibition against publishing by continuing to publish Inonu's speeches. One speech of note by Inönü, presaging future events, stated, "'It is a dangerous undertaking to deflect this democratic regime from its true course, turning it into a regime of oppression. If you persist on this path, even I will not be able to save you. . . . When conditions demand it, revolution is the lawful right of nations'" (Aksin 2007, 263). At this point, demonstrations by university students at the University of Istanbul on April 28, 1960, forced the DP government to impose martial law and suspend classes. The army took notice and forced senior commanders to make a choice between defending the Menderes government or taking alternative action (Hale 1994, 107).

On May 27, 1960, the DP government was overthrown and its leaders arrested in a military coup led by a group of middle-ranking officers who had opposed the Democrat regime for some time and were convinced that Menderes was undermining Kemalism. The officers' junta was known as the National Unity Committee (NUC) and was led by General Cemal Gürsel. The NUC would rule Turkey from 1960 to 1961 and was beset with divisions between "those officers—mostly at the upper end of the age/rank scale—who favored a return to elected civilian government, and a group of younger radicals, who wished to set up a long-term authoritarian reformist regime" (Hale 1991, x). The Turkish army would return to the barracks in 1961 because of its strong sense of professionalism and the conviction that a long-term involvement in politics would harm the army's homogeneity (Birand 1991).

The first few months of the NUC in power was a time of conflict between the NUC and the remaining politicians of the DP and CHP. President Bayar, Prime Minister Menderes, and most of the DP representatives in the TGNA were arrested and charged with "abrogating the constitution and instituting a dictatorship" (Glazer 1996, 42). The NUC then spent the next few months purging members of the armed forces (thirty-five thousand officers) to restore the pyramid structure of the ranks (Hale 1994, 125). One of the more pressing problems faced by the NUC was the economy. According to Glazer (1996), "The ousted regime had been responsible for inflation and heavy debt, and emergency austerity measures had to be taken to stabilize the economy. An economic planning agency, the State Planning Organization, was established to study social and economic conditions and to draw up the country's five-year development plans" (43). Most importantly a constituent assembly was created in January 1961 and produced a new constitution. As Birand (1987) notes, "Out of an alliance of the secular intelligentsia, 'Kemalist' civil servants, the . . . [CHP] politicians and a pliable military junta comprised mainly middle-ranking officers, there emerged a new and remarkably liberal constitution prepared by a Constitutive Assembly dominated by the RPP" (11).

Accordingly, throughout the next few years (1961–1963), there were repeated rumors of unrest and plotting within the Turkish armed forces, but the democratic transition still went forward. The NUC executed Menderes and shut down the DP. There was debate about whether the execution of Menderes was justified. Hale (1994) contends the NUC "was under strong pressure from the AFU to confirm the sentences" since there was a likelihood of serious unrest with army and a possibility Menderes could return to the political stage (145). In short, by executing Menderes, the NUC could forestall a return to politics by Menderes and retribution against the NUC officers.

Elections held on October 15 would bring further challenges to the NUC. The CHP failed to win a majority of seats, winning 173 of the 450 seats in the lower House of Representatives and thirty-six in the Senate. A new party, the Justice Party, led by General Gümüspala, representing the interests of DP supporters, came in second winning 158 seats in the House and won a majority of seats (70) in the Senate (Hale 1994, 145). According to Zürcher (1997), "Parts of the army wanted to intervene after the disappointing election result . . . but the army's most senior officers and the AFU prevented it" (261). The AFU, specifically the hawks led by Aydemir, "decided that the results had 'not completely realized the national will' (which presumably meant their own will) and that they would have to intervene" (Hale 1994, 145). Consequently, seven generals, four admirals and twenty-seven colonels met in Istanbul to sign the 21 October Protocol. This protocol was "the manifesto of a coup which was otherwise unprepared", which meant that "the authors of the protocol only seem to have had the vaguest idea of what sort of regime they wanted to install" (Hale 1994, 146).

Ultimately, the protocol called for the annulment of the election results with new elections to be held at the end of October. Top commanders, though, had a choice to make. The NUC could prevent Menderes's supporters from taking power, or they could annul the election results. If the latter happened, the NUC would be in an untenable position domestically and internationally for interfering in the democratic process (Hale 1994, 146). Subsequently, negotiations began between the JP and CHP to form a coalition government. Gümüspala and Inönü agreed that Inönü would become prime minister and both would support Gürsel as president. On November 29, 1961, Inönü's government was sworn in and the NUC was dissolved (Hale 1994, 147).

Inönü's government, however, was in a very untenable situation. Internal strife continued within the JP and the military. Gümüspala, as a former general, was encouraged by the previous military regime to head the party, since his stature as a general could keep extremists elements within the party in line. For the military, a majority of the senior commanders were in agreement with Chief of the General Staff Sunay, who believed that another coup would not be justified. Their main concern would be to prevent the junior officers from subverting the normal chain-of-command (Hale 1994, 154).

After 1963, the generals and politicians settled into a period of cohabitation that lasted until 1971. With the two coup attempts behind them, multi-party politics moved forward, albeit with continued shaky coalitions. In October 1965, the JP won a landslide victory under new leader Suleyman Demirel, who became prime minister. Demirel was a self-made man from a small village in the province of Isparta and his emergence on the scene symbolized the emergence of a new elite in Turkey. As Zürcher (1997) notes, "The DP had managed to capture the vote in the more developed parts of the countryside, but it had its origins in a split within the Unionist/Kemalist elite, which had, it is true, always coopted members of the traditional landowning elite, but was itself city-based. The JP by contrast was a party in which, and through which, self-made men from the countryside and from the smaller (but fast-growing) provincial towns became a dominant force" (263).

The mid-to-late 1960s in Turkey saw an increase in both economic growth and the average income of Turkish citizens by an average of twenty percent (Zürcher 1997, 263). For many Turks, Demirel "was an orator who could speak the language of the mass of the people—something Inonu and the other Kemalist political leaders, or for that matter socialists such as Aybar, had never been able to do" (Zurcher 1997, 263). Owing to this popularity, Demirel sought to reconcile with the army. One of the first issues on the table was the issue of limited amnesty for the former Democrat leaders. Commander of the Land Forces, General Cemal Tural wrote a letter to the Defense Minister, Ahmet Topaloglu, adamantly opposing amnesty. Demirel stated that the decision on amnesty rested with the TGNA not with the army. After discussions between President Gürsel and three former members of the NUC, the army decided it would not intervene further and parliamentary procedures should run their course. Accordingly, an amnesty bill was passed pardoning over twenty thousand people including Bayar (Hale 1994, 172–73).

A second step on the road to reconciliation between the army and government occurred on March 1966 when Gürsel became ill after suffering several strokes and resigned the presidency (Hale 1994, 173). At this point, his successor was to be chosen by the TGNA in an election, but the election never occurred. Instead, the TGNA accepted the army's choice, Cevdet Sunay, the Chief of the General Staff. Sunay retired from the army and was elected to the TGNA. He won the required two-thirds majority over his only competitor, Alparslan Türkes, with Cemal Tural becoming Chief of the General Staff (Hale 1994, 173). Sunay's presidency was important for civilian-military rapprochement, since a former military man would be in politics giving the army a recognized voice and make both sides likely to preserve the status quo (Hale 1994, 173). For Demirel, Hale (1994) argues, "Not only did it [the rapprochement] help to stabilize his relations with the armed forces, it also meant that the NSC could act as a sort of substitute cabinet, which could bypass the normal constitutional machinery and thus, it is alleged, overcome opposition from his party colleagues" (173–74). In effect, Demirel was trying to appeal to two con- stituencies—Democrat supports whom the JP needed to stay in office and the army—a position that was not sustainable, as the events of 1968 to 1971 will demonstrate.

Before discussing the events of 1968 to 1971, a third step in civ- il–military reconciliation during the 1960s concerned economics. Specifi- cally, throughout the 1960s, the government sought to ensure army offi- cers received better pay and conditions to forestall another coup, since the May 27 coup was brought about because of said conditions. (Hale 1994, 174). Accordingly, Demirel encouraged private enterprise to rival the state sector. The army participated in this process through the estab- lishment of the Armed Forces Mutual Assistance Fund (or OYAK) by the NUC. OYAK took 10 percent of serving military officers and civilian employees of the Ministry of Defense, deposited the funds into OYAK, and then invested the money into various enterprises. The proceeds were used to provide benefits to subscribers, which included pensions, low- cost mortgages, and subsidized consumer goods (Hale 1994, 174). The presence of OYAK, Hale (1994) argues, allows "the armed forces . . . [to] becom[e] conservative supporters of the capitalist system which Demirel and his party espoused . . . [Also], among most of the senior officers, there was now a degree of acceptance of the economic status quo which had been absent during the 1950s" (175).

Despite the efforts mentioned above, Demirel would face repeated opposition from a number of different sources. According to Glazer (1996), "He was opposed on some issues and prodded on others by a traditionalist wing that was socially conservative, more agrarian in its orientation, and had ties to the Islamic movement" (45). Consequently, Demirel tried to emphasize the Islamic character of his party and its stand for traditional values, as well as continuing to attack parties on the left with anti-communist propaganda (Zürcher 1997, 264). In contrast, the CHP, under its new leader, Bülent Ecevit, sought to identify the CHP as a left-of-center party similar to social democrats in Western Europe (Zürcher 1997, 265). The CHP party platform "favored state-directed in- vestment over private investment and recommended limits on foreign participation in the Turkish economy" (Glazer 1996, 45). Glazer (1996) notes, "As a party leader, Ecevit attempted to transform the CHP from an elitist party seeking to guide the nation from above into a mass move- ment involving a broadly based constituency in the political process. Ecevit's socialist rhetoric was compatible with the Kemalist principles of state direction of the economy, but the shift to the left . . . caused dissen- tion in the party (46).

In 1967, dissension within the CHP resulted in sixty-seven party mem- bers leaving the party as well as the rise of extreme left and extreme right parties. Ideologically, during the 1960s, the extreme left in Turkey represented a small number of trade unionists and leftist intellectuals who were a part of the Turkish Workers' Party (TWP). Its platform "called for the redistribution of land, nationalization of industry and financial institutions, and the expansion of foreign capital, and urged closer cooperation with the Soviet Union" (Glazer 1996, 46). On the extreme right was the Republican Peasants' Nation Party led by Türkes (changing its name in 1969 to the Nationalist Action Party, hereafter MHP). The MHP believed in strong state influence in the economy making it hostile toward capitalism and foreign investment (Glazer 1996, 46). More importantly, Türkes incorporated Islam as part of his ultra-nationalist platform; this was an attempt to garner votes, but Türkes also formed a youth organization called the "Grey Wolves." After receiving paramilitary training the Grey Wolves ran an intimidation campaign against leftist students, teachers, publicists, booksellers, and, finally, politicians, with the expressed mission "to conquer the streets (and the campuses) on the left" (Zürcher 1997, 270). One other conservative party of note was Professor Necmettin Erbakan's National Order Party (NOP). The NOP believed that the JP had moved away from Islam and was an instrument of Freemasons and Zionists. Ultimately, the appearance of these extreme political parties on the fringes of the Turkish political spectrum would incite conflict between politicians and the army necessitating the army's intervention once again into politics in March 1971.

On March 12, 1971, the Turkish Armed Forces intervened to overthrow the Demirel government. The 1971 coup came together due to three elements: First, senior, conservative generals believed Demirel had lost grip on power and his government was unable to deal with violence and the rise in political terrorism so law and order had to be restored; Second, officers appeared to be unwilling to "carry the can" for perceived government misdeeds; Third, a new group of reformist officers believed that progress was not possible within a liberal democratic system of government and advocated an "egalitarian, more independent and more 'modern'" authoritarian regime (Hale 1994, 185–86).

Effectively, the coup was planned by the senior, conservative generals in an ad hoc group known as the Enlarged Council of Commanders. The generals in the Council wanted to ensure that they carried their subordinates with them and, rumor was, to prevent a "leftist" coup by the younger reformist officers (Aksin 2007, 272). According to Aksin (2007), "This rumor was substantiated by the fact that immediately after the coup took place, the officers had prepared the leftist coup—five generals, one admiral, and thirty-five colonels—were relieved from duty" (272–73). Ultimately, both groups compromised by issuing the memorandum which forced Demirel's government to resign, putting in its place an administration which took direction from the military chiefs (Hale 1991, x).

The "Coup by memorandum" imposed national government under Nihat Erim, who was a member of the CHP and a former professor of constitutional law. Martial law was declared and the generals focused on the 1961 Constitution "which was perceived to be 'tailored too loose to fit Turkish society'" (Birand 1987, 14). However, Hale (1994) argues, "[T]he 12 March regime rested on an unstable balance of power between civilian politicians and the military" (195). This relationship would continue long after March 12. Within Erim's cabinet there were divisions between progressives, such as Kocas and Karaosmanoglu, and conservatives within the JP.

Consequently, Erim's efforts at implementing land reform, financial reforms, and a reorganization of the public sector would be difficult to achieve (Hale 1994, 199). Throughout the first year of the military-backed Erim government, debate continued on what reforms should be a priority. Protest came from both the reformist and conservative members of parliament, as well as within the "Brain Trust" who were created to implement reforms. As a result, Erim "was in the position of having to satisfy the left while catering to the right, since the government still had to answer to and have laws passed by the National Assembly in which the Justice Party was the majority" (Askin 2007, 273). By October 1971, Erim's government was breaking down. He submitted his resignation to President Sunay, who refused to accept it, but eventually accepted the resignation. In effect, both conservative and reformist members of parliament at different points resigned from government due to Erim's inability to implement reforms.

Additionally, Hale (1994) notes that the collapse of the first Erim government "caused profound disillusionment for . . . those members of the armed forces who had hoped that the post-memorandum administration could implement egalitarian reforms" (200). At this point, President Sunay called a meeting, attended by Erim, Tagmac and the force commanders, whereby the president proposed that Erim be invited to form a new government. One of the reformists, Muhsin Batur, protested that this would be handing power to the JP, which had the majority, and he urged the inclusion of more reformist ministers, but was overruled by the President Sunay and the other commanders (Hale 1994, 201). Erim's second government would be the caretaker government until elections could be held in October 1973.

In February 1973, the Supreme Command Council (the Chief of the General Staff, and the commanders of the army, navy, and air force) met with all the party leaders, except Demirel (who refused to attend) and put forth General Faruk Gürler, the Chief of the General Staff. Gürler subsequently resigned and was appointed to the Senate by Sunay. Askin (2007) notes, "Ecevit and Demirel joined forces to ensure that retired Admiral Fahri Korutürk was elected rather than Gürler, signaling the end of the 12 March regime" (274). The Generals realized "that this kind of quasi-military regime was an unworkable alternative to either outright military rule, or freely elected civilian government. Unwilling to take over power openly, they retired to their barracks in October 1973, to give way to a series of weak, but at least elected, coalition governments" (Hale 1991, xi).

From September 1974 until March 1975, a transitional government formed by Sadi Irmak took over. After continued negotiations, the first Nationalist Front coalition formed under Demirel of the JP and the Nationalist Action Party led by Turkes. The Nationalist Front Coalition was a center-right coalition and its win was "a turning point in the left-right polarization of Turkish politics characteristic of the 1975–1980 period" (Birand 1987, 19). In particular, Birand (1987) argues, "In the run up to 1980, government crises would increasingly come to be interpreted as crises of the regime. That Nationalist Front, with its hard-right rhetoric and unstable amalgam of extremist parties, added to the polarization and the growing crisis of legitimacy" (19).

The June 5, 1977, elections resulted in a victory for the CHP with 41.4 percent of the vote; however, this was not enough to form a government on its own (Aksin 2007, 277). Ecevit formed a minority administration with independents, but this government failed after one month in office and was succeeded by a second Nationalist Front Coalition under Demirel. The second Nationalist Front lasted approximately seven months and was replaced in January 1978. At this point, Ecevit formed a government of CHP and independents, but was not able to accomplish much due to opposition attacks and the purging of ministries by previous Nationalist Front governments. In October 1979, senate elections saw a drop in CHP support resulting in Demirel's return to power, albeit just with support from JP and without the NSP and NAP (Zurcher 1997, 275).

Violence, as mentioned above, was occurring from groups on the left and right of the political spectrum since the late 1960s and early 1970s. Although the violence was suppressed during the martial law administration after the 1971 coup, incidences of armed robbery, kidnapping, and bombings increased to the point that the public was in a state of fear (Hale 1994, 224). The perpetrators are divided into three broad categories: ideological, sectarian, and ethnic. Groups on the left included the Turkish People's Liberation Front and the Maoist-inspired Turkish Workers and Peasants Liberation Army "who carried out selected assassinations of prominent victims, particularly high-level university administrators and professors" while members of the extreme-left teachers association (TÖB-DER) and the Federation of Revolutionary Youth (Dev-Genç) conducted armed clashes as "soldiers in a war rather than specifically selected targets" against groups on the right, such as the Grey Wolves and the Association of Idealist Youth (Hale 1994, 225).

The second cause of the violence was sectarianism, specifically between Sunni and Shi'a Islam. A majority of the population are Sunni

Muslims, while approximately 15 percent are Shi'ites, known in Turkey as Alevis (Hale 1994, 225). Alevi Muslims are either Arabs or Turks and are concentrated along the Syrian Border in Southeastern Turkey in isolated mountain communities. Additionally, there is also a small minority of Shi'a who are Kurdish and "the competition between Alevi and Sunni Turks for urban jobs led to a revival of traditional sectarian tensions by the mid-1970s" (Hooglund 1996, 101).

The most well-known example of ethnic conflict in Turkey is the conflict between the Kurds and the state. Although the Kurds are a distinct ethnic group, according to Eric Hooglund (1996), "[T]hey are divided by class, regional, and sectarian differences similar to those affecting ethnic Turks. . . . Although the government of Turkey does not compile official data on religious affiliation, scholars estimate that at least two-thirds of the Kurds in Turkey nominally are Sunni Muslims, and that as many as one-third are Shi'a Muslims of the Alevi sect" (100). Prior to 1980, the state's policy vis-à-vis the Kurds included the banning of the Kurdish language in all government institutions, including courts and schools (Hooglund 1996, 98). Consequently, from as far back as 1925, organizations have emerged to challenge the state. The most militant was the Kurdistan Worker's Party (PKK), led by Abdullah Öçalan, which subscribes to both Marxist-Leninism and nationalism (Hale 1994, 226).

Concomitantly with the political violence described above, the economic crisis came to a head during the three years prior to the 1980 coup. Beginning in 1973 with an increase in oil prices, Turkey was beset with cascading economic difficulties into the early 1980s. As Birand (1987) notes, "There is no doubt that the crisis was structural and represented the accumulation over a period of many years of all the problems associated with rapid economic growth and unequal social distribution in a developing country" (45). More specifically, a combination of loans coming due, industry that depended on foreign investment, and the availability of foreign reserves made Turkey especially vulnerable (Zürcher 1997, 280).

The National Front governments continually met the economic crisis by working out loans first with Europe and then the IMF and World Bank. In fact, after prolonged negotiations with these creditors due to demands placed on Turkey, in July 1979 an agreement was reached to provide $1.8 billion in new credits dependent on the Turkish government instituting a reform package consisting of the removal of import and export controls, cutting subsidies, freeing interest rates, raising prices, and cutting government spending (Zürcher 1997, 281). The delay in working out the loan package by the West is best explained by the fact that a number of Third World countries were likely to default on their loans. As a result, an agreement emerged regarding how to deal with possible defaulters and the need to refer these cases to the IMF, where further stabilization and austerity measures would be implemented. Put simply, this would be a "new economic order" put into practice throughout the 1980s (Hale 1994, 46). Consequently, with Demirel returning to office in November 1979, a new economic stabilization plan was approved by parliament after consultation with international banks and led by an economist, Turgut Özal (more on his efforts later).

Despite the effort to meet their international economic obligations, the increasing violence caused the imposition of martial law. The military "became increasingly uneasy over the continued criticism of the armed force in the Grand National Assembly" and "[t]he apparent inability of successive governments to deal with problems of the economy and public order led many in the military to conclude that the 1961 constitution was defective" (Hooglund 1996, 60). In fact, by the summer of 1979, General Evren was receiving messages from several MPs and Senators that military intervention would be the only way to end the crisis (Hale 1994, 233). General Evren, however, decided that the situation had not reached the point where the army would need to intervene. Nevertheless, a "Special Planning Group" had already been set up by General Evren in 1978 and was under the direction of the Deputy Chief of Staff, General Haydar Saltik (Birand 1987, 137). Saltik and two staff officers were tasked by Evren to investigate whether the time for intervention had come or whether a warning to government would be sufficient. Accordingly, Saltik reported back "suggesting that it would be impossible to defeat anarchy and terrorism under the present regime. Hence, the army should take over the government and dissolve the Grand National Assembly" (Hale 1994, 234).

The repeated turnover in power between Ecevit and Demirel convinced General Evren that the time was not ripe for intervention in 1979 so shortly after Senate elections were held. The decision to intervene would be postponed to see the efficacy of Demirel's government. Instead of a full-scale takeover, a warning letter was sent to President Korutürk by General Evren and the force commanders calling for politicians to cooperate in restoring order (Hale 1994, 234). Unfortunately for the politicians, in the spring of 1980, they were unable to come to agreement on a successor to President Korutürk when his term expired. Accordingly, "parliament's failure to elect any permanent successor to Korutürk served as a sharp and bitter reminder [to the army] of the effective paralysis of government" (Hale 1994, 236).

By the summer of 1980, Ecevit and Demirel attempted to form a grand coalition government to placate General Evren and the General Staff. Talks continued throughout July and resulted in a summit at the end of July where the two leaders attempted to work through their differences as violence and sectarian unrest continued to build in the cities and spread to the countryside (Glazer 1996, 60). Accordingly, on August 9, 1980, General Evren convened a meeting of the Supreme Military Council, which included the General Staff plus the force commanders, and the date of the coup was set to September 12, 1980. There was some debate about what the coup should look like, considering that the operation had already been canceled once before.

Confident that a coup was not imminent, Ecevit aligned the CHP with Erbakan and the NSP to force the resignation of Demirel's foreign minister, Hayrettin Erkman. The next day, the NSP sponsored a massive rally at Konya, "where Islamists . . . demonstrated to demand the reinstatement of Islamic law in Turkey, reportedly showing disrespect for the flag and the national anthem" (Glazer 1996, 60). As a result, the generals were "particularly incensed by the open defiance of secularism now being shown by Erbakan" (Hale 1994, 237). Moreover, Hale (1994) notes, "On August 31, 1980, the NSP leader refused to appear at the annual Victory Day parade (which includes a ritual homage at Ataturk's mausoleum). This was taken as a grave insult to the army and to Ataturk's memory" (237). Finally, on September 6, Ecevit delivered a speech to a meeting of the petroleum worker's union comparing the political struggle to a soccer match by appealing to the workers to get out of the stands and onto the pitch (Hale 1994, 238). Thus, on September 7, 1980, General Evren met secretly with the armed forces and police commanders and gave the go-ahead for the September 12th coup (Birand 1987, 171).

The September 12 coup occurred in the early morning hours. According to Glazer (1996), "There was no organized resistance to the coup; indeed, many Turks welcomed it as the only alternative to anarchy" (60). Whereas the 1960 and 1971 military coups had institutional reform as their objective, the small group of officers who took over in 1980, had straightforward aims: "to end the appalling terrorist bloodshed, right the economy and return Turkey to elected civilian government in conditions which, they hoped, would make yet another intervention unnecessary." (Hale 1994, 246).

The military's first task was to reestablish law and order. The martial law commanders were given enhanced powers, specifically the right to ban strikes, public meetings and demonstrations, suspend newspapers and other publications, and to dismiss local and central government staff whose employment was deemed undesirable (Hale 1994, 251). Accordingly, violence decreased over the next year, ending by 1982. Also, with the increased power of the state terrorists networks collapsed (Hale 1994, 252).

Although the violence was quelled, there were costs; namely, that anyone who expressed leftist or Islamist views before 1980 could be arrested. The generals created an enemies list which included trade unionists, legal politicians, university professors, teachers, journalists and lawyers (Aksin 2007, 283). The actions described above can be explained by an important ideological dimension to the regime, according to Aksin (2007):

We saw earlier that during the 12 March 1971 coup there had been a left-right struggle within the army, with the right gaining preponderance. Apparently this swing had continued in the 1970s, with the result that Evren and most of the army were now thinking, probably with encouragement from the United States, that Islam was the best remedy for communism. Thus, the suppression of the left was accompanied by an effort to fabricate a new ideology, the so-called 'Turkish-Islamic' synthesis (283).

The "Turkish-Islamic synthesis" was an ideology introduced by the group, Aydinlar Ocagi (Hearths of the Enlightened), whose membership counted influential people from the business world, universities, and politics; its purpose was to counter a perceived monopoly of the social, politica,l and cultural debate by left-wing intellectuals (Zürcher 1997, 303). The tenet of the Turkish-Islamic Synthesis centered on Islam holding a special attraction for Turks because of similarities between their pre-Islamic culture and Islamic civilization. Through a shared sense of justice, monotheism, a belief in the immortal soul, and a strong emphasis on family life and morality, Turks were to be the soldiers of Islam (Zürcher 1997, 303).

Support for the Turkish-Islamic Synthesis, in the late 1970s, came most prominently from the Nationalist Salvation Party and Nationalist Action Party of Türkes. Interestingly, support also came from prominent military leaders, including General Kenan Evren. It must be remembered that during this period the Cold War was in full swing and the military was trained to view socialism and communism as Turkey's foes. To counter this, fierce nationalism and Islam would be used. Thus, under Evren and the NSC's military rule from 1980 to 1983, religion and ethics became a part of the basic curriculum in schools that was "exclusively Sunni in content and patriotism and love for parents, the state and the army . . . was presented as a religious duty" (Zürcher 1997, 303). After 1983, Özal would use the Synthesis as a driving force behind his Motherland Party (MP). Essentially, at this point in Turkey's development, Islam gained traction as a political force that spoke for the poor and would continue to build discontent within society into the 1990s and 2000s.

Before returning power to the civilians, the military regime also drew up a new constitution, which aimed to install a more restricted version of democracy than had been sanctioned since 1961. To accomplish this task, a Constituent Assembly was convened consisting of a Consultative Assembly and the NSC. As Hale (1994) notes, "In theory, the Consultative Assembly shared legislative powers with the NSC, though in practice the final say rested with Evren and his colleagues. Moreover, the 160 members of the Assembly were either handpicked by the junta or else nominated by the provincial governors" (256). The Assembly then elected a fifteen-member committee to draft the new constitution. The constitution placed power in the hand of the NSC and restricted civil liberties—namely, freedom of the press, freedom of trade unions (effectively banning political strikes), as well as individual rights such as freedom of speech and freedom of association (Zürcher 1997, 295). In fact, the constitution included clauses protecting rights and liberties, but there was also a stipulation that they could be annulled, suspended or limited based on the national interest, public order, national security, danger to the republican order, and public health (Zürcher 1997, 295).

Next, the constitution was put to a referendum on November 7, 1982, with the vote tied to Evren becoming president for seven years after the constitution's adoption. The vote was also made compulsory (Zürcher 1997, 295–96). While the constitution passed with 91.4 percent, there were, not surprisingly, "no" votes from Kurds in southeast Turkey. In sum, despite the defects of the constitution and other laws introduced by the generals, the ability for the generals to work with the politicians was still proving to be difficult (Hale 1994, 259–60).

As mentioned earlier, the NSC banned all politicians who had been active in politics prior to September 1980 for ten years. Now that the military had essentially rewritten the rules with the Political Parties Law, political elites found it difficult to establish new political parties. New parties were subjected to bureaucratic restrictions (Hale 1994, 262). Effectively this meant that of the fifteen parties found, twelve were deemed unacceptable by the military. The three parties who participated in the November 6, 1983 election were the *Milliyetçi Demokrasi Partisi* (Party of Nationalist Democracy [PND]), a party supported by the generals; the *Halkçi Parti* (Populist Party [PP]), a party very similar to the Kemalist wing of the CHP; and the *Anavatan Partisi* (Motherland Party [ANAP]), led by Turgut Özal, the man behind the economic reform program launched in 1979–80 (Zürcher 1997, 296).

From the outset, the NSC came out in favor of the PND and, in fact, according to Hale (1994), "It was apparently part of the junta's design that a moderate leftist party should be encouraged to run against the NDP, to give legitimacy to the elections" (263). Evren "observed that while the civilian authority had to act responsively to the people, the military should also act in that manner. . . . [Evren] and his co-intervenors wanted . . . Ulusu to found a political party because they thought Ulusu was liked and respected by the people" (Heper and Güney 1996, 626).

In effect, the military's overt support for the PP allowed Özal to campaign "as the only genuine democrat and thus to attract the votes of those who, after three years, wanted the military out of politics" (Zürcher 1997, 297). These developments left Turkey with a host of unanswered questions: Would the return to civilian government under Prime Minister Turgut Özal in 1983 be a genuine one, or would the military continue to control the country's political destinies from behind the scenes? (Hale 1991, xi).

Before the March 1984 municipal election, the ANAP was facing growing criticism from opposition parties that were excluded from the 1983 election. Consequently, the ANAP-controlled TGNA voted to allow these opposition parties to participate in the 1984 municipal election. The Social Democratic Party (SDP) led by Professor Erdal Inonu, the son of the late Ismet Inönü, the True Path Party (DYP), led by political cronies of Demirel, and the Refah Party, a reincarnation of Erbakan's NSP, were allowed to participate, essentially, to divide the votes of the opposition parties and thereby improve ANAP's majority in the assembly (Zurcher 1997, 298). Accordingly, the ANAP won 41.5 percent, followed by the SDP with 23.5 percent and the DYP with 13.5 percent and the Welfare (*Refah*) Party with 4.5 percent (Zurcher 1997, 298). Thus, the elections created conditions whereby the opposition parties had lost their legitimacy. As a result, in November 1985, the PP merged with the SDP and the NDP voted to dissolve itself (Glazer 1996, 63). Furthermore, in national elections for local government officials on September 28, 1986, ANAP received 32 percent of the votes, the DYP won 23.7 percent, and the new Social Democratic Populist Party (Sosyal Demokrat Halkçi Parti—SHP) won 22.7 percent of the votes (Glazer 1996, 63). At this point, pressure was building against the army to restore the pre-1980 political leaders, whom the army had tried to exclude from the system.

Following a national referendum on September 6, 1987, these leaders regained their political rights. One way or another, these leaders were still able to control proxy parties (Hale 1991, xii; Hale 1994, 279). Demirel became head of True Path Party (DYP); Bulent Ecevit refused to cooperate with Inönü and formed the Democratic Left Party (DSP); Necmettin Erbakan assumed leadership of the Welfare Party (Refah); Alpsan Turkes resumed control of his party which after an interval reverted to the name of MHP. The result of the above moved Özal to announce early national elections for November 1987.

Özal's campaign focused on the government's economic achievements. In particular, Turkey had an average growth rate of 6.6 percent GNP between 1984 and 1987 (Hale 1994, 280). This success rested on policies implemented by Özal during the Demirel government—opening the economy to foreign markets, the application of market principles internally and reducing the role of the state sector—however, he was unable to control public expenditure and inflation (Hale 1994, 280). Nevertheless, the November 1987 elections saw the ANAP get 36 percent, the SDPP 25 percent, and the DYP 19 percent of the vote (Aksin 2007, 288). The next four years would see a number of domestic events impact on civil–military relations in Turkey: concessions to Islamists, ethnic conflict, economics,

From 1987 to 1991, within Özal's ANAP, there was dissension over the role of Islam in politics. More specifically, the government, to retain its grass roots support from rural Turkey, made concessions to fundamentalists which included: the expansion of religious education and Friday prayer, and gave permission to female students to wear Islamic headscarves to university classes (Hale 1994, 281). The headscarf issue would become the "hot-button" issue in the debate on secularism that would continue into the 1990s and 2000s with the electoral wins of Refah and the Justice and Development Party.

Next, ethnic conflict was continuing in southeastern Turkey. Between 1984 and 1994, attacks by the PKK on security forces and pro-government Kurdish villages challenged government authority. Banned by the Turkish government, the PKK began a sustained guerrilla war against the state. The PKK attacked a variety of government installations throughout the southeast of Turkey from their training camps in the mountains separating Northern Iraq from Turkey (the same mountains where Operation Provide Comfort would take place after the 1990 Persian Gulf War). The violence of the PKK could be described as "the use of indiscriminate violence, and PKK guerrillas did not hesitate to kill Kurds whom they considered collaborators. Targeted in particular were the government's paid militia, known as village guards, and schoolteachers accused of promoting assimilation" (Hooglund 1996, 281). As a result, the PKK was declared a terrorist organization by the government "to justify its own policies, which included the destruction of about 850 border villages and the forced removal of their populations to western Turkey" (Hooglund 1996, 281).

Third, the economy played a major role in the ANAP electoral campaign, but would just as easily bring about its decline between 1987 and 1991. Özal had campaigned on his efforts to implement a "neo-liberal" restructuring of the economy emphasizing decentralization, privatization, export-led growth, and a redistribution of power away from the state toward a market economy (Nasr 2009, 237). The restructuring required loans from the World Bank and IMF as well as a new emphasis on social openness and citizen participation (Nasr 2009, 237). However, the effects of Özal's effort would not become apparent for some time. As Nasr (2009) notes, "The economic transformation ran wide and deep as globalization transformed Turkish economic and social life. Economic power shifted to small and medium-sized businesses and the Anatolian heartland overshadowed Istanbul as engine of growth. These changes over time produced both a new business elite and a new middle class, of the same basic persuasion as that of the rising middle class all over the region" (Nasr 2009, 238).

However, the decline in Özal's and ANAP's popularity was due to continued high inflation (Zürcher 1997, 301). Moreover, Özal's economic policies were accompanied by nepotism and corruption. Consequently, a number of business scandals developed involving ANAP ministers and party leaders. For instance, the Özal family was criticized for nepotism and corruption in their business activities: "When one of the president's sons made vast sums of money on the Istanbul stock exchange, dealing in stocks of firms which were given government contracts soon afterwards, there was a suspicion that more than just foresight was involved. After the 1989 elections, Özal countered some of the criticism by removing his family members from the cabinet" (Zürcher 1997, 301).

A watershed moment in Turkish politics occurred in the fall of 1989. President Evren was about to retire as president. Since 1961, the presidency was designed to be neutral, nonpartisan and held by retired senior military (Hale 1994, 282). However, upon President Evren's retirement, Özal became Turkey's first fully civilian head of state since 1960. Under the 1982 Constitution, the TGNA can elect whomever it likes, as long as he or she meets certain minimum qualifications, and receives two-thirds majority in the Assembly on the first two ballots (Hale 1994, 282). Özal's election to the presidency created a new dynamic between the president and prime minister. In effect, as founder of the ruling party and having experience as prime minister, allowed him greater influence than any previous president, thereby creating "an active, dominating presidency" giving him more power than previous presidents (Hale 1994, 282).

In sum, the events of 1987–1991 took their toll on the popularity of Özal. Aksin (2007) argues, "His unconstitutional, high-handed and adventurous conduct was causing an uproar. The opposition and many newspapers were criticizing him. There was unrest not only in the cabinet, but also in the [ANAP]. Last but not least, the army was against him" (295). General Necip Torumtay, who became chief of the general staff on August 31, 1987, believed Özal and other civilians did not pay much attention to matters pertaining to the military: "His [Torumtay's] perception of the military's display of professional traits and civilian's lack of them led him to think that the military 1) should have as much autonomy as possible from the civilian authority; 2) should be consulted on matters that also have military aspects; and 3) should have the last word on solely military issues" (Heper and Güney 1996, 627–28).

Torumtay was upset from the moment he became Chief of the General Staff. For him, the military was a professional organization "through constant and careful training" (Heper and Güney 1996, 627). During the Gulf War, Torumtay "complained that for four months the military could not obtain from the government any guidelines on the basis of which to determine military strategy. He thought, however, that the military had the sole responsibility for formulating military strategy, and added that the Turkish Armed Forces are led by highly qualified generals and admirals who were promoted to those ranks after proving their competence in previous ranks" (Heper and Güney 1996, 628–29). In effect, Torumtay was upset that Özal did not consult others when making decisions; in this case, regarding foreign policy. Heper and Güney (1996) provide a telling illustration from Torumay's memoirs:

At the crisis management meetings . . . the president came up with novel ideas based on his frequent telephone conversations with political leaders of other countries and his constant watching of the CNN. Even on military issues outside of his expertise and experience, the president persistently made suggestions and demands, including a military operation against Iraq, which conformed to neither the basic principles of the military warfare nor the military strategy (629).

Consequently, Torumtay believed that Özal and other civilian politicians were violating the rule of law by not respecting their posts and the "sublimity of the nation" and chose to retire in December 1990 (Heper and Güney 1996, 629). His retirement did not cause any discussion of coup; instead, General Dogan Gures, a former commander of the land forces, took over as Chief of the General Staff and made several statements about the Turkish military not intervening in politics and respecting democracy: "'The Turkish Armed Forces is an admirer of democracy; 'the military is a democratic-constitutional institution; it holds in high esteem democratic principles; it is in a subordinate position to the civilian government; 'the chief commander of the Turkish Armed Forces is the Turkish Grand National Assembly; the military has great respect for the Assembly'" (Heper and Güney 1996, 630). Although these statements might reflect his belief in the democratic process, Gures' faith in politicians would be tested following the 1991 general election.

The October 20, 1991, parliamentary election was significant, as the ANAP lost the elections to Demirel's DYP. The DYP won 27 percent or the vote and ANAP came in second with 24 percent of the vote (Aksin 2007, 295). DYP emerged as strongest party, and Demirel formed a coalition with Erdal Inönü's SHP. The new government sought to continue President Özal's liberalization policies.

However, suddenly on April 17, 1993, President Özal suffered a massive heart attack and passed away. Despite the economic problems and scandals, Zürcher (1997) argues, "[T]here was a general feeling that he had a unique place in the modern history of Turkey and in many commentaries he was called the second great modernizer (after Atatürk) of the country" (309). A month later, Demirel became president and was succeeded as ANAP leader and prime minister by Tansu Ciller who continued the coalition with SHP.

Ciller, a former professor of economics and minister of state for the economy in Demirel's last cabinet, has been described as having politics closer to Özal than Demirel "both in content (extremely pro-American with an almost blind faith in the workings of the free market) and in style (dramatic, adventurous and publicity-seeking)" (Zürcher 1997, 310). Ciller's coalition governments were consistently under threat from parties on the left and right. The left challenged Ciller's government to prove its social democratic credentials, while on the right, the business community and the army (Zürcher 1997, 310). Ciller's government would consistently deal with three issues: the economy, the Kurdish question, and the relationship with the EU.

During her time in office, from 1991 to 1994, the economy took a downturn. As Aksin (2007) notes, "The irresponsible economic and fiscal policies of Özal governments, involving deficit spending and heavy borrowing (between 1988 and 1993 the external debt rose from $41 to 67 billion), provoked major crisis, the dollar suddenly rose from fifteen thousand to thirty-eight thousand liras and there was a run on the banks" (298–299). Consequently, the IMF was called in and an agreement was reached to implement a neo-liberal economic principles. The economic recovery was slow-going and its effect would not be felt until late 1995 and throughout 1996 (Zürcher 1997, 324). In fact, the effect of these policies would help Refah win both local elections in March 1994 and the general election of December 1995.

Ironically, the fundamentalists would come to power in the December 1995 general elections. Ciller hoped that the signing of the Customs Union Treaty would endear her to voters, many of whom suffered from the 1994 recession which was a result of Ciller's development policy (Mango 2006, 96). However, in the March 1994 local elections, Erbakan's Refah Party was able to win the mayoralties in twenty-nine large cities around the country, including Ankara and Istanbul, from the SDPP, who subsequently merged with the CHP led by Deniz Baykal (Momayezi 1998, 16; Mango 2006, 95). The decline of the SDPP and even the CHP "can be explained by rather weak leadership and the fact that the SDPP seemed to be properly championing neither the welfare of the lower classes nor the principles of Kemalism" (Aksin 2007, 299). Aksin (2007) argues, "Even though Inonu had an aura, he, Karayalcin and Hikmet Cetin were on the whole rather weak political personalities. Deniz Baykal, leader of the RPP, seemed to have a strong personality, but he was out to please everybody and in the process he was turning his back on leftist policies, including Kemalism. This meant that he was pleasing almost nobody, because by enunciating rightist policies he could not hope to compete with rightist parties" (299).

While Refah's victory was, in part, due to ineffective leadership of the DYP and SDPP, the rise in the Islamic vote was also attributed to four factors: First, the win was attributed as a protest vote against the parties in power for failing to provide employment, economic, and social benefits to the people. Second, Islamists received significant financial support from within Turkey and in Europe, including from Saudi Arabia and Libya. Third, the Islamists were effective in local voter mobilization by conducting door-to-door election campaigns. Fourth, votes were received for purely religious reasons (Aksin 2007, 300). In short, Refah's electoral victory would begin a six month period of internecine conflict which would catch the attention of the General Staff and culminate in Turkey's first post-modern coup

The December 1995 elections gave Refah 21.4 percent of the national vote and "[i]n the political horsetrading which followed, the main concern of party leaders was to block a parliamentary investigation into corruption charges leveled against them by their political rivals" (Mango 2006, 96). Erbakan negotiated with Ciller to form a coalition government, despite Ciller being an outspoken secularist. During the night of the election she stated, "'[Y]our decision is to choose civilization over darkness'" (Momayezi 1998, 17). She was accused of allying with Erbakan to shield herself from investigations by parliament into her finances and, in fact, Erbakan's supporters in parliament helped to defeat proposals that would have referred the issue of her finances and handling of the discretionary fund to the Supreme Court (Aksin 2007, 301; Momayezi 1998, 17).

Moreover, on foreign policy, Erbakan's election rhetoric was perceived as radical. Political scientist Nasser Momayezi (1998) notes, "It [election rhetoric] was anti-Western, anti-NATO, and anti-Israel, and he opposed the U.S.-led Operation Provide Comfort. . . . He was also opposed to Turkey joining the European Economic Community" (17). Refah wanted to strengthen the ties between Turkey and the rest of the Islamic world with a foreign policy that "reflected a curious mixture of nationalism and Islamic transnationalism" (Momayezi 1998, 17). The General Staff, however, took steps once Erbakan took office to ensure that Turkish foreign policy, the military's purview, would not be harmed. The three security portfolios—defense, foreign affairs, and interior—were given to Ciller, who became foreign minister, at the suggestion of the military (Momayezi 1998, 18). In effect, the generals and other officers had "strong suspicions about Refah's secular as well as democratic credentials" (Heper and Güney 2000, 639–40). At this point, the Turkish General Staff adopted a strategy of "wait-and-see" (Heper and Güney 2000, 640).

The "wait-and-see" period occurred between July and December 1996, with the military observing the actions of Erbakan and Refah (Heper and Güney. 640). What events were causing such disquiet among the generals? The generals' concerns, first expressed in August 1996 at a meeting of the National Security Council, concerned the threat of militant Islam toward secularism (Heper and Güney 2000, 642). To this end, a number of events influenced a report issued in January 1997 to the National Security Council by the National Intelligence Agency. First, the military was concerned that "a number of religious orders and associations were trying to create 'alternative state structures . . . trying to bring back to Turkey an order based on Shari'a'" (Heper and Güney 2000, 640). Second, the military was concerned with radical Turkish Islamic organizations receiving funds collected from Turkish workers abroad and channeled to Islamic holding companies to support political Islam in Turkey. Third, there were a number of students graduating from the Prayer Leader and Preacher Schools; in particular, "[a]ccording to military intelligence, even though the annual need for religious functionaries in the late 1990s was around 3,000, every year more than 50,000 students graduated from these schools" (Heper and Güney 2000, 640).

Finally, the most immediate concern of the military included Refah staffing the bureaucracy with co-ideologists who would implement the following projects: 1) only those who knew Arabic were to be admitted to the Foreign Ministry, 2) diplomats were to practice their religion at foreign posts, and 3) every Turkish representative abroad was to act as a missionary for Islam (Heper and Güney 2000, 641). Also, Erbakan visited a number of militantly Islamic states, including Iran and Libya, but "his tours of Muslim countries [did not] produce the money to build an 'Islamic car,' and 'Islamic submarine,' even less an 'Islamic aircraft-carrier'" (Mango 2006, 96). President Demirel warned Erbakan and other Refah leaders to act prudently but these warnings went unheeded.

Consequently, at the December 26, 1996, National Security Council meeting, "the commanders noted that since August of 1996, the Islamic threat had become greater by the day and reiterated their request that this matter be placed on the agenda of the MGK" (Heper and Güney 2000, 643). Chief of the General Staff Ismail Hakki Karadayi stated, "[B]oth secularism, 'which is the very essence of intellectual progress, liberty of conscience, and democracy,' and liberal democracy, 'which is the lifestyle of free, civilized, and modern individuals,' are the fundamental characteristics of the Turkish Republic" (Heper and Güney 2000, 643). General Karadayi and President Demirel were in close contact and Demirel tried for four weeks to dissuade Erbakan and Ciller's government from continuing down the road it was on. According to Heper and Güney (2000), "The commanders' response was that they were well aware of the president's earnest endeavors concerning this matter, but Prime Minister Erbakan and Deputy Prime Minister Ciller were refraining from taking the necessary measures; worse still, they were acting against the laws enacted to safeguard secularism" (644). Therefore, the General Staff set in motion their carefully orchestrated "post-modern coup."

At a meeting of the National Security Council on February 28, 1997, the military demanded that "'the forces of reaction' should be confronted'" (Mango 2006, 260). Accordingly, the General Staff "urged the members of the council to recommend to the government the necessary measures, adding that otherwise a critical threshold would be crossed, the implication being that then the military would be obliged to deal with the threat unilaterally" (Heper and Güney 2000, 645). Refah declared its purposes were to achieve social justice, a "just economic order," and the promotion of Muslim values in Turkey through education; however, the General Staff, and other critics, argued that "from the beginning that it had a hidden agenda: the conversion of Turkey into a state governed by *sharia* (Islamic law)" (Salt 1999, 72). According to Mango (2006), "Thus began what became known in Turkey as 'the process of 28 February'—a campaign, concerted by the military, to eradicate political Islam from education, business and other activities" (97).

The National Security Council issued a memorandum demanding Erbakan take steps to "protect the secular nature of the state, including changing the education laws to force the closure of . . . prayer leader and preacher . . . schools" (Salt 1999, 74). Erbakan and Ciller, however, were not going to go quietly. Ciller attempted a defense of the government stating "that religion could not be used for political purposes because she and her colleagues in her party—DYP—stood guard for secularism" (Heper and Güney 2000, 645). The General Staff remarked that Ciller's comments were only words and they (politicians) were not backing their words up with action (Heper and Güney 2000, 645).

Moreover, the West Working Group was established by the General Staff to monitor suspected fundamentalists, senior bureaucrats, and judges whom the generals believed had links to political Islam. To increase the pressure on Erbakan, the military also called in academics and journalists to meetings of the National Security Council to give them briefings on the dangers posed by "fundamentalism" and the "terrorism" of the PKK (Salt 1999, 74). As Professor Jeremy Salt (1999) recounts, "[T]he general staff warned that 'giving freedom of movement to religious extremism and to the outlawed [PKK] in the context of democracy would be tantamount to the state committing suicide. There cannot be any such concept of democracy" (75).

Next, the National Security Council gave the prime minister a list of 18 directives written in a "tense communiqué" which was worked out in a nine-hour meeting with the five senior officers and four civilian ministers and chaired by the president (Momayezi 1998, 19–20). Momayesi (1998) notes, "Among the demands were those to cut the number of students being trained at religious academies, crack down on Muslim groups who are believed to be accumulating weapons, close unlicensed 'Koran schools' and end his party's recruitment of officers cashiered from the army because of their fundamentalist sympathies" (19). Erbakan dragged his feet and was hoping to ride out the military's criticism of his government. The military was upset at the influence Islam had on Erbakan's government and were worried how the WP would be perceived by the European Union: "'It has been decided that in Turkey, secularism is not only a form of government but a way of life and the guarantee of democracy and social peace. . . . It is necessary to end all speculation which may lead to suspicions about our democracy and damage Turkey's image and prestige abroad'" (Momayezi 1998, 20). Therefore, it was not only the threat to Kemalism and the state, but international influence and recognition of one day belonging to the EU that was behind the 1997 military intervention.

By May 1997, the conflict between the military and the Erbakan-Ciller government came to a head. Under pressure from the military, Erbakan stepped down as prime minister. President Demirel favored Yilmaz's ANAP. Yilmaz, a secularist, was a close ally of the military and he formed a coalition with DSP and DYP dissidents. According to Momayezi (1998), "The generals did not want to see the Refah Party with any power, even in a government led by Ciller whom they consider[ed] corrupt and willing to deal with anyone who will protect her from prosecution" (21). Subsequently, on January 16, 1998, Turkey's Constitutional Court dissolved the Refah Party and ruled that Erbakan was banned from politics for five years with Refah losing its 152 seats in parliament (Aksin 2007, 308; Momayezi 1998, 21). Refah reconstituted itself as the Virtue Party under Recai Kutan, but after its dissolution, Erbakan's followers formed the Felicity Party.

By fall 1998, Yilmaz's government would be accused of corruption. According to Aksin (2007), "[T]apes of telephone conversations between a mafia leader and an [ANAP] . . . minister found their way to the press. Their content indicated that the Deputy was trying to 'fix' the sale of a bank, using the services of the mafia for this purpose" (309). Consequently, when the incident was brought before the TGNA and the CHP supported a motion of inquiry, Yilmaz resigned. Ecevit and the DSP formed a minority government in run-up to elections in April 1999. Ecevit's DSP and Turkes's MHP emerged as the strongest two parties. Ecevit formed a coalition with MHP and ANAP that served for two years. Mango (2006) describes these two years, as follows: "At first all went well. But success in defeating the insurgency of Kurdish separatists was matched by a growing realization that a decade of short-lived coalition governments, not to say half a century of vote-seeking policies, interrupted only by brief intervals of military rule, had left the administration in tatters" (98). Specifically, Turkey's economy, under Ecevit, "was in free fall"; Ecevit's government increased interest rates, but this supposed cure in effect made three million Turks jobless (Nasr 2009, 238). Consequently, an agreement was reached with the IMF to implement a stabilization program "designed to stop politicians from playing fast and loose with the economy" (Mango 2006, 100).

In May 2000, President Demirel's seven year term was up and despite Ecevit's efforts to persuade parliament to extend his term, the TGNA refused to do so citing public pressure for change (Mango 2006, 101). Ahmet Necdet Sezer, president of the constitutional court, was elected as the next president of Turkey after Ecevit persuaded parliament to vote for someone outside of politics and the army (Mango 2006, 101). Sezer was "[a] stickler for rules and regulations" and in a meeting of the National Security Council in February 2001 he "accused the government of covering up corruption scandals" (Mango 2006, 101). A public quarrel between Sezer and Ecevit led to economic crisis in February, because markets were already shaken by events the previous fall. The Turkish Lira was floated and lost half of its value with GNP falling by nearly 10 percent (Nasr 2009, 238). Credits were secured from the IMF under a new stabilization program. World Bank vice-president Kemal Derivs was called in by Ecevit to implement it. According to Mango (2006), "Its immediate aim was to cut back public expenditure and produce a large and continuing surplus which would serve to reduce the public debt. . . . The program worked, and by the following year the economy had begun to recover. But confidence was not easily restored and new jobs were slow in coming" (101–2).

By the summer of 2002, Ecevit fell ill and a number of his ministers quit, led by his right-hand man Husamettin Ozkan, Ismail Cem and Kemal Dervis. Consequently, the DLP lost sixty-three deputies, who formed the New Turkey Party. Moreover, Nationalist Action Party leader, Devlet Bahceli, "had already broken ranks by opposing the abolition of the death penalty, cultural rights or the Kurds and concessions in Cyprus as the price of EU membership[,] now declared that he would leave the coalition unless elections, due in April 2004, were advanced to November 2002" (Mango 2006, 102).

Ecevit gave in and elections were scheduled for November 2002. Mango (2006) notes, "In the elections held in November 2002, none of the three coalition parties—Ecevit's Democratic Left, Bahceli's Nationalists and Yilmaz's Motherland Party—could win the minimum of 10 percent of the total poll, which under Turkish electoral law a party needs in order to qualify for representation in parliament" (102–3). The winner was the Justice and Development Party (AKP), which emerged on the political scene after the Virtue Party and Felicity Party were banned. The AKP, which is short for "Adalet ve Kalkinma Partisi", and means "clean party," was led by Erdogan and "promised good and clean government and a fresh start" (Nasr 2009, 239). Due to its Islamist roots, Nasr (2009) argues, "The fear has been of a fundamentalist takeover, through from the start, the leaders of Turkey's Islamic political revival have been a very different breed from the fundamentalists who have wreaked so much havoc around the region" (239). Next, we turn to the AKP and its relationship with the Turkish military and society.

The AKP was founded in 2001 from members of Felicity who "softened their Islamic message" by touting "a pro-Western outlook, conservative but also favorable to democracy and markets" (Nasr 2009, 240). Additionally, the AKP accepted secularism and made a firm commitment to Ataturk's legacy of modernization, especially with its continued goal of joining the EU. Because Erdogan was still banned from politics, AKP deputy leader Abdullah Gül became prime minister. The AKP built its base from the Anatolian heartland focusing on conservative family values (Nasr 2009, 241). As Nasr (2009) notes, "Party leaders prefer to be called 'conservative' rather than 'Muslim' or 'Islamic' democrats. To them, the term 'conservative' evokes in equal measure national-patriotic values, a high regard for the family, religious piety, and a respect for

Ottoman as well as local traditions" (241). Kemalists, however, were opposed to the AKP and their interpretation of secularism.

Two important factors to consider as this period is discussed are the influence of the economy and continued goal of joining the EU. Between 2002 and 2007, the economy began to revive. First, Turkey implemented neo-liberal austerity measures, as part of a foreign debt restructuring package. Next, the AKP privatized many industries and promoted globalization to deepen economic and political ties to Europe (Nasr 2009, 239). As a result, thanks to Turkey's "fiscal discipline and wise macroeconomic management, GDP nearly tripled, going from $230 billion to $660 billion and raising Turkey to number seven in the size rankings of European economies and number sixteen in the world. Over the same period . . . Foreign Direct Investment grew at a mind-boggling rate, skyrocketing from just $1 billion to $42 billion by the end of 2007" (Nasr 2009, 239).

In December 2002, the EU granted Turkey candidate status and would decide in December 2004 whether to set a date for accession negotiations (Mango 2006, 261). Since the November 2002 elections, the TGNA passed "no less than seven comprehensive legislative reform packages and a variety of major constitutional amendments under the . . . broad categories of judicial, human rights, economic, minority rights, and foreign policy reforms" (Cook 2007, 127). Of note, was the AKP's amending of Articles 76 and 78 of the constitution which made it more difficult to ban a politician and political party. Consequently, Erdogan was able to return to politics and oversaw AKP electoral victories in 2004, 2007, 2013, and 2014.

Essentially, "[p]ressure from the EU for Turkey to comply with the Copenhagen criteria for civilian control of the military" instigated a number of reforms by the AKP to military institutions or mechanisms by which the military influenced politics (Cook 2007, 128). A December 2003 amendment to the Law on Public Financial Management and Control establishment oversight and control over the Defense Industry Support Fund and strengthened the civilian-controlled under secretariat of defense "to identify priorities for defense expenditures" whereas in the past, the civilian leadership in the Ministry of Defense would just carry out the wishes of the general staff (Cook 2007, 128). Next, the TGNA made changes to several government boards where the military exercised its influence; namely, military representatives were removed from the Higher Education Board and High Audio-Visual Board. According to Cook (2007), "Established after the 1980 coup, the senior command used these boards to ensure Kemalist orthodoxy by prohibiting anything other than official interpretations of Islam (reactionaryism), Kurdish nationalism (separatism), and socialism in university curricula and the media" (128). In short, the AKP was attempting to put in place civilian control of the military and limit the military's ability to "use nationalism" to bring the country in line with the EU's Copenhagen Criteria.

The most significant institutional changes in the civil–military relationship were the changes made to the National Security Council. First, the composition of the National Security Council was amended in October 2001 to include more civilian members. Cook (2007) argues, "In fact . . . 'civilianizing' the MGK was little more than a cosmetic change, the military signaled its willingness to accede to this change a year before the amendment was adopted" (128–29).

Moreover, by January 2004, the MGK's only military officer was the Chief of the General Staff and a civilian secretary-general was appointed reporting directly to the prime minister and president. Previously the position was a military officer reporting to the Chief of the General Staff (Cook 2007, 129).

Second, the MGK's meetings were reduced from monthly to bimonthly unless a special session is convened at the request of the prime minister or president. Finally, the duty of the MGK was redefined as "'[r]eaching advisory decisions regarding the designation, determination and implementations of the state's security policies within the prescribed frameworks, determining a method for providing the necessary coordination, and reporting these advisory decisions to the Cabinet Council'" (Cook 2007, 129). Consequently, the Commission of the European Union found that the Turks had met the Copenhagen Criteria and accession talks began in 2005. Put simply, the importance of the above for Turkey's future, can be described as: "Beyond the details of the government's reform drive, the EU project produced something much more profound and important for the country's future political trajectory—a shift in the interests and constraints of its most important political actors, Islamists and officers" (Cook 2007, 130).

At this point, an important question must be asked: Why did the military not intervene again after these overt intrusions into the military domain? In part, the answer can be found through an examination of the "conflict" between progressive Pashas and the conservative Pashas on the General Staff.

From 1998 to2002, the Chief of the General Staff was General Huseyin Kivrikoglu. He was an outspoken general, who as head of the General Staff, "primarily exerted political influence through informal means, setting parameters for government policy by informing governments of its 'concerns' at monthly meetings of the NSC and in private meetings with government officials or via the media through statements at public functions and in briefings to chosen journalists" (Jenkins 2006, 192). In other words, the General Staff used a number of informal contacts within government, as well as high-level meetings between a member of the general staff and the prime minister, to influence policy. Jenkins (2006) notes, "Although these channels were sometimes used to exert pressure on the government and to ensure that policy remained within what the [General Staff] saw as acceptable parameters, the two-way flow of information often served to alleviate—if never completely eradicate—mutual suspicions" (192).

The AKP's November 2002 electoral victory coincided with the appointment of a relatively "circumspect" chief of staff in August 2002— Hilmi Özkök (Jenkins 2006, 193). Özkök avoided being seen as influencing the political process, because of the importance of the EU accession process to Turkey's future. In particular, Özkök, in the first statement issued by the General Staff, "vowed that the Turkish military would continue to 'protect the Republic against every kind of threat, particularly fundamentalism and separatism'" (Jenkins 2006, 194). During Özkök's tenure, the General Staff dealt with two policy issues of note, both foreign and domestic—the 2003 Iraq War and the headscarf. In both cases, Jenkins (2006) argues that Özkök "has pursued a more subtle strategy that tries to ensure that the [General Staff] adopts a low a political profile as possible and intervening to warn the government only if he believes that the Kemalist interpretation of secularism is in imminent danger" (193).

For example, in the build-up to the 2003 Iraq War, Turkey was asked by the United States if it could use its territory to transit troops to Iraq to establish a northern front. The AKP decided to put the issue to a vote in the TGNA on March 1 with the NSC scheduled to meet on February 28. According to Jenkins (2006), "The JDP appears to have calculated that the [General Staff] would use the NSC meeting to issue a public recommendation to Parliament to pass the motion and allow the government to shift the responsibility for the U.S. troop deployment onto the military. But Özkök declined to insist on any reference to the motion in the communiqué issued at the end of the meeting" (Jenkins 2006, 196). When the motion passed by 264 to 250 with nineteen abstentions "[t]he result was a humiliation for the government but was greeted with elation by most of the Turkish public, and with angry dismay by Washington" (Jenkins 2006, 197). Conservative Generals in the General Staff openly complained that Özkök should have been more assertive, as they were concerned about the fallout affecting defense procurement from the United States, Turkey's largest supplier of weapons and military equipment (Jenkins 2006, 197).

The second issue concerned the headscarf ban, specifically that women could not wear headscarves in schools and government buildings. On April 23, 2003, the General Staff boycotted a reception held by Bülent Arinc to celebrate National Sovereignty and Children's Day "when it learned that it would be co-hosted by his headscarved wife" (Jenkins 2006, 197). At the NSC meeting on April 30, 2003, the General Staff "stepped up the pressure on the government, accusing it of trying to foster links with what it described as 'fundamentalist organizations' amongst the Turkish diaspora in Europe" by stressing that it was doing so to protect secularism (Jenkins 2006, 197). Ultimately, the government was unwilling to confront the generals directly and Jenkins (2006) notes, "JDP leaders, such as Erdogan and Gül, adopted a compromise policy of taking their headscarved wives with them when they traveled abroad on official trips, but pointedly leaving them at home when they attended official functions inside Turkey" (198).

Nevertheless, there are still a number of generals who believed that the AKP was attempting to erode Kemalism gradually. From 2002 to 2004, Özkök attempted to resist the influence of the conservative generals to intervene more overtly. However, in 2007, with the AKP's resounding victory and the election of Abdullah Gül as president, "the Kemalist establishment reacted viscerally" (Nasr 2009, 248). The chief of the general staff during this period was General Yasar Büyükant. Many conservatives favored General Büyükant (chief of staff, 2006–2009) hoping he would reverse the progressive momentum initiated by his predecessor Özkök (Aydinli 2009, 591). In fact, the dispute over the AKP's encroachment upon secularism drew up to one million people at an anti-government rally in Istanbul (Spiegel, 4/30/2007).

Shortly thereafter, on April 27, 2007, General Büyükant issued an "e-ultimatum" on the army's webpage on behalf of the NSC stating: "'Arguments over secularism are becoming a focus during the presidential election process and the Turkish armed forces are following the situation with concern. It must not be forgotten that the armed forces are the determined defenders of secularism'" (Aydinli 2009, 591; Spiegel, 4/30/2007). While initially many were unsure of whom within the General Staff wrote the memo; upon the end of his tenure, Büyükant stated, "I myself wrote this. . . . It was Friday evening and I personally wrote it. The April (2007) declaration puts emphasis on the Turkish armed forces' sensitivity toward secularism'" (Reuters, 5/8/2009).

After several court challenges, the AKP government called elections in July 2007, which produced an overwhelming victory for the AKP and on August 28, 2007, Gül was elected president (Reuters, 5/8/2009). Throughout the campaign, the AKP campaigned on their success in managing the economy and focus on Turkey's prosperity and sound governance instead of Islam and secularism (Nasr 2009, 249). Subsequently, in 2008, Turkey's Constitutional Court fined the AKP for anti-secular activities, which Büyükant said justified the military's position (Reuters, 5/8/2009). Therefore, the army maintained its position on the headscarf ban, but agreed to work with the president "whose legitimacy was 'unquestionable'" (Aydinli 2009, 591). However, not all conservatives were comfortable with this position taken by Büyükant and the NSC. An ultra-nationalist group, Ergenekon, which consisted of writers, members of civil society organizations, and former military officers, was indicted for plotting a coup against the AKP government. Eighty-six people were charged in April 2010 after the arrests of retired generals, Sener Eruygur and Hursit

Tolon, uncovered a cache of weapons, explosives and illegal documents in these officers' homes (Arsu, 7/15/2008). The military has continually sought to distance itself from the Ergenekon group.

Under General Büyükant's successor, General Ilker Basbug cooperation with the justice system continued. Overall, the military leadership "is growing more consolidated within a progressive agenda, and . . . the conservative argument is losing its centrality . . . [as] the attitudes and actions of these three generals...reveal their dissociation from the conservative discourse and their proactive efforts to help remove the remaining agents of securitization which have provided a vital infrastructure for the military's conservative figures" (Aydinli 2009, 594).

General Basbug was Chief of the General Staff from August 2008-August 2010 and in his speeches he "stressed that the priority of the Turkish Armed Forces was the 'fight against terrorism,' a sign that the military would be prioritizing its 'regular,' externally oriented military mission, and nothing else" (Aydinli 2009, 593). In effect, Basburg and the military leadership, were concerned with the military's relationship with society. Basburg stated that the military would only express its views through the NSC and reiterated that the military's power derived from soft power rather than hard power: "'The Turkish military is not getting its power from its weapons but from the Turkish society's love and trust in its armed forces'" (Aydinli 2009, 593). Nevertheless, Basbug would be arrested in 2012 as part of the Ergenekon case, but was later released in 2014 after the Turkish Court found that his rights had been violated (Hurryiet, 3/7/14).

Turkey's civil–military relationship cannot be understood without "understanding the dynamics of the Turkish societal instincts such as its deep fears of (in)security and disorder, which are at the core of its existential bond with the army" (Aydinli 2009, 595). Consequently, Turkish military officers benefit from Turkey's amalgam of democratic practices and quasi-democratic institutions. For the officers and their civilian allies, this seeming convergence between principle and practice helps to reinforce the legitimacy of the regime. According to Cook (2007), "[T]he officers use Turkey's pseudodemocratic institutions to insulate themselves from politics. . . . [T]he pseudo-democratic institutions give the military the respect and admiration of large majorites of the Turkish people. Although the officers are responsible for the political order, the presence of institutions resembling a democratic polity effectively shields them from public dissatisfaction" (105).

While the military has been the guarantor of the nation, in recent years, as the AKP consolidated its position in government, the military's influence waned. There are both domestic and international factors impacting the military's influence. First, the AKP's consolidation of power as a single party government allowed AKP's use of the Turkish legal system to amend the functions and powers of the military vis-à-vis the government. In particular, by the AKP's second term in office, the role of the NSC was curtailed by abolishing the Protocol on Cooperation for Security and Public Order (EMAYSA) in January 2010 and putting a constitutional reform referendum on the ballot in September 2010, giving civilians increased power to oversee discharges from the military and further restricted the jurisdiction of military courts (Gürsoy 2012, 193–94).

Second, the 2007 "e-ultimatum" against the presidency of Abdullah Gül and the AKP resulted in a period of conflict between civilian and military leaders lasting until 2011, but whose effects are still prevalent in Turkish society. *Ergenekon* and *Balyoz* (Sledgehammer), on one hand, were considered by the government, media groups, and intellectual supporters of the AKP, as a crucial moment in Turkish history since it brought coup plotters to justice and contributed to the democratization of Turkish civil–military relations. While, on the other hand, the government opposition, believed the cases "rested on shaky, even sometimes planted, evidence" and were used as "mechanisms for the government to eliminate its political rivals and to create a more authoritarian environment in which the media and intellectuals would be afraid to freely voice their opinions" (Gürsoy 2012, 194–95).

Third, NGOs and interest groups have increased their role in politics. The presence of civil society in Turkey allows for groups such as the Turkish Industrialists' and Businessmen's Association (TÜSIAD) and the Chambers of Commerce (TOBB) to advocate for the economy to be considered more fully in discussions of national security (Kaya 2011, 7). The increased presence of civil society in Turkey stems from Turkey's effort to become a full member of the EU. By achieving candidate status in 2005, the AKP achieved reforms which improved Turkish hegemony within the Middle East; namely, Turkish economic growth has averaged 5 percent, inflation tamed, and the army brought under greater civilian control with the military chain of command going through the prime minister's office instead of the defense minister (as in every other NATO country) (Kaya 2011, 3; The Economist 8/16/14). Even the military recognizes the importance the economy plays in Turkey's future, as Chief of the General Staff Isik Kosaner mentioned upon taking office in 2010: "'The concept of security is expanding from one being based solely on defending the country's territory to one being based on economic, diplomatic, cultural and technological aspects" (Kaya 2011, 8–9).

However, with the presidential election of August 10, 2014, Erdogan became Turkey's first popularly elected president after winning 52 percent of the vote (The Economist, 8/30/14). Historically, the presidency is a ceremonial role, but Erdogan declared the "start of a new era" to capitalize on his popularity among his base in rural parts of Turkey. If the AKP wins two-thirds of parliamentary seats, Erdogan has said he would seek to rewrite the constitution to enhance the executive powers of the presidency (BBC News, 9/10/14). The AKP would need another party's votes to achieve this objective and, if he were to secure such a deal, an enhanced presidency could allow Erdogan to stay in power beyond 2023, which is the 100th anniversary of Ataturk's republic (The Economist, 8/16/14).

In the summer 2015 parliamentary elections, the AKP won 258 seats, below the 276 seats necessary to form a single-party government. The CHP, Nationalist Movement Party (MHP) and the People's Democracy Party (HDP) won 132, 81, and 79 seats, respectively (Uras, 6/7/15). The elections were held at a time of increasing anxiety for the Turkish public after violence in Southeastern Turkey between PKK militants and the Turkish military in addition to suicide bombings in Ankara and along the Turkish-Syrian border, which the government said is linked to ISIS militants (BBC News, 11/2/15). Consequently, given the increased militancy, Erdogan called new parliamentary elections for November 2015. The AKP regained its parliamentary majority after winning 49.4 percent of the vote or 316 seats. The AKP's opponents said the vote was a "chance to curb what it sees as the increasingly authoritarian tendencies of Mr. Erdogan" (BBC News, 11/2/15).

The AKP, since 2002, has used the legal system to increase government's ability to control the army and cow political opposition. Most recently, there have been charges of corruption against him, which resulted in Erdgoan taking firmer control of the judiciary and responding to criticism, such as last summer's Gezi Park protests, with assaults on free media, on individual journalists, and the censoring of the Internet (The Economist, 8/16/04). The next few years will be important for Turkey, as it is caught in a "'middle-income trap.'" according to The Economist, "losing competitveness in the basic goods it produces, but unable to move up to higher-tech ones" (The Economist, 8/16/14). Therefore, Turkish civil–military relations will be influenced by economic forces and how Erdogan and the AKP respond: "To keep growing, Turkey needs both liberalizing reforms and foreign capital. Mr. Erdogan has shown scant interest in reform. And although foreign investors stomach autocratic regimes around the world, they don't much care for social instability of the sort that Mr. Erdogan's type of polarizing politics usually portends" (The Economist, 8/16/14).

## REGIONAL AND INTERNATIONAL RELATIONS

Turkey's geographical position straddling both Europe and the Middle East make it an important state for geostrategic reasons. At the end of World War II, Turkey allied with Britain, France, and the United States and over the next several years participated in the establishment of the Council of Europe, became a full member of NATO, became an associate member of the European Common Market, and participated in the General Agreement on Tariffs and Trade (GATT) and the World Trade Organization (WTO) (Eder 2014, 861). These multilateral institutions were designed during the Cold War to balance the power of the Soviet Union. In fact, during the Cold War, one of the most important relationships Turkey had was with the United States. Below, this section will detail the Turkish-U.S. relationship and then discuss issues of regional and international concern for Turkey affecting Turkish civil–military relations. The issues discussed will be: the Turkish-U.S. strategic partnership/foreign aid, the influence of the EU, and Turkey as a regional power.

The Turkish-U.S. relationship dates back to the creation of NATO in 1952. As part of the United States's containment policy toward the Soviet Union, Turkey received extensive economic and military aid. 80 percent of its arms and defense-related purchases were from the US (Eder 2014, 862). In addition, over the years the US has $5 billion worth of FDI in Turkey's banking and manufacturing sectors (Eder 2014, 862). By the 1960s, Turkey experienced rapid industrialization and international economic development, which Esposito, Sonn and Voll (2016) say incited left-wing politics and "increased fears of a communist threat, contributing to the reassertion of Islam in Turkish politics" and Turkey being one of the largest recipients in the Middle East of foreign aid by the end of the Cold War (30; Eder 2014, 861).

Before the end of the Cold War, though, the Turkish-U.S. relationship was tested as a result of the Cuban Missile Crisis and the United States banning the use of its weapons, and imposing an arms embargo after the Turkish invasion of Cyprus. Although, the overthrow of the Iranian shah and the Soviet invasion of Afghanistan would bring reconciliation. Under Özal, Turkey signed a defense and economic cooperation agreement with the United States and on April 14, 1987, Özal applied for membership in the European Community (EC).

The EC report, which came out at the end of 1989, and adopted by the EC Council of Ministers, advised that neither party was ready for EC membership stressing the problems of the Turkish economy (inflation, unemployment, structural differences, etc.) and the political problems (human rights, problems of democracy, unresolved issues with Greece) (Aksin 2007, 292–93). Aksin (2007) notes, "The sheer size of Turkey and the great cultural and religious differences from the European norm which it represented also probably played an important part in the European decision" (293). Instead, Turkey would be allowed to take part in a custom union to establish further economic ties with Europe.

Not to be deterred, after Saddam Hussein invaded Kuwait, Özal "hoped that Turkey's willing participation in the United States-led coalition would strengthen the country's image abroad as a crucial ally, a particular concern in the post-Cold War world" (Glazer 1996, 65). The government authorized the use of Incirlik air base for the bombing campaign against Iraq and deployed troops along the Turkish-Iraqi border.

Glazer (1996) notes that after the Persian Gulf War, "The Turkish government was unable or unwilling to permit several hundred thousand refugees to enter the country. The coalition allies, together with Turkey, proposed the creation of a 'security zone' in northern Iraq. By mid-May 1991, some 200,000 Kurdish refugees had been persuaded to return to Iraq" (65–66).

The collapse of the Soviet Union and its East European bloc was significant for Turkish foreign policy. As Aksin (2007) adroitly states, "In the first place it freed the Turkish psyche from an almost pathological obsession, the danger of Communism, which had been the result of intense internal and external 'cultivation.' In the second place, it opened up the perspective of warm and mutually beneficial relations with Russia in all areas. Thirdly, it opened the door of close cooperation with the Turkic Republics of the former Soviet Union" (293). Essentially, the end of the Cold War would force Turkey to alter its defense planning. Hale (1994) notes, "Previous defense planning had been based on the maintenance of very large conventional forces in the First and Third Armies, which had been designed to block any attempt by the Warsaw Pact to take over the straits or eastern Anatolia, and hence the Middle East" (293). The United States and Turkey were both aware of Turkey's strategic position next to areas of potential and actual conflict—the Balkans, Central Asia, and the Middle East. Therefore, Turkey participated in the Conference of Security and Cooperation in Europe and agreed to reduce the number of conventional forces facing the Warsaw Pact. However, Turkey was given leeway on troop reductions due to its strategic position in the Middle East. The border with Syria and Iraq was excluded from the troop reductions given the nature of the PKK threat (Hale 1994, 293).

The Kurdish problem intensified throughout the 1990s. More specifically, the PKK continued to mount attacks forcing the Turkish army to undertake a classic counterinsurgency against the group (Zürcher 1997, 326). As mentioned earlier, the PKK fled into northern Iraq and were conducting operations across the border, resulting in continuous operations to rout out PKK guerillas. To cut the PKK off from its bases, a scorched earth policy was used and the battle regularly flowed over the border into Iraq (Zürcher 1997, 326–27). In a sense, the continued conflict with the PKK and the Kurds as an ethnic community in Turkey can best be explained by the fact that the "Kurds' status in Turkey's (national) political community always has been ambiguous" (Yegen 2009, 597).

Yegen (2009) defines this ambiguity as a result of several factors: "First, legal citizenship as a formal status has never been the sole marker of Turkishness in Turkey. . . . Secondly, Turkish citizenship itself has not been a firm category. Instead . . . Turkish citizenship has, from the beginning of the Republic, oscillated between an ethnic and a political definition of the (Turkish) nation" (597). Therefore, the ambiguity of the Kurds is a result of the main actors of the Turkish state—the army, bureaucracy, bourgeoisie, mainstream political parties, and mainstream media—continually shifting their image of the Kurds depending on the times (Yegen 2009).

The continuing conflict with the Kurds had a direct bearing on Turkey's relationship with the EU. Specifically, many in Europe began questioning Turkey's human rights record. Turkey had applied for membership in April 1987, but was only offered membership in a customs union instead of full membership. For Turkey, "This unique construction was seen . . . as the next step towards full membership, but in the eyes of the Europeans it was really a consolation prize, although all European politicians took care not to say so openly to the Turks" (Zürcher 1997, 331). Moreover, the trial of Kurdish parliamentarians in Turkey whose parties were banned from parliament caught the attention of the European parliament, and shone a light on Turkey's human rights records. In October 1994, the Council of Europe started exclusion proceedings against Turkey and suspended negotiations over the customs union until March 1995 with ratification by the European parliament dependent upon further political liberalization (Zürcher 1997, 331). After constitutional changes the EU Customs Union treaty was signed, but it took lobbying from the United States on behalf of the Turks that the Customs Union "would anchor Turkey firmly in Europe and prevent the 'fundamentalists' from gaining power" (Zürcher 1997, 33).

While anchoring Turkey in Europe, Özal also had his eye on the Middle East. More specifically, according to Mine Eder (2014), "Turgut Özal started the transformation of Turkey's foreign policy toward the Middle East in the 1980s and early 1990s, emphasizing economic ties, trade, and relationships by playing a positive role in the return of Egypt to the OIC [Organization of Islamic Countries], in which Turkey became very active" (863). Additionally, Turkey signed military and industrial agreements with Israel and Turkey becoming "one of the few countries in the region that had close contacts with both Israel and the Arab world" (Eder 2014, 863).

The AKP's election in 2002 saw the ascendence of a party committed to a social contract based on the principles of democracy, human rights, social justice and underlying ethical and moral principles (Esposito, et al. 2016, 37). As Esposito, Sonn and Voll (2016) note, "This engendered a worldview that was built on the overlap of tradition and modernity. . . . The result was a hybrid party identity—simultaneously Turkish, Muslim, and Western" (38).

Under the AKP, Turkey sought more regional influence in the Middle East. In its early years, the Erdogan government sought closer relations with Iraq and to play the role of mediator between Israel and the Palestinian Authority and Syria. However, the May 2010 Mavi Marmara flotilla affair, "where nine aid workers heading to Israeli-blocked Gaza were killed by Israeli naval commandos," led to criticisms from Erdogan of the

Israeli operation and an increase in his popularity throughout the Arab world (Eder 2014, 863). Also, since the Arab Spring in 2011, Turkey's foreign policy strategy was called "zero problems with neighbors" and used "democracy promotion, Islamic solidarity, and intensification of economic relations" to increase influence throughout the Middle East (Eder 2014, 863).

Nevertheless, the Syrian Civil War and subsequent refugee crisis will impact the future of the region. Turkey, which has been held up as an example of successful democratization and democratic consolidation in the Middle East, has recently seen backsliding with Erdogan's responses to domestic opposition from the Ergenkon case and Gezi protests, as well as the crackdown following the failed coup of July 15, 2016. Therefore, Turkey's democratic future "is dependent on fostering a more pluralist political culture and values of power sharing, preserving a meaningful system of checks and balances, and strengthening institutional safeguards of checks and balances as well as freedoms that enable the public to protest and . . . express their discontent without fear of suppression of rights" (Esposito et al. 2016, 49).

## CONCLUSION

The Turkish Armed Forces are the defenders of the Kemalist flame. Since Turkey's founding in 1920, the military has intervened four times when the officers felt politicians were straying from Kemalism, specifically secularism. Despite their disdain for politicians, the military preferred to stay out of the day to day operations of government and wanted to be involved only as long as necessary to establish a "clean slate" and hold elections. Essentially, the military is seen as the ultimate guarantor of the nation by Turkish society.

The military's relationship with Turkish society weighed heavily on each decision to intervene. The reverse of that decision, the withdrawal of the military, and return to electoral democracy, was influenced in later years by the West, specifically the EU accession process and the "paradigmatic divide" that has developed in the officer corps between conservative generals who were strident defenders of Kemalism and progressive generals who were more open to the ongoing transformation and modernization occurring in Turkey. Since the AKP's electoral victory in 2002, the military has kept a watchful eye on the government fearful that its Islamist roots were harmful to the Kemalist order established by Atatürk.

However, the progressive generals have grown confident in the NSC and the democratic institutions and processes in place. As the AKP's popularity has grown, the likelihood of future military interventions in Turkey has waned; namely, because the military cannot be seen ceding the label of modernizer of the nation to the Islamists. Thus, Turkey's civil–military relations has matured to allow for some civilian control, due to the influence of the West, but the military will continue to be an institutional check on the power of government. As Esposito, Sonn and Voll (2016) point out, "[T]he military, secular elites, and other opposition are challenged to accept the role of a 'loyal opposition' and not use political differences and discontent as an excuse to topple a democratically elected government through military intervention or violence rather than through the electoral process" (49). Turkey developed in the shadow of the Cold War influenced by the West, but is now confronted with the challenges of the East. How Turkey responds to the political, ideological and cultural challenges will be a bellwether for how other Middle Eastern states confront similar challenges.

# SIX
## Conclusion

This study of military interventions and withdrawals serves as a useful starting point for understanding the endurance of authoritarianism in the Middle East and South Asia. More specifically, the Algerian, Egyptian, Pakistani, and Turkish militaries were the strongest institution at the birth of the nation. Throughout Algerian, Egyptian, Pakistani, and Turkish history, there were severe socioeconomic problems and contradictions, internal conflicts, war, and international influence. These factors necessitated the militaries coming to the defense of the nation and protecting their interests from politicians.

This chapter will compare and contrast the similarities and differences in civil–military relations of the Middle East and South Asia and offer implications for democracy in the Middle East and South Asia. Since the Arab Spring, the Middle East witnessed increased activity within civil society in the form of protests against authoritarianism in the region. In fact, what we see in the Middle East and South Asia today are authoritarian-democratic hybrids (Stepan and Linz 2014; Rutherford 2014). Ultimately, the success or failure of democratic transitions and consolidation in the Middle East can be determined by a civil–military relations framework described below.

### COMPARING MILITARY INTERVENTIONS AND WITHDRAWALS

At the start, two questions drove this study: Why do militaries intervene in politics; and what factors are necessary for the military to "return to the barracks"? Algeria, Egypt, Pakistan, and Turkey offer four of the most recent cases of military intervention and withdrawal from politics. Therefore, taking the cases of Algeria, Egypt, Pakistan, and Turkey as a whole, this study has shown that within the Middle East and South Asia one can argue that militaries intervene in politics because of the conflict that is present throughout history between political elites and the military, inter-party conflict among elites, inter-military conflict among officers, and conflict between military/political elites and internal societal actors.

Algeria, a state with a strongly egalitarian, nationalist people, has been in conflict for much of its existence since the end of colonialism. At that point, the political system was defined by clan politics, as the ALN, FLN and FIS were subsumed in interclan rivalry. These rivalries started within the FLN during the war of independence and continued within the ANP as well.

After the war, there were two groups within the military, the "old guard," who were members of the interior ALN, and an "external group" of officers who were based during the war in Tunisia and Morocco. These officers came from various clans around the state and were led by Ben Bella and Boumedienne, respectively. Ben Bella became president with the support of Boumedienne, but this support was short lived. Conflict abounded between politicians within the FLN and between the military and politicians. Ben Bella would spend three years prior to Boumedienne's coup pitting factions against one another to attempt to hold on to power. Subsequently, the military intervened in 1965, when Boumedienne felt that Ben Bella's government was interfering with the professional development and control of the army.

Once in power, Boumedienne consolidated his hold on power by placing members of his Oujda clan in the bureaucracy to help in the political administration of the country. Boumedienne used socialism and support from the Soviet Union to win acquiescence from the population with the promotion of rapid development and the creation of a strong industrial base. This top-down modernization resulted in new industries and an increase in literacy, but by the 1980s, Algeria witnessed a new generation born after the war of independence begin to come of age.

As with any youth bulge, and especially one within a Middle Eastern society, there was dissatisfaction with the one-party rule established by Boumedienne and the generals that succeeded him. In Algeria, conflict against the regime came from two ideological movements: the communists (including Berber identity movements) and Islamists, most notably the FIS. As such, from the 1970s through today, conflict between these groups and conflict directed toward the military regime have been ever present.

After Boumedienne's death in 1978, the Military High Command continually put forth its preferred candidate for the presidency. With Chadli in office, the military withdrew from the day-to-day running of the country and would hold elections to appeal to societal pressure. A combination of violence, a deteriorating economy, and the emergence of the Islamists forced the ANP to cancel the second round of parliamentary elections in 1992 after the FIS victory. The army would then be caught in the middle of a vicious civil war. During this period, while conflict raged across the country, a younger group of officers was coming of age and attempted to influence the direction of the country. The conflict between the "eradicators" and "concilators" concerned how best to deal with Islamism. The eradicators favored all-out repression of political Islam, while the conciliators sought a political solution based on compromise.

As part of the negotiations undertaken by the conciliators under General Zeroual, who became president, the High Security Council was established to allow the military to influence Algeria's return to electoral politics. A new constitution was written which reinforced the military's role in the political process through the High Security Council, a strong presidency, and the creation of a political party, the National Rally for Democracy, to counter the influence of the FLN and FIS. As a result, Algeria's president has been the ANP's man.

President Bouteflika, Algeria's current president, has been in power since 1999 and the longevity of his reign is due in part to economic support received from the West, specifically the IMF and the United States. Algeria is a major supplier of oil and natural gas to the international community, and the instability currently present is a direct result of the Bouteflika regime siphoning profits and fuels the discontent Islamists, who are now part of AQMI, have toward the regime and contributing to the military's need to maintain its role in government, albeit from behind the scenes.

In Egypt, on July 1, 2013, Egyptian President Mohamad Morsi was given forty-eight hours to resign after months of violence engulfed Egypt. The coup by Field Marshal Abdel Fattah al-Sisi was the culmination of a year of conflict between the Egyptian military and the Muslim Brotherhood and its political party—the Freedom and Justice Party. Conflict between the military and politicians effectively began after the momentous events of January 2011. The Egyptian military formed an institution, the Supreme Council of the Armed Forces (SCAF), to guide Egypt's transition to democracy; however, once the Muslim Brotherhood (MB) won and Morsi took office, Morsi appointed MB loyalists and replaced the head of the SCAF Field Marshal Mohammed Tantawi with a pious Muslim general whom Morsi felt would assist in Morsi's Islamist agenda for Egypt.

As protests increased throughout the country and Morsi excluded his political opponents, the Egyptian military, as defender of Egyptian nationalism, stepped in. Al-Sisi's election as president in May 2014 saw an increase in conflict between the state and its political opponents; namely, the Muslim Brotherhood. While it can be argued that the democratic transition is still ongoing in Egypt, al-Sisi's election as president portends not further democratization but an endurance of authoritarianism. History, conflict between politicians and the military, and external support from international actors such as the United States, Soviet Union or IMF assisted the Egyptian military in consolidating its influence in the country.

In Pakistan, conflict was present from the outset. The death of Jinnah, left the political elites without their leader and the forceful personality needed to help build the compromise needed between the various ethnic and sectarian groups within the new Pakistani state. The military, the state's strongest institution, intervened after ethnic and sectarian violence was engulfing multiple provinces and the politicians were unable to quell this violence. This produced the five-step dance where the military warns "incompetent" politicians that they are encroaching on the military's institutional and elite self-interests, a crisis occurs resulting in the intervention, followed by the military junta introducing constitutional changes to "straighten out" Pakistan. This occurred in 1958, 1969, 1977, and 1999.

Once the military is satisfied that their interests will not be encroached upon they will withdraw from politics. However, in Pakistan, political elites were in constant conflict with one another as well as the military. When the military would withdraw, politicians in the PPP and PML attempted reforms to try and improve their position vis-à-vis the military, even encroaching on policy issues perceived as vital to military institutional and elite self-interest. This occurred three times: 1956–1958, 1988–1999, and 2008–Present.

Most importantly, both politicians and the military sought to manage Islamism, which sprang up as a result of political and economic policies of the various military and political regimes. Each regime used Islam in its attempts to nation-build, but it must be noted, that the use of Islam was not used for the benefit of the Pakistani people; instead the military protected its interests. Consequently, the Pakistani people have suffered. The state is in a continuing battle with religious extremist groups, which at various times throughout its history, were used in ideological struggles against communism and now Salafism. Pakistan's geostrategic position between the Middle East and South Asia make it an important frontline state and the recipient of huge sums of economic and military assistance from the United States. Thus, as the battle against Al-Qaeda and the Pakistani Taliban continues, and with the U.S. war in Afghanistan winding down, the Pakistani military will continue to influence politics, as each of these are vital military interests that threaten the security of the Pakistani state.

Turkey, under the leadership of Atatürk, implemented a top-down modernization through an ideology known as Kemalism. Through the promotion of secularism and assimilationaist nationalism, the Turkish military were the guardians of Kemalism and Atatürk's legacy. Since the founding of the Republic, the military has intervened four times when the General Staff, and even a group of junior officers, felt the politicians were straying from Kemalism.

As part of Kemalism, Turkey moved toward a multi-party democracy with the influence of the international community, specifically the United States and NATO. The end of World War II and Marshall Plan funds helped influence Inönü to continue multi-party politics and moved the military's focus to a conflict between the left and right on the political spectrum—socialism and Islamism. Despite a disdain for politicians, whom the military viewed as corrupt and a threat to the secular, Kemalist order, the military preferred to be removed from the day-to-day operations of government and only remained involved as long as necessary to establish a "clean slate" and hold elections. Each time, the military was conscious of how the intervention would be perceived by Turkish society.

Therefore, the military established institutions, such as the National Security Council to provide input to politicians, but there was also a tremendous amount of influence from the West. Both the military and politicians were mindful of the benefit EU membership would have on Turkey. Since the last intervention in 1997, there has been a "paradigmatic divide" between conservative generals who sought to protect Kemalism and more reform-minded generals who embraced the transformation and modernization occurring in Turkey. More importantly, the AKP's victories in 2002 and 2007 demonstrate a unique situation; namely, that Islamist political elites' established a compromise to work with the reformist generals, whom had installed institutions that would protect their interests. The military cannot be seen as ceding the label of modernizer to the Islamists, so for the foreseeable future, the military will continue to be an institutional check on the power of government.

## IMPLICATIONS FOR POLICY: MILITARIES AS DEMOCRATIZERS?

Scholars such as Janowitz (1977), Nordlinger (1979), Welch (1980) and Hale (1994) developed descriptive typologies defining the characteristics of military rule, however there has been a lack of literature on how these military regimes could move away from military rule and toward civilian rule. A civil–military relationship in the Western sense, as defined by Huntington (1957), is still years away. It is important to remember that states in the Global North developed their civil–military relationships, in some cases, over hundreds of years. In the case of the Middle East and South Asia, the political development of Algeria, Egypt, Pakistan, and Turkey's civil–military relationships are still in their infancy—at fifty-four, sixty-eight, sixty-nine, and ninety-three years, respectively. Therefore, this study is a first step at understanding the international and domestic factors influencing conflict between various individuals and institutions in the Middle East and South Asia that will continue to impact the future of nation-building in the Islamic World.

What will democratization look like in a post-Arab Spring Islamic world? Democracy includes participation and contestation with all citizens having equal access to the political process and certain issues being decided through competition (Dahl 1971). However, in the Middle East, Quandt (1998) argues "While democratization is still a debatable concept in much of the Arab world, most analysts would agree that a substantial degree of liberalization has taken place. . . . The crucial question is whether these measures are an important component of the democratization process, or whether they may become a substitute for it" (154). The cases of Algeria, Egypt, Pakistan and Turkey are symbolic of similar trajectories taken by states in the Middle East and South Asia. There is a history of colonialism, the creation of institutions, conflict both internal and external, the influence of the international community, a youth bulge which leads to a demand for change, a political opening, and conflict between politicians and the military to defend their interests. In short, democratization in the Middle East will be an incremental process where, because of history, militaries, and elites will protect their positions in society. These causes of the endurance of authoritarianism allow us to begin thinking about what factors will be necessary for a transition to and consolidation of democracy.

Historically, democratic transitions in the Middle East have been influenced by colonialism's role in the development of the state. In Egypt with the British and in Algeria with the French, the military was established as the strongest institution in the state. Accordingly, both societies viewed service in the military as a means for upward mobility. As anticolonial nationalism became an ideological force in both states, the Free Officers overthrew King Farouk in July 1952 and the FLN and ALN fought a war to end French colonialism. In both cases, the result was the creation of authoritarian regimes with militaries as their guarantor.

As the Egyptian and Algerian states developed throughout the Cold War and the post-9/11 era, the militaries of each state were influenced by foreign economic and military aid from the Soviet Union and the United States. Nasser and Boumedienne used socialism and support from the Soviet Union to win acquiescence from the population with the promotion of rapid development and the creation of a strong industrial base. This top-down modernization resulted in new industries and an increase in literacy, but by the 1970s in Egypt and the 1980s in Algeria, their economies could not keep up and both states relied on policies that gradually opened up their economies to western aid from the IMF. For Egypt and Algeria, as with any developing state receiving loans from the IMF, the state must: reduce their budget deficit, remove subsidies, float the exchange rate, raise interest rates, and eventually privatize some of the state-owned industries (Quandt 1998, 153). Although, with the continued receipt of loans from the West, military run industries were often exempt from privatizing and resulted in an increase in corruption and the continuation of cronyism by senior military officers (Yildirium 2013, 61). In effect, this entwined the state's economy as part of the military's interests moving forward. The international support of the Soviet Union, United States, and IMF provided support for authoritarian regimes, but the Egyptian, Algerian, Pakistani and Turkish state did not make this largesse available to their respective societies.

Consequently, opposition movements and later political parties sprang up to challenge state authority. In Egypt, this movement was the Muslim Brotherhood and in Algeria, the FIS, GIA, and smaller Berber movements, in Pakistan it was the JI and Pakistan Taliban, and in Turkey, the WP, AKP, and most recently the Gülen Movement. These states' histories are replete with periods of accommodation and repression toward these actors. For the purposes of our discussion surrounding democratic transitions, both the Muslim Brotherhood and FIS used strikes and protests to call attention to the deteriorating economic situation for ordinary Egyptians and Algerians. Moreover, during the late 1980s and early 1990s in Algeria and from 2011 to 2013 in Egypt a generational shift was occurring both within society but, more importantly, within the military. The significance defined the transition process for Algeria and appears to be doing the same at present in Egypt.

The result of this new youth generation coming of age was dissatisfaction with one party rule and with the deteriorating economy in both Algeria and Egypt the timing was ripe for a political opening. In Algeria, this opening was the Black October Riots of 1988 that forced Chadli to end one party rule and accede to multi-party elections, while in Egypt the Arab Spring brought about the overthrow of the Mubarak regime and the election of Morsi. The result for both Algeria and Egypt were rocky democratic transitions. This rockiness stems from political leaders' "internecine fighting, disagreements, and resoluteness" (Gerbaudo 2013, 110). Both the Algerian and Egyptian militaries used conflict between politicians to step in and protect the interests of the regime, with a military leader attempting to fill the leadership vacuum—Nezzar in Algeria against the FIS and al-Sisi against Morsi in 2013. The result in Algeria was continued fighting between politicians and the military, but also an increase in terrorism from excluded groups, which led to a civil war.

In Egypt, al-Sisi banned the Muslim Brotherhood from politics due to Morsi's ideological and authoritarian policies against the institutions of the state. Violence increased throughout Egypt since Morsi's overthrow in July 2013. Also, the absence of secular political forces and weakness of the labor movement in Egypt allowed for youth subcultures to develop that al-Sisi has used to portray himself as the savior of the nation. The effect of this on the success or failure of democratization in the long run for Egypt is aptly stated by Paulo Gerbaudo (2013): "[W]hen people refuse to engage with the state, the space they thereby vacate offers an opportunity for the state's worst autocratic tendencies" (112). In short, the military has sought to occupy this space in Egypt to "guide" the democratic transition.

If the military will guide democratic transitions for the foreseeable future in the Middle East and South Asia, how will this affect their relationship with politicians and civil society? In their study on the transitions from authoritarian rule in Latin America, Guillermo O'Donnell and Philippe C. Schmitter (1986) argue that for the military to cede control and move toward a western civil–military relationship, "they must somehow be induced to modify their messianic self-image; they must be given a creditable and honorable role in accomplishing (but not setting) national goals; and they must be made more impervious to the enticements of civilian politicians who turn to them when frustrated in the advancement of their interests by democratic means" (32). A useful analogy to describe the transition process is that of a multi-layered chessboard where the property rights of the bourgeoise must be protected and leftist parties (or rightist parties in the case of the Middle East and South Asia) must accept playing the central part of the board. Furthermore, players must be compelled to compete for spaces and pieces rather than trying to elimate opposing players, since the players may not have attained consensus on democratic values and must respect the rules emerging from the game (O'Donnell and Schmitter 1986, 69).

Indonesia's transition post-Soeharto offers lessons that are applicable vis-à-vis states in the Middle East and South Asia. In "Successful and Failed Democratic Transitions from Military Rule in Majority Muslim Societies," Marcus Mietzner (2014), describes the similarities between Indonesia and Egypt: "'[B]oth are nations with large Muslim populations, but significant religious minorities; both traditionally witnessed deep military involvement in politics; both had anti-Western ideologues as presidents in the 1960s and turned into allies of the West in the 1970s; both recorded similar GDP-per capita levels; both saw thirty-year presidencies by increasingly sultanistic ex-generals; and in both countries, these autocracies ended after popular protest and the military's withdrawal of support from their former leaders'" (Mietzner, 436, quoting Brownlee et al 2013, 38). However, after the overthrow of Morsi by al-Sisi, this is when the similarities end. More specifically, Mietzner (2014) argues the dissimilarties in the patterns of authoritarian rule, military organization, intra-civilian conflict and international support create a divergence between the Indonesian and Egyptian cases with Indonesia sidelining its military from politics becoming one of Southeast Asia's most democratic societies, while Egypt regressed to military-backed rule (Mietzner 2014, 448).

These diverging trajectories occurred because of pre-existing institutional structures and legacies as well as the decisions civilian leaders and groups made at various junctures in the transition process (Mietzner 2014, 448). In Egypt the military was excluded by Mubarak from repression, while in Indonesia, Suharto placed the armed forces at the center of repression. This gave the military the upper-hand in the early years of the transition process in Egypt, whereas in Indonesia the military was discredited and forced into reforms, such as the strict imposition of a retirement age of fifty-five. Therefore, Mietzner (2014) argues, "[C]ivilian protest leaders and elites in Indonesia were adamant that the military should not lead the first post-Suharto government—they were not convinced that it was sincerely committed to democracy. In Egypt, on the other hand, civilians—including many critical civil society groups—entrusted the military with the management of the democratic transition, with predictable results" (448).

Furthermore, state-society relations differed in that the Muslim Brotherhood's exclusion from Egyptian politics for many years created a secretive nature and once in power their desire to implement an Islamist agenda threatened military interests, while Indonesia's leading Muslim organizations "had 'softened' through effective regime cooptation" (Mietzner 2014, 448). In other words, since politicians in Indonesia had the upper-hand, they worked through intra-civilian conflict over a four year period to settle on a compromise on the role of Islam in the state and issues of democratic governance, while in Egypt there was a lack of compromise as "neither the MB nor the largely Cairo-based liberal-secular elite were prepared to compromise on their positions: the former rushed a pro-Islamic constitution through formal-legal channels without much consultation, while the latter dragged the military into what should have been an exclusively intracivilian discourse" (Mietzner 2014, 448).

Do repeated confrontations between Islamist parties and militaries of the Middle East and South Asia portend the death knell of democracy? In short, not yet. However, "'the difficulties of shifting from an autocratic to a democratic model for protecting different societal interests will preoccupy the Arab world for the coming decade and beyond'" (Diamond, Plattner and Grubman 2014, xix, quoting Brumberg 2013). Middle Eastern and South Asian militaries intervene in politics to protect their interests, especially when intra-civilian and military-civilian conflict is persistent or threatens military interests.

The influence of the international community through ideological and economic support since the Cold War has strengthened militaries at the expense of the civil. Accordingly, given the continued strategic importance of the Middle East and South Asia for the United States and Russia, Middle East and South Asian civilian and military leaders' decision-making will be made with an eye on how to maximize the benefits of a relationship with the international community. Military withdrawal and a democratic transition were successful if military interests were protected and consensus reached through dialogue, as in the case of Turkey. However, Turkey's history had more than a modicum of secularism, which influenced the military's positioning vis-à-vis politicians. The pull of the EU was strong in the Turkish case. Algerian, Egyptian, and Pakistani political culture, however, has not embraced secularism to the same degree. Therefore, the development of an "Islamic civil–military relations" at this time is not possible, given the varying degrees of political and military institutional strength in Algeria, Egypt, and Pakistan, as well as how the militaries are influenced by an international/regional politics still coming to terms with Islamist politics in the liberal international order.

In conclusion, understanding the process of military intervention and withdrawal is important because democratization and nation-building cannot happen unless one addresses the failure of political institutions. It is this failure that brings the military in on horseback, so to prevent this or, to hasten the return to the barracks, the strengthening of civil society, political institutions and processes is paramount. As Larry Diamond and Marc Plattner (1996) argue, "Above all, military role expansion and military coups are *politically* driven processes; by the same token, the achievement of civilian supremacy over the military must be *politically* led. Military establishments do not seize power from successful and legitimate civilian regimes. They intervene in politics . . . when civilian politicians are weak and divided, and when their divisions and manifest failures of governance have generated a vacuum of authority" (xxix). How this vacuum of authority was created in Algeria, Egypt, Pakistan, and Turkey offers insight into how we might begin to understand not only the role of the military moving forward in the Middle East and South Asia, but what factors will end the endurance of authoritarianism and offer hope for democracy.

# Bibliography

Abbas, Hassan. *Pakistan's Drift into Extremism: Allah, the Army, and America's War on Terror.* (2005).

Addi, Lahouari. "Algeria," in Ellen Lust, ed., *The Middle East,* 13th edn. Thousand Oaks, CA: CQ Press, 2014, 367–95.

Ahmad, Khurshid. "Pakistan: Vision and Reality, Past and Future," *The Muslim World* 96, no. 2. (April 2006): 363–79.

Agüero, Felipe. "Legacies of Transitions: Institutionalization, the Military, and Democracy in South America," *Mershon International Studies Review* 42, (1998): 383–404.

AkParti. Official English Website of Turkey's Justice and Development Party. https://www.akparti.org.tr/english. Accessed May 10, 2016.

Aksin, Sina. *Turkey, From Empire to Revolutionary Republic: The Emergence of the Turkish Nation from 1789 to Present.* New York: New York University Press, 2007.

Albecht, Holger and Dina Bishara. "Back on Horseback: The Military and Political Transformation in Egypt," *Middle East Law and Governance,* 3, (2011): 13–23.

*Al-Jazeera.* "US Suspends F-16 Fighter Jet Delivery to Egypt." July, 24, 2013. http://america.aljazeera.com/articles/2013/7/24/us-suspends-f-16fighterjetdeliverytoegypt.html. Accessed March 15, 2016.

Al-Sisi, Abdel Fattah Gen. "Democracy in the Middle East." Strategy Research Report submitted to the U.S. Army War College. March 15, 2006. https://www.scribd.com/doc/158975076/1878-001. Accessed via Judicial Watch, August 4, 2014.

Amin, Galal. *Egypt in the Age of Hosni Mubarak, 1981–2011.* Cairo: American University in Cairo Press, 2011.

Anderson, Lisa. "Demystifying the Arab Spring: Parsing the Differences Between Tunisia, Egypt, and Libya," in Gideon Rose, ed., *The New Arab Revolt.* New York: Council on Foreign Relations, (May/June 2011): 320–28.

Arsu, Sebnem. "86 Charged in Turkey Coup Plot," *New York Times,* July 15, 2008. http://www.nytimes.com/2008/07/15/world/europe/15turkey.html. Accessed August 15, 2015.

Aydinli, Ersel. "A Paradigmatic Shift for the Turkish Generals and an End to the Coup Era in Turkey," *The Middle East Journal* 63, no. 4 (2009): 581–96.

Banerji, Rana. "Pakistan 2013: Civil–Military Relations." Institute of Peace and Conflict Studies, no. 4245. January 10, 2014. http://www.ipcs.org/article/pakistan/pakistan-2013-civil-military-relations-4245.html. Accessed June 10, 2015.

Barany, Zoltan. *How Armies Respond to Revolutions and Why.* Princeton, NJ: Princeton University Press, 2016.

———. *The Soldier and the Changing State: Building Democratic Armies in Africa, Asia, Europe and the Americas.* Princeton, NJ: Princeton University Press, 2012.

Baxter, Craig. *Pakistan: A Country Study.* Washington, DC: Federal Research Division, Library of Congress, 1995.

BBC News. "Egypt: Abdul Fattah al-Sisi Profile." May 16, 2014. http://www.bbc.com/news/world-middle-east-19256730. Accessed August 10, 2015.

———. "Egypt Army Chief al-Sisi: Room for all in Egypt." August 2013. http://www.bbc.com/news/world-middle-east-23744435. Accessed September 18, 2013.

———. "Egypt election: Sisi secures landslide win." May 29, 2014. http://www.bbc.com/news/world-middle-east-27614776?print=true. Accessed June 20, 2014.

Bellin, Eva. "Reconsidering the Robustness of Authoritarianism in the Middle East: Lessons from the Arab Spring," *Comparative Politics* 44, no. 2 (January 2012): 127–49.

Birand, Mehmet Ali. *Shirts of Steel: An Anatomy of the Turkish Armed Forces*. New York: I.B. Tauris & Co. Ltd., 1991.

———. "The Robustness of Authoritarianism in the Middle East," *Comparative Politics* 36, (January 2004): 139–57.

Bonner, Michael, Megain Reif, and Mark Tessler, eds., *Islam, Democracy and the State in Algeria: Lessons for the Western Mediterranean and Beyond*. New York: Routledge, 2005.

Brooker, Paul. *Non-Democratic Regimes: Theory, Government & Politics*. New York: St. Martin's Press, 2000.

Brownlee, Jason. "The Transnational Challenge to Arab Freedom," *Current History* 110, no. 739 (November 2011): 317–23.

Brownlee, Jason, Tarek Masoud, and Andrew Reynolds. *The Arab Spring: Pathways of Repression and Reform*. Oxford: Oxford University Press, 2015.

———. "Why the Modest Harvest?" in Larry Diamond and Marc Plattner, eds., *Democratization and Authoritarianism in the Arab World*, Baltimore: Johns Hopkins University Press, 2014, 127–41.

Brynen, Rex, Pete W. Moore, Bassel F. Salloukh, and Marie-Jöelle Zahar. *Beyond the Arab Spring: Authoritarianism & Democratization in the Arab World*. Boulder & London: Lynne Rienner Publishers, 2012.

Buhmiller, Elisabeth. "Stability of Egypt Hinges on a Divided Military," *New York Times*. February 5, 2011. http://www.nytimes.com/2011/02/06/world/middleeast/06military.html?_r=2&hp"http://www.nytimes.com/2011/02/06/world/middleeast/06military.html?_r=2&hp. Accessed February 5, 2011.

Capezza, D. "Turkey's Military Is a Catalyst for Reform," *The Middle East Quarterly* XVI, no. 3 (Summer 2009). Retrieved from "http://www.meforum.org/2160/turkey-military-catalyst-for-reform "http://www.meforum.org/2160/turkey-military-catalyst-for-reform.

Chapin Metz, Helen, ed. *Algeria: A Country Study*. Washington, DC: Federal Research Division, Library of Congress, 1993.

Childress, Sarah. "The Deep State: How Egypt's Shadow State Won Out." September 17, 2013. http://www.pbs.org/wgbh/frontline/article/the-deep-state-how-egypts-shadow-state-won-out/. Accessed March 17, 2016.

Cizre, U. "Problems of Democratic Governance of Civil–military Relations in Turkey and the European Union Enlargement Zone," *European Journal Of Political Research* 43, no. 1 (2004): 107–25.

Cloughley, Brian. *War, Coups & Terror: Pakistan's Army in Years of Turmoil*. New York: Skyhorse Publishing, 2008.

Cohen, Stephen Philip. *The Idea of Pakistan*. Washington, DC: Brookings Institution Press, 2004.

———. *The Pakistan Army*. Berkeley, CA: University of California Press, 1984.

Cole, Juan. "Egypt's New Left versus the Military Junta," *Social Research* 79, no. 2 (Summer 2012): 487–510.

———. "Pakistan and Afghanistan: Beyond the Taliban." *Political Science Quarterly* 124, no. 2 (2009): 221–49.

Coll, Steve. *Ghost Wars: The Secret History of the CIA, Afghanistan, and Bin Laden, from the Soviet Invasion to September 10, 2001*. New York: Penguin Books, 2004.

Cook, Steven A. *Ruling But Not Governing: The Military and Political Development in Egypt, Algeria, and Turkey*. Baltimore: Johns Hopkins University Press, 2007.

———. *The Struggle for Egypt: From Nasser to Tahrir Square*. Oxford and New York: Oxford University Press, 2011.

Cottam, Martha L. and Richard W. Cottam. *Nationalism and Politics: The Political Behavior of Nation States*. Boulder, CO: Lynne-Rienner Publishers, 2001.

Diamond, Larry and Marc F. Plattner, eds., *Civil–Military Relations and Democracy*. Baltimore: Johns Hopkins University Press, 1996.

———. *Democratization and Authoritarianism in the Arab World*, Baltimore: Johns Hopkins University Press, 2014.

Diamond, Larry, Marc. F. Plattner, and Nate Grubman. "Introduction," in Larry Diamond and Marc F. Plattner, eds., *Democratization and Authoritarianism in the Arab World*. Baltimore: Johns Hopkins University Press, 2014, viv–xxxiii.

Doran, Michael Scott. "The Heirs of Nasser: Who Will Benefit From the Second Arab Revolution?" in Gideon Rose, ed., *The New Arab Revolt*. New York: Council on Foreign Relations, (May/June 2011): 344–58.

The Economist. "The Turkish Army: Coups Away." February 11, 2010. Accessed April 10, 2014.

———. "Turkey's New Government: Davutoglu's Moment," August 30, 2014. http://www.economist.com/node/21614191/print. Accessed August 20, 2015.

———. "Turkey's President: Erdogan On Top," August 16, 2014. http://www.economist.com/news/leaders/21612154-it-would-be-better-turkey-if-presidency-remained-mainly-ceremonial-erdogan-top"http://www.economist.com/news/leaders/21612154-it-would-be-better-turkey-if-presidency-remained-mainly-ceremonial-erdogan-top. Accessed August 20, 2014.

———. "Turkey's Presidential Elections: The Next Sultan?" August 16, 2014. http://www.economist.com/news/europe/21612237-recep-tayyip-erdogans-plans-presidency-next-sultan"http://www.economist.com/news/europe/21612237-recep-tayyip-erdogans-plans-presidency-next-sultan. Accessed August 20, 2014.

Eder, Mine. "Turkey," in Ellen Lust, ed., *The Middle East*, 13th edn. Thousand Oaks, CA: CQ Press, 2014, 367–95.

Elgindy, Khaled. "Egypt's Troubled Transition: Elections without Democracy," *The Washington Quarterly* 35, no. 2, (Spring 2012): 89–104.

El-Khawas, Mohamed. "Egypt's Unfinished Revolution," *Mediterranean Quarterly* 23, no. 1 (Winter 2012): 52–66.

El Sherif, Ashraf. "Islamism After the Arab Spring," *Current History* 110, no. 740 (December 2011): 358–63.

Entelis, John P., ed., *Islam, Democracy and the State in North Africa*. Bloomington and Indianapolis, IN: Indiana University Press, 1997.

Esposito, John L., Tamara Sonn, and John O. Voll. *Islam and Democracy After The Arab Spring*. Oxford and New York: Oxford University Press, 2016.

Evin, Ahmet. "Changing Patterns of Cleavages Before and After 1980" in Metin Heper and Ahmet Evin, eds., *State, Democracy and the Military: Turkey in the 1980s*. Berlin and New York: Walter De Gruyter, 1988, 201–213.

Fahim, Kareem and Mayy El Sheikh. "Egypt Lifts a Junior Corps Impatient Over Military Failure," *New York Times*. August 13, 2012. http://www.nytimes.com/2012/08/14/world/middleeast/purge-by-morsi-shows-impatience-within-egypts-military.html?_r=1. Accessed on June 13, 2013.

Fair, Christine C. *Fighting to the End: The Pakistan Army's Way of War*. Oxford and New York: Oxford University Press, 2014.

———. "Pakistan's Own War on Terror: What the Pakistani Public Thinks," *Journal of International Affairs* 63, no. 1, (Fall/Winter 2009): 39–55.

Finer, S. E. *The Man On Horseback: The Role of the Military in Politics*, 2nd edn. Middlesex: Peregrine Books, 1975.

Frisch, Hillel. "The Egyptian Army and Egypt's 'Spring,'" *The Journal of Strategic Studies* 36, no. 2 (2013): 180–204.

Gerbaudo, Paulo. "The Impermanent Revolution: The Organizational Fragility of the Egyptian Prodemocracy Movement in the Troubled Transition," *Social Justice* 39, no. 1 (2013): 8–23.

———. "The Roots of the Coup," *Soundings: A Journal of Politics and Culture* 54, no. 1 (2013): 104–113.

Giglio, Mike and Christopher Dickey. "The Quiet General: What does Egypt's ruler want?" *Newsweek*, August 16, 2013. http://mag.newsweek.com/2013/08/16/general-al-sisi-the-man-who-now-runs-egypt.html. Accessed November 12, 2013.

Glazer, Brian. *Turkey: A Country Study*. Washington, DC: Federal Research Division, Library of Congress, 1996.

GlobalSecurity.org, "Army: Egypt," January 29, 2011. http://www.globalsecurity.org/military/world/egypt/army.htm. Accessed February 1, 2011.

———. "Egypt: Military in Politics," January 29, 2011. http://www.globalsecurity.org/military/world/egypt/politics-military.htm. Accessed February 1, 2011.

Goldstone, Jack A. "Understanding the Revolutions of 2011: Weakness and Resilience in Middle Eastern Autocracies," in Gideon Rose, ed., *The New Arab Revolt*. New York: Council on Foreign Relations, (May/June 2011): 329–43.

Grare, Frédéric. "Pakistan's Foreign and Security Policies after the 2013 General Election: The Judge, the Politician and the Military," *International Affairs* 89, no. 4 (2013): 987–1001.

Güney, Aylin. "The Military, Politics and Post-Cold War Dilemmas in Turkey," in Kees Krooning and Dirk Kruijt, eds., *Political Armies: The Military and Nation Building in the Age of Democracy*. London: Zed Books, 2002, 162–78.

Güney, A. & Petek Karatekelioglu. "Turkey's EU Candidacy and Civil–Military Relations: Challenges and Prospects," *Armed Forces & Society* 31, no. 3, (2005): 439–62.

Gürsoy, Yaprak. "The Final Curtain for the Turkish Armed Forces? Civil–Military Relations in View of the 2011 General Elections," *Turkish Studies* 13, no. 2 (2012): 191–211.

Hale, William. *The Turkish Military and Politics*. London: Routledge, 1994.

———. "Transition to Civilian Governments in Turkey: The Military Perspective," in Metin Heper and Ahmet Evin, eds., *State, Democracy and the Military: Turkey in the 1980s*. Berlin and New York: Walter De Gruyter, 1988, 159–75.

———. "Foreword," in Mehmet Ali Birand, *Shirts of Steel: An Anatomy of the Turkish Armed Forces*. New York: I.B. Tauris & Co. Ltd., 1991, vii–xv.

Haqqani, Husain. *Magnificent Delusions: Pakistan, The United States, and an Epic History of Misunderstanding*. New York: Public Affairs, 2013.

———. *Pakistan: Between Mosque and Military*. Washington, DC: Carnegie Endowment for International Peace, 2005.

Harris, George S. "The Role of the Military in Turkey in the 1980s: Guardians or Decision-Makers?" in Metin Heper and Ahmet Evin, eds., *State, Democracy and the Military: Turkey in the 1980s*. Berlin and New York: Walter De Gruyter, 1988, 177–200.

Hasan, Syed Shoaib. "Rise of Pakistan's 'Quiet Man'," *BBC News*. June 17, 2009. http://news.bbc.co.uk/2/hi/south_asia/7024719.stm. Accessed August 4, 2014.

Heiduk, Felix. "From Guardians to Democrats? Attempts to Explain Change and Continuity in the Civil–military Relations of Post-authoritarian Indonesia, Thailand and the Philippines," *The Pacific Review* 24, no. 2 (May 2011): 249–71.

Heper, Metin and Aylin Guney. "The Military and Democracy in the Third Turkish Republic," *Armed Forces and Society*, (Summer 1996): 619–42.

Heper, Metin and Ahmet Evin. *Politics in the Third Turkish Republic*. Boulder, CO: Westview Press, 1994.

Hermida, Alfred. "Algeria: Democracy Derailed," *Africa Report* 37, no, 2 (March/April 1992): 13–17.

Hilali, A. Z. "The Challenges to Pakistan's Domestic Security," *Journal of Third World Studies* 19, no. 1 (Spring 2002): 65–100.

Hill, JNC. "Islamism and Democracy in the Modern Maghreb," *Third World Quarterly* 32, no. 6 (2011): 1089–1105.

Honna, Jun. *Military Politics and Democratization in Indonesia*. London and New York: RoutlegeCurzon, 2003.

Hooglund, E. "The Society and its Environment," in Helen C. Metz, ed., *Turkey: A Country Study*. Washington, DC: Federal Research Division, Library of Congress, 1996, 71–143.

Horne, Alistair. *A Savage War of Peace: Algeria 1954–1962*, 4th edn. New York: New York Review of Books, 2006.

Huntington, Samuel P. *Political Order in Changing Societies*. New Haven and London: Yale University Press, 1968.

————. *Soldier and the State: A Theory and Politics of Civil–Military Relations*. Cambridge, MA: Harvard University Press, 1957.

Jaffrelot, Christophe. "Nationalism without a Nation: Pakistan Searching for its Identity," in Christophe Jaffrelot, ed., *Pakistan: Nationalism without a Nation?* London: Zed Books, Ltd., 2002.

Janowitz, Morris. *Military Institutions and Coercion in the Developing Nations*. Chicago: University of Chicago Press, 1977.

————. "The Military in the Political Development of New Nations," *Bulletin of the Atomic Scientists*, (October 1964): 6–9.

Jenkins, Gareth. *Context and Circumstance: The Turkish Military and Politics*. Adelphi Paper 337. Oxford: The International Institute for Strategic Studies, 2001.

————. "Continuity and Change: Prospects for Civil–Military Relations in Turkey," *International Affairs* 83, no. 2 (2006): 339–55.

Jones, Owen Bennett. *Pakistan: In the Eye of the Storm*. New Haven, CT: Yale University Press, 2002.

Kahn Kundi, Abdul. "Civil–Military Relations and the Balance of Power," *Pakistan Today*. January 9, 2014, http://www.pakistantoday.com.pk/2014/01/09/comment/civil-military-relations. Accessed March 2, 2014.

Kandil, Hazem. "Back on Horse? The Military between Two Revolutions," in Bahgat Korany and Rabab El-Mahdi, eds., *Arab Spring in Egypt: Revolution and Beyond*. Cairo: American University in Cairo Press, 2012, 175–97.

————. *Soldiers, Spies, and Statesmen: Egypt's Road to Revolt*. Verso Books, 2014.

Karabelias, Gerassimos. "The Evolution of Civil–Military Relations in Post-War Turkey, 1980–1995," *Middle Eastern Studies* 35, no. 4 (October 1999): 130–51.

Karaosmanoğlu, A. L. "Transformation of Turkey's Civil–Military Relations Culture and International Environment," *Turkish Studies* 12, no. 2 (2011): 253–64.

Karawan, Ibrahim A. "Egypt," in Constantine P. Danopoulos and Cynthia Watson, eds., *The Political Role of the Military: An International Handbook*. Westport, CT: Greenwood Press, 1996, 107–121.

————. "Politics and the Army in Egypt," *Survival* 53, no. 2 (April/May 2011): 43–50.

Karpat, Kemal H. "Military Interventions: Army-Civilian Relations in Turkey Before and After 1980," in Metin Heper and Ahmet Evin, eds., *State, Democracy and the Military: Turkey in the 1980s*. Berlin and New York: Walter De Gruyter, 1988, 137–58.

Kårtveit, Bård and Maria Gabrielsen Jumbert. "Civil–Military Relations in the Middle East: A Literature Review," *Working Paper—Chr. Michelsen Institute*, no. 5 (June 2014): 1–26. http://www.cmi.no/publications/search/?pubtype=cmi-working-papers.

Kaya, Karen. "Turkey and the Arab Spring," *Military Review* (July/August (2012): 26–32.

King, Stephen J. *The New Authoritarianism in the Middle East and North Africa*. Bloomington and Indianapolis, IN: Indiana University Press, 2009.

Krooning, Kees and Dirk Kruijt, eds., *Political Armies: The Military and Nation Building in the Age of Democracy*. London: Zed Books, 2002.

Kuehn, David and Philip Lorenz. "Explaining Civil–Military Relations in New Democracies: Structure, Agency, and Theory Development," *Asian Journal of Political Science* 19, no. 3 (December 2011): 231–49.

Lenze, Paul E., Jr. "Civil–Military Relations in Islamic 'Democracies'": Comparative Dynamics Affecting Military Intervention and Withdrawal in Algeria, Pakistan & Turkey. PhD Dissertation. Washington State University, May 2011.

Lewis, Bernard. *The Emergence of Modern Turkey, Third Edition*. Oxford: Oxford University Press, 2002.

Londono, Ernesto. "Protesters Death Latest in Egypt Unrest," *The Washington Post*. November 26, 2011. http://www.washingtonpost.com/world/middle_east/protesters-death-latest-in-egypt-unrest/2011/11/26/gIQAZm8BzN_story.html"http://www.washingtonpost.com/world/middle_east/protesters-death-latest-in-egypt-unrest/2011/11/26/gIQAZm8BzN_story.html.

Luttwak, Edward. *Coup d'Etat: A Practical Handbook.* Cambridge, MA: Harvard University Press, 1968.

Lynch, Marc. "Regional and International Relations," in Ellen Lust, ed., *The Middle East,* 13th edn. Thousand Oaks, CA: CQ Press, 2014, 367–95.

Mackenzie, Kenneth. "Turkey Under The Generals," *Conflict Studies,* no. 126 (January 1981): 3–31. Institute for the Study of Conflict.

MacMillan, Margaret. *Paris 1919: Six Months That Changed the World.* New York: Random House, 2003.

Martinez, Luis. *The Algerian Civil War: 1990–1998.* New York: Columbia University Press, 2000.

Martini, Jeff and Julie Taylor. "Commanding Democracy in Egypt: The Military's Attempt to Manage the Future," *Foreign Affairs* 90, no. 5 (September/October 2011): 127–37.

Masoud, Tarek. "Egypt," in Ellen Lust, ed., *The Middle East,* 13th edn. Thousand Oaks, CA: CQ Press, 2014, 367–95.

Maswood, Javed and Usha Natarajan. In Bahgat Korany and Rabab El-Mahdi, eds., *Arab Spring in Egypt: Revolution and Beyond.* Cairo: American University in Cairo Press, 2012, 223–49.

Mietzner, Marcus. "Successful and Failed Democratic Transitions from Military Rule in Majority Muslim Societies: The Cases of Indonesia and Egypt," *Contemporary Politics* 20, no. 4 (2014): 435–52.

The Military Balance. "Chapter Four: Europe," 116:1, 2016.

———. "Chapter Seven: Middle East and North Africa," 116:1, 2016.

———. "Chapter Six: Asia," 116:1, 2016.

———. "Chapter Ten: Country Comparisons-commitments, Force Levels and Economics," 116:1, 2016.

Momayezi, Nasser. "Civil–Military Relations in Turkey," *International Journal on World Peace* (September 1998): 3–28.

Mortimer, Robert. "Algeria: The Clash between Islam, Democracy, and the Military," *Current History* 92, no. 570 (January 1993): 37–41.

———. "Islamists, Soldiers, and Democrats: The Second Algerian War," *The Middle East Journal* 50, no. 1 (Winter 1996): 18–39.

Musharraf, Pervez. *In the Line of Fire: A Memoir.* New York: Simon & Schuster, 2006.

The Muslim Brotherhood. *The English Language Site of the Muslim Brotherhood,* Ikhwanweb.com, 2016.

Nassif, Hicham Bou. "Why the Egyptian Army Didn't Shoot," *Middle East Report,* no. 265 (Winter 2012): 18-21.

Nasr, Vali. *Forces of Fortune: The Rise of the New Muslim Middle Class and What It Will Mean for Our World.* New York: The Free Press, 2009.

———. "Islamic Opposition in the Political Process: Lessons from Pakistan," in *Political Islam: Revolution, Radicalism, or Reform,* 1997, 135–56.

———. "Military Rule, Islamism, and Democracy in Pakistan," *The Middle East Journal* 58, no. 2 (Spring 2004): 195–209.

Naviwala, Nadia. "Playing Hardball with Aid to Pakistan," *Foreign Policy.* September 4, 2015. http://foreignpolicy.com/2015/09/04/playing-hardball-with-aid-to-pakistan/ . Accessed May 16, 2016.

Nordlinger, Eric A. *Soldiers in Politics: Military Coups and Governments.* Englewood Cliffs, NJ: Prentice Hall, 1977.

O'Donnell, Guillermo and Philippe C. Schmitter. *Transitions from Authoritarian Rule: Tentative Conclusions about Uncertain Democracies.* Baltimore and London: The Johns Hopkins University Press, 1986.

Osman, Tarek. *Egypt on the Brink: From Nasser to Mubarak.* New Haven and London: Yale University Press, 2010.

Ottaway, David and Marina Ottaway. *Algeria: the Politics of a Socialist Revolution.* Berkeley, CA: University of California Press, 1973.

Özbudun, Ergun. *Contemporary Turkish Politics: Challenges to Democratic Consolidation.* Boulder, CO: Lynne Rienner Publishers, 2000.

Perlmutter, Amos. *The Military in Politics: On Professionals, Praetorians, and Revolutionary Soldiers.* New Haven, CT: Yale University Press, 1977.

Perlez, Jane. "Pakistan's Chief of Army Fights to Keep His Job," *New York Times.* June 16, 2011. http://www.nytimes.com/2011/06/16/world/asia/16pakistan.html?_r=0& pagewanted=print. Accessed May 10, 2012.

Phillips, David L. "Turkey's Dreams of Accession," *Foreign Affairs* 83, no. 5 (September/October 2004): 86–97.

Pierre, Andrew J. and William B. Quandt. "Algeria's War on Itself," *Foreign Policy* 99 (Summer 1995): 131–48.

Pion-Berlin, David. "The Study of Civil–Military Relations in New Democracies," *Asian Journal of Political Science* 19, no. 3 (December 2011): 222–30.

Pratt, Nicola. *Democracy and Authoritarianism in the Arab World.* Boulder, CO: Lynne Rienner Publishers, 2007.

Pripstein Posusney, Marsha. "Enduring Authoritarianism: Middle East Lessons for Comparative Theory," *Comparative Politics* 36, no. 2 (January 2004): 127–38.

Quandt, William B. *Between Ballots & Bullets: Algeria's Transition from Authoritarianism.* Washington, DC: Brookings Institution Press, 1998.

Reidel, Bruce. "Are We Losing in Afghanistan?" Brookings Institution, July 5, 2009.

Reuters. "Text of Sisi Interview with Reuters." May 15, 2014. Accessed May 23, 2014.

Rivzi, Hasan-Askari. *Military, State and Society in Pakistan.* Boulder, CO: Westview Press, 2000.

Roberts, Hugh. "The Algerian State and the Challenge of Democracy," *Government and Opposition* 27, (Summer 1992): 433–54.

———. *The Battlefield Algeria, 1998–2002: Studies in a Broken Polity.* London and New York: Verso Books, 2003.

Rosefsky Wickham, Carrie. *Mobilizing Islam: Religion, Activism, and Political Change in Egypt.* New York: Columbia University Press, 2002.

———. "The Muslim Brotherhood After Mubarak: What the Brotherhood Is and How It Will Shape the Future," in Gideon Rose, ed., *The New Arab Revolt.* New York: Council on Foreign Relations, February 3, 2011, 91–97.

———. "The Muslim Brotherhood and Democratic Transition in Egypt," *Middle East Law & Governance* 3.1, no. 2 (2011): 204–23.

Roy, Olivier. *The Failure of Political Islam.* Cambridge, MA: Harvard University Press, 1994.

Ruedy, John. *Modern Algeria: The Origins and Development of a Nation.* Bloomington, IN: Indiana University Press, 1992.

Rutherford, Bruce K. *Egypt after Mubarak: Liberalism, Islam, and Democracy in the Arab World,* 2nd edn. Princeton, NJ: Princeton University Press, 2011.

———. "Egypt: The Origins and Consequences of the January 25 Uprising," in Mark L. Haas and David W. Lesch, eds., *The Arab Spring: Change & Resistance in the Middle East.* Boulder, CO: Westview Press, 2013, 35–63.

Said, Atef. "The Paradox of Transition to 'Democracy' under Military Rule," *Social Research* 79, no. 2 (Summer 2012): 397–433.

Salt, Jeremy. "Turkey's Military 'Democracy,'" *Current History* (February 1999): 72–78.

Satana, Nil S. "Civil–Military Relations in Europe, the Middle East and Turkey," *Turkish Studies* 12, no. 2 (June 2011): 279–92.

Searle-White, Joshua. *The Psychology of Nationalism.* New York: Palgrave, 2001.

Shah, Aquil. *The Army and Democracy: Military Politics in Pakistan.* Cambridge, MA: Harvard University Press, 2014.

Sharp, Jeremy M. "Egypt in Transition," *Congressional Research Service,* February 8, ]2012. 2012. http://www.fas.org/sgp/crs/mideast/RL33003.pdf"www.fas.org/sgp/ crs/mideast/RL33003.pdf. Accessed March 5, 2012.

Shehata, Dina. "The Fall of the Pharaoh: How Hosni Mubarak's Reign Came to an End," in Gideon Rose, ed., *The New Arab Revolt*. New York: Council on Foreign Relations, (May/June, 2011): 137–48.

———. "Youth Movements and the 25 January Revolution," in Bahgat Korany and Rabab El-Mahdi, eds., *Arab Spring in Egypt: Revolution and Beyond*, Cairo: American University in Cairo Press, 2012), 105–24.

Siddiqa, Ayesha. *Military Inc.: Inside Pakistan's Military Economy*. London and Ann Arbor: Pluto Press, 2007.

Sinaisky, Sergey. "USSR-Egypt Military Cooperation Revisited," *International Affairs* (n.d.): 150–61.

Singh, Chaitram and John Hickman. "Soldiers as Saviors of the Staet: The Cases of Turkey and Pakistan Contrasted," *Journal of Third World Studies* XXX, no. 1 (Spring 2013): 39–54.

Sorenson, David S."Civil–Military Relations in North Africa," *Middle East Policy* XIV, no. 4 (Winter 2007): 99–114.

Spiegel Online. "Threat of Coup by Secularist Army: Alarm Grows Over Political Crisis in Turkey," April 30, 2007. http://www.spiegel.de/international/world/threat-of-coup-by-secularist-army-alarm-grows-over-political-crisis-in-turkey-a-480235. html. Accessed July 10, 2008.

Springborg, Robert. "Sisi's Islamist Agenda for Egypt," *Foreign Affairs*, July 25, 2013. https://www.foreignaffairs.com/articles/middle-east/2013-07-25/sisis-islamist-agenda-egypt. Accessed August 15, 2014.

———. *Mubarak's Egypt: Fragmentation of the Political Order*. Boulder and London: Westview Press, 1989.

Stacher, Joshua. "Egypt's Democratic Mirage: How Cairo's Authoritarian Regime is Adapting and Preserving Itself," in Gideon Rose, ed., *The New Arab Revolt*. New York: Council on Foreign Relations, February 7, 2011, 98–103.

———. "Establishment Morsi," *The Middle East Report*, no. 265 (Winter 2012): 10–11.

Stone, Martin. *The Agony of Algeria*. New York: Columbia University Press, 1997.

Stora, Benjamin. *Algeria, 1830–2000: A Short History*. Ithaca and London: Cornell University Press, 2001.

Tahi, Mohand Salah. "The Arduous Democratisation Process in Algeria," *The Journal of Modern African Studies* 30, no. 3 (1992): 397–419.

Talbot, Ian. *Pakistan: A Modern History, Expanded and Updated Edition*. New York: Palgrave MacMillan, 2005.

Taspinar, Omer. "The Old Turks' Revolt," *Foreign Affairs* 86, no. 6 (November/December 2007): 114–30.

Taysi, Tanyel Bedia. *For The People, In Spite Of The People? Official Turkish Identity From 1960*. PhD Dissertation, Washington State University, May 2004.

Tibi, Bassam. "Islamism and Democracy: On the Compatibility of Institutional Islamism and the Political Culture of Democracy," *Totalitarian Movements and Political Religions* 10, no. 2 (June 2009): 135–64.

Tlemcani, Rachid and William W. Hansen. "Development and the State in Post-Colonial Algeria," *Journal of Asian and African Studies* XXIV, nos. 1 and 2 (1989): 114–33.

Toth, A. "Historical Setting," *Algeria: A Country Study*. 1994.

Trager, Eric. "Letter from Cairo: The People's Military in Egypt?" in Gideon Rose, ed., *The New Arab Revolt*. New York: Council on Foreign Relations, January 30, 2011, 81–85.

Uras, Umut. "Ruling party loses majority in Turkish elections," Al-Jazeera, http://www.aljazeera.com/news/2015/06/ak-party-leads-turkish-parliamentary-polls-150607161827232.html, June 7, 2015, accessed on November 15, 2015.

Vatikiotis, P. J. *The History of Modern Egypt: From Muhammad Ali to Mubarak*, 4th edn. Baltimore: Johns Hopkins University Press, 1991.

Volpi, Frederic. "Democracy in Algeria: Continuity and Change in the Organisation of Political Representation," *The Journal of North African Studies* 5, no. 2 (Summer 2000): 25–40.

———. *Islam and Democracy: The Failure of Dialogue in Algeria.* London: Pluto Press, 2003.

Walsh, Declan. "Sharif vs. Army, Round 3," *New York Times.* May 13, 2013. http://www.nytimes.com/2013/05/14/world/asia/pakistan-vote-revives-premiers-rivalry-with-army.html. Accessed February 2, 2014.

Wan, William and Ernesto Londono. "Egypt's Aid From US in Peril Amid Crackdown on Pro-Democracy Groups," *The Washington Post.* February 3, 2012. Accessed March 5, 2012. "http://www.washingtonpost.com/world/national-security/egypts-aid-from-us-in-peril-amid-crackdown-on-pro-democracy-groups/2012/02/03/gI-QAp5GQqQ_story.html"http://www.washingtonpost.com/world/national-security/egypts-aid-from-us-in-peril-amid-crackdown-on-pro-democracy-groups/2012/02/03/gIQAp5GQqQ_story.html.

Weinbaum, Marvin G. "Hard Choices in Countering Insurgency and Terrorism along Pakistan's North-West Frontier," *Journal of International Affairs* 63, no. 1 (2009): 73–88.

Welch, Claude E. Jr. "Military Disengagement from Politics: Paradigms, Processes, or Random Events," *Armed Forces and Society* 18, no. 3 (Spring 1992): 323–42.

———. *No Farewell to Arms?: Military Disengagement from Politics in Africa and Latin America.* Boulder, CO: Westview Press, 1987.

Willis, Michael. *Islamist Challenge in Algeria: A Political History.* New York: New York University Press, 1997.

Yegen, Mesut. "Prospective-Turks or Pseudo-Citizens: Kurds in Turkey," *Middle East Journal* 63, no. 4 (2009): 597–615.

Yildirim, Kadir A. "Military, Political Islam, and the Future of Democracy in Egypt," *Insight Turkey* 15, no. 4 (Fall 2013): 61.

Zahab, Mariam Abou and Olivier Roy. *Islamist Networks: The Afghan-Pakistan Connection.* New York: Columbia University Press, 2006.

Zartman, I. William, "The Algerian Army in Politics," *Soldier and State in Africa.* 1970.

Zoubir, Yahia H. "Stalled Democratization of an Authoritarian Regime: The Case of Algeria," *Democratization* 2, no. 2 (Summer 1995): 109–39.

Zürcher, Erik J. *Turkey: A Modern History.* London and New York: I.B. Tauris & Co. Ltd., 2004.

# Index

# About the Author

**Paul E. Lenze Jr.**, PhD is currently senior lecturer in the Department of Politics and International Affairs at Northern Arizona University in Flagstaff, Arizona. His teaching and research interests are in international relations and comparative politics with a focus on civil–military relations, Middle East politics, U.S. foreign policy, and national security.